INTRODUCING
THE PSALMS

INTRODUCING
THE PSALMS

by

Klaus Seybold

Translated by

R. Graeme Dunphy

T & T CLARK
A Continuum imprint
LONDON • NEW YORK

T&T CLARK LTD
A Continuum Imprint

The Tower Building   15 East 26th Street
11 York Road   New York 10010
London SE1 7NX, UK   USA

www.continuumbooks.com

First published 1990
Reprinted 1997, 2003, 2004

ISBN 0 567 29174 X

British Library Cataloguing-in-Publication Data
A catalogue record for this book is available from the British Library

Printed and bound in Great Britain by Biddles Ltd, *www.biddles.co.uk*

PREFACE

'He who preserves your life from ruin,
He who crowns you with grace and mercy,
He who satisfies your desires with good things,
In order that your youth might be renewed . . .'

'As far as the rising is from the setting,
So far will he remove our transgressions from us.
As a father is merciful to his children,
So YHWH is merciful to those who fear him . . .'

The text fragment reproduced on the cover contains these lines from Ps.103. It was found in a cave near the ruins of Qumran in the Judean desert, and is known as 4QPs[b]. The Psalter manuscript to which the two columns belong was written about the time of the birth of Christ (50–0). It is one of the oldest pieces to have survived.

This fragment might be seen as a symbol of our fragmentary knowledge of the Psalms. A certain amount is clear to see, and more can be deduced, but there is a great deal which is no longer available to us. This introduction to the Psalms sets itself the aim of pointing out what is visible, explaining what may be derived from it, and hinting at what must have been lost. It attempts to come as close as possible to the Biblical Psalms. It does so by sketching out what has come to light in the long history of research into the Psalms; questions, answers and problems. In this way it seeks to contribute to a historical understanding of this ancient book.

Our study will not deal with the use of the Psalter as a volume of meditation and prayer. Nor will it offer any new approach to the Psalms for which the author alone may claim credit. Rather, it builds on the results of scholarly exegesis and the accumulated knowledge which this has made available. It seeks to bring its readers to read the

Psalms for themselves, and to make their own observations and discoveries. It is therefore assumed that readers will have an open Bible, and will be following for themselves the texts under discussion. When texts are cited, these lean for the most part on the wordings of *Zürcher Bibel*, with a number of exceptions, eg the rendering of the Tetragrammaton as 'YHWH' (read as 'Yahweh') rather than 'The LORD'.

Klaus Seybold,
Basle,
Switzerland,
Autumn 1986.

TRANSLATOR'S PREFACE

This book has had to be adapted in a number of ways to meet the needs of its new readership. In Chapter X, I have added two paragraphs on English-language song-psalters (X.4). The section on the history of German Bible translation (X.6) has been partly retained because of the importance of German scholarship for our understanding of the Old Testament. Hopefully it has been rendered in such a way that readers without a knowledge of German will also find it useful. A corresponding section on the history of English Bible translation has been added (X.7). Much of the bibliographical material has been omitted as it would be inaccessible to the English reader, but suggestions for further reading will be found in XI.7 and 8.

Bible quotations have been translated from the German edition, but with a careful eye on the Hebrew text (BHS) and on the major English versions (particularly NIV, RSV). Chapter and verse numbers follow the usual English system. Quotations from ancient texts outwith the Bible have, where possible, been taken from existing English translations.

I am indebted to my wife, Rhona, for reading the texts, and to Dr Brian Murdoch, Dr James Martin and Mr Kai Funkschmidt for their helpful comments and advice.

R. Graeme Dunphy,
Culloden,
Scotland,
Winter 1989.

CONTENTS

Chapter I

THE PSALTER AND ITS TRANSMISSION

1. Terminology

'Psalm' and 'Psalter', the terms by which the Biblical book is known, are of Greek origin. ψαλμός, 'the playing of a stringed instrument' (from ψάλλειν, 'to pluck strings', 'to play'), is equivalent to the Hebrew *mizmôr*, which also means a song accompanied by stringed instruments. In the plural it serves as a title for the entire collection, and thus for the 'song-book', as for instance in the most important Greek manuscript B, the so-called *Codex Vaticanus* of the 4th century AD. Through the Latin form *psalmus* it became the usual term for the texts of that Biblical book, and has come into common use in literature and music.

ψαλτήριον refers to a stringed instrument, and translates the corresponding Hebrew expressions for lyre and harp. Manuscript A, the 5th century *Codex Alexandrinus*, uses this term as a title for the book, on the same assumption, that these are songs which are to be sung to the lyre. Under these titles, Psalms, ψαλμοί, *psalmi*, and Psalter, ψαλτήριον, *psalterium*, the book is to be found in the early canons of the Greek and Latin Church, often expanded by βίβλος or *liber*, 'book'. Examples of this are to be found in Luke 20,42 and Acts 1,20, and the title page of *Codex B*, where 'Psalms' can stand *pars pro toto* for the whole third section of the canon; this is confirmed by Luke 24,44 in the speech of the risen Christ: '... everything must be fulfilled that is written about me in the Law of Moses (I), the Prophets (II) and the Psalms (III)'.

The early canons of the Church occasionally contain parallel titles or definitions which give us an insight into the Hebrew terms of the Jewish tradition. For example, the list in the *Codex Hierosolymitanus* (1st century AD?), which lists the Biblical books bilingually, gives at No. 10 the equation: σφερτελίμ = ψαλτήριον, the former being without doubt the Hebrew *sēpher* *t^ehillîm*, 'Book of praise-songs', 'Hymnary', 'Book of Laudations' or 'Praises' (thus Martin Buber: *Buch der Preisungen*). Indeed, this seems to have been the usual term in the old synagogues. In his commentary on the Psalms, Origen transcribes *spharthelleim*, and Jerome writes in the *Psalterium juxta Hebraeos*: '... *titulus ipse hebraicus sephar tallîm, quod interpretatur volumen hymnorum.*'[1] It is not quite clear when the book first came by this title. In the oldest manuscript fragments, titles for whole books are apparently not used. Even the Hebrew manuscripts *Codex Aleppo* and *Codex Leningradensis*, for example, have no titles. Ps. 1 follows, after a blank line, directly from the closing masora (a note of the number of verses) of the Book of Chronicles (Fig. 1). Philo of Alexandria and the Jewish historian Flavius Josephus (both mid-1st century AD) speak generally of 'Hymns' (ὕμνοι) which, after the 'Laws' and the 'Prophecies', dominate the third part of the Scripture. This could go back to Hebrew *t^ehillîm*, commonly translated by ὕμνοι. In each case, the collection is characterised by this term as the ('Book of') 'Songs', no doubt following the contemporary custom – as again Philo bears witness – of performing the Psalms as 'hymns' in the classical sense, that is, with a choir and precentor, and a circular dance. This term, not normally used in the plural, draws the texts together in one group, a structured entity.

It is striking that these old titles, the oldest known, appear to conceive of the Psalter from the musical point of view, as a song-book, while they fail to take account of the large number of prayer texts which it contains. Collections of cult-lyrics

[1] J. P. Migne (ed.), *Patrologiae gr.* (1857ff.), XII 1084; *lat.* (1844ff.), XXVIII 1124.

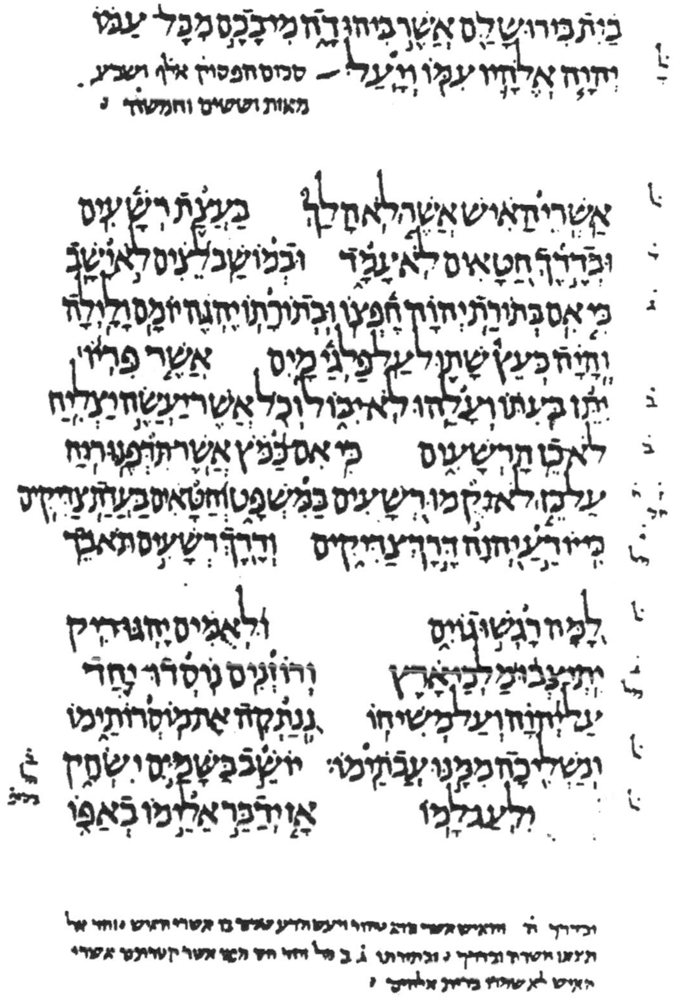

Fig. 1. The beginning of the Psalter in the *Codex Aleppo* (10th century). Notice the transition from Chronicles to Psalms. After the closing masora there is an empty line, and then Ps. 1 begins without a heading. Notice also the gap between Pss. 1 and 2. No numbering is to be seen. It is interesting that Ps. 1 is laid out as prose, whereas Ps. 2 is written as poetry (in stichs).

3

from the large body of cuneiform and hieroglyphic literature tend to take account of both aspects with the title 'Hymns and Prayers'. The scribes who bring us the Biblical cult-lyrics apparently preferred the musical nomenclature. Certainly, we are entitled to conclude that for them the hymnodic use of the Psalms as choir pieces – perhaps also with instrumental music – was the most salient characteristic feature of this Biblical book.

2. The History of the Psalter

In the tractate *Baba bathra* ('Last Gate') of the Babylonian Talmud, details are given of the origins of the canonical writings:

> 'Moses wrote his own book, the Balaam pericope, and Job. Joshua wrote his own book and eight verses in the Torah (Deut. 34,5–12). Samuel wrote his own book, the book of Judges, and Ruth. David wrote the book of Psalms, bringing us the ten elders, that is, Adam, Melchizedek, Abraham, Moses, Heman, Jeduthun, Asaph and the three sons of Korah. Jeremiah wrote his own book, Kings and Lamentations. Hezekiah and his people wrote Isaiah, Proverbs, the Song of Songs and Ecclesiastes . . .' (14b.15a)[2]

So David is presented as the author of the Book of Psalms. As in the old headings, care is taken not to refer to it as 'his own book', in contrast to the apocryphal collection 'The Psalms of Solomon'. Nevertheless, given the details of authorship of the individual psalms, it is a small step to conceive of the whole book as his work. The same tractate goes on to justify its preferred order of the biblical books in the third part of the canon (Ruth, Pss., Job, Prov., Eccles., S. of S., Lam., Dan., Esther, Ezra (Ne), Chr.), in which Ruth is placed before the Psalms, on the grounds that the story told in Ruth belongs to the biography of David, who wrote the Psalms. Also important is the

[2] Cf. R. Smend, *Die Entstehung des ATs*, 1984 (3rd ed.), pp. 15ff.

4

reference to the 'ten elders', a source which roots the Psalter right back in the earliest part of the *Heilsgeschichte*, in the creation story. This testifies to the particularly high standing which this book was accorded, even by the standards of Holy Scripture.

This view of the origin of the book has been brought into question by the historical examination of the Biblical writings, and in particular of the Psalms and the Psalter itself. Distinctions which had been made as early as the Talmud have been taken up and pursued. It seems that the simple picture of the writing and redacting king is not applicable to the Psalter as a book, that in reality the development of the book ran along far more complicated lines than this model of authorship would suggest. Let us attempt to reconstruct the history of the text from those points which prove to be firm and reliable.

(1) The texts discovered in the caves in the vicinity of *Khirbet Qumran*, the settlement of an Essene monastic community on the north-west bank of the Dead Sea, have given a whole new insight into the textual history of the Old Testament writings. They offer us a glimpse of a decisive phase in the development of, among other texts, the Psalms, which can serve as a starting point for our historical reconstruction.

During the turmoil of the years 66–70 AD, the library of the Essene community was taken from its store and hidden, and thus, by a stroke of fortune, fragments were preserved. Among them were found extracts and remains of all the Old Testament Scriptures, or rather, of the books which a little later were brought together to form the Hebrew canon, with the significant exception of the book of Esther. The fragments belonged to scrolls of parchment and leather, representing more or less the full range of the Scriptures which were later to be canonised and catalogued, but which at this point were still being transmitted separately. The discoveries produced thirty-one copies of the Psalter, which, interestingly, differ at various points. The experts are no doubt correct in concluding that, while in content and order the central core of the Psalms already existed in Qumran at that time, neither the final selection nor the final order of the texts, particularly of the texts in the last third of the Psalter, had been determined. Specimens were found which deviate from the 'standard' (established later, but also attested at Qumran) in the order of their texts (4QPs^{abd}), or which offer additional texts (4QPs^f; 11QPs^a; 11QPs^d), later counted as 'apocryphal', and either omitted from the Hebrew canon or included elsewhere; e.g. Ps. 151 (LXX), the Syrian Psalms, etc. (Fig. 2).

While various Psalters were in use, all of them were clearly regarded by their users as Holy Scripture. They became the subject of exegesis in the so-called *Pešarim* (singular: *Pešer*), along with the prophetic writings, and they enjoyed particular popularity and esteem. No other Biblical book was represented by so many manuscripts in the cave library: Compare Pss. 31; Deut. 25; Isa. 18; Gen., Exod. 14; . . . Jer., Job, Ruth, S. of S., Lam. 4 – Commentaries: five on Isa., three on Pss., two on Hos., Mic., Zeph., one on Hab. Texts quoted as Holy Scripture and introduced with the usual formula come most frequently from Isaiah, then from Deuteronomy and the Psalms.[3]

It must therefore be assumed that in the first half of the 1st century AD the Psalter had not yet found its final and universally acknowledged form; it was open-ended, and was still flexible in the arrangement of the texts, particularly in the last section (11QPs^a). Nonetheless it was universally accepted

[3] Following D. Barthélemy in: S. Amsler, etc., *Le canon de l'AT: Sa formation et son histoire*, 1984, pp. 9–45.

as Holy Scripture and was esteemed at least as highly as the book of the prophet Isaiah or the books of Moses (Deut., Gen., Exod.). And needless to say it was held that David had compiled the book. Indeed, according to one text from the Psalm scroll found in the 11th cave, he was the author of 3600 hymns (*thlym*) and 450 liturgical songs (*šyr* sing.) (11QPS[a] column 27). The 150 or so texts are only a small selection. What is of particular interest is the distinction between hymns and liturgies, in which – the figures imply *it*, and the text specifies the latter – by hymns we should understand the

Fig. 2. The last column, column 28, of the Psalter manuscript 11QPs[a] (1st century AD). This column, which is damaged at the bottom, contains Ps.134,1–3, and after a blank line, Ps.151, David's Hebrew autograph text, which was previously known only in the Greek and Syriac versions. Notice that the tetragrammaton is written in the old Hebrew script (eg in the top two lines).

7

freely available lyric material (in quantity), while by cultic texts we should think of set formulae (collectively, a *corpus*) (Chapter II.1).

If the desert library of the Essene community of Qumran owned thirty-one Psalter manuscripts, then, reasoning *a minore ad maius*, one must assume a far wider distribution for the real centres of the 'orthodox' Judaism of the 1st century. The fact that around 100 AD the Pharisaic movement established and enforced the standard form, also attested at Qumran, as the sole text of the Psalter, led to the stabilisation of a fixed text, the Masoretic Text, and may have limited the richness and variety of the pre-Masoretic forms. However, we no longer have any direct witness to these Rabbinic-Pharisaic specimens and their successors. With the close of the canon around 100 AD, and in particular with the ultimate codification, that is, the assembling of the individual writings for transmission in codex or scroll, the era of the independent Psalm Book comes to an end, and the history of its exegesis, which is every bit as important, begins (Chapter XI).

(2) The fact that the history of the Greek translation of the Psalms runs more or less parallel with that of the Hebrew Psalter is most revealing. A discovery like Qumran has, of course, not yet been granted us in this field of research, but the New Testament writings can take the place of the Essene library in this respect, in so far as it is possible to evaluate the Scriptural quotations which are found there. For the library of the synagogue in Capernaum, for example, or the archives of the school in which Paul studied, are irretrievably lost. The discovery and publication of the Bodmer Papyrus XXIV has shed some light on what has been lost. This is a Greek Psalter manuscript, probably from the 2nd, or possibly the 3rd century AD, which represents an upper-Egyptian textual tradition previously only known in part.[4] Pss. 17–118 have

[4] R. Kasser – M. Testuz, *Psalmen. Papyrus Bodmer XXIV*, 1967.

Fig. 3. A page from the Bodmer Papyrus XXIV (2nd–4th century?).
This leaf contains Pss. 57,12–59,5. The Psalms are run together without
gaps, but a number is given at the top of each Psalm, eg l.3: NH (=58);
l.27: NΘ (=59) (cf. the other method of counting found in the large
manuscripts of the Septuagint).

been preserved (Fig. 3).

Some surprising parallels appear here. Judging from the frequency of quotations, the New Testament communities had quite similar preferences in their choice of Scripture readings. In first place with around fifty-four New Testament references we again find the Psalms; then come Isaiah with forty-eight, Deuteronomy with forty-two, Exodus with twenty-four, Lamentations/Proverbs with twenty-two, Genesis with nineteen ...[5] Only the second and third positions have been reversed. The New Testament communities also cited the Psalms as Scripture. In Acts 1,20 Peter argues: 'For it is written in the Book of Psalms . . .'; and he makes use of two texts from two different Psalms as 'Scripture which the Holy Spirit prophesied through the mouth of David', and which now finds its 'fulfilment' (cf. Acts 1,16; Luke 20,42; 24,44; Acts 13,33). Similarly at Qumran the Psalms were regarded as prophetic texts which became relevant when one related them to the present.[6] This is exactly what we observe in Acts 1,16, and again in 2,30 where David is designated as 'prophet' and Ps. 132,11 is quoted; and most notably in the passion narratives of the Gospels and their use of Ps. 22 (cf. John 19,24.28).[7] In this context it is important to notice that according to Mark 14,26 (Matt. 26,30) after the Last Supper Jesus and his disciples 'sang a hymn', (Greek ὑμνεῖν) that is, recited the *Hallel* (probably Pss. 114–18) in Psalmodic fashion, before they went up onto the Mount of Olives. This was no doubt their custom, familiar from temple and synagogue worship, and from their religious up-bringing.

In their appraisal of the Psalms – and in the use of the Psalter scrolls which this presupposes – the early Christian

[5] Following Barthélemy, op. cit.

[6] Cf. the *Pešer* on Ps. 37 (4QpPs37).

[7] Cf. Ps. 14 in Rom. 3; Ps. 2 in Acts and Hebrews; Ps. 95 in Heb. 3&4; Ps. 69 in Revelation; cf. also Chapter XI.1.

communities followed their Jewish predecessors. According to the Mishnah tractate *Tamid* (7,4), the singing of Psalms was part of the temple cult and accompanied the sacrifices, particular Psalms being prescribed for each day of the week: Shabbat Ps. 92, I 24, II 48, III 82, IV 94, V 81, VI 93 (in the Greek translation). This was recorded as early as the Books of the Maccabees (II, 1,30; I 4,54), and it is described in detail by Josephus (Ant. 7,364.305; 8,124; 9,269). He also makes mention of stringed music which accompanies the temple singing of the Levites. On the coins of the Bar-Cochba period (*c.*132 AD) musical instruments appear as symbols of the temple cult (Fig. 17).[8]

In religious education the Psalms also played their part. According to 4 Macc. 18,18, fathers in the diaspora would teach their children 'the' song of Moses (Deut. 32) – also revered by Philo of Alexandria and Eusebius of Caesarea – and sing Psalms to them.

Philo may be taken as a representative of the Greek-speaking diaspora communities of Alexandria at the beginning of the 1st century. And this brings us full circle. For Philo's work is close both to the Qumran writings and to the early Christian literature, and again parallels arise. To Philo, as to the Qumran community and the New Testament, the Psalms ('Hymns') are Holy Scripture, and they are his main source for quotations after the *Torah*(!). Here he encounters prophetic utterances: these hymns (ὑμνῳδίαι) were written by a prophet. Thus quotations from the Psalms and quotations from the *Torah* can be combined, something which also happens in the New Testament.

(3) The light which these three libraries, the writings of Qumran, the New Testament and Philo, shed on the history of the Psalter, certainly illuminates the situation in the mid-1st

---

[8] Cf. also the description of the Feast of Tabernacles in *Succoth* 5,4.

century AD, but it is not sufficient to clarify the earlier phase of the transmission and distribution of the book, far less its origins. Nevertheless, we have here a definite starting point, or more precisely two, the Hebrew and the Greek Psalter. From both of these the way back into the origins can be traced in a very rough and ready manner. At this stage we must also take into account the point at which the two strands of tradition parted and began their separate lives, that is to say, the translation of the Psalter into Greek. The triangle which is created by these three points illustrates the various aspects of the problem.

What can we make of this phase of the Psalter's history?

Assuming that the critically reconstructed text of our editions of the Septuagint, which rely mainly on the large *codices*, corresponds roughly to the text of the period in question, and that the (pre)-masoretic Qumran version represents the Hebrew text in the middle of the diagram, we find that the two strands of textual history, when compared, for the most part concur. The basic shape of the texts is more or less determined. The order is parallel, though the divisions and the resulting numbering systems, added later, do differ. The reasons for the comparatively insignificant discrepancies can generally be recognised; usually an erroneous linking with the preceding or following text (eg. Pss. 9/10 = Ψ9).[9] We must assume that the two versions, later regulated within the

[9] As a rule of thumb, for Pss. 10–112 & 116–145, MT = LXX + 1. Or: MT 11–113 = LXX 10–112, and MT 117–147 = LXX 116–145.

Hebrew-Jewish canon and the Greek-Christian canon, lay very close to one another even in their early stages. Since in their origin they are, so to speak, twins, it is safe to assume that they at no point diverged far from one another, but rather, have always been quite similar.

Despite major areas of similarity, however, there are a number of peculiarities which point to their separate development. For example, the Greek Psalter does not end with Ps. 150, which seeks at once to close the words of praise and to open a cosmic praise without words. Instead, it adds Ps. 151. 'An independent Psalm of David, outwith the count' – reads the heading to the Greek version of this psalm, the Hebrew 'original' of which was found recently in the 11th cave at Qumran (11QPs^a) (Fig. 2). Ps. 151 is something of an autobiographical text. As such, it closes the book with details of the identity of the author. And as in 11QPs^a, this *subscriptio* explicitly declares the book to be the Psalter of David, the framework of which is formed by Psalms 2 and 151. The received title of the Hebrew version on the other hand, *t^ehillîm* (Hymns), matches better the Psalter closing with the cosmic *Hallelu-Yah* of Ps. 150. Clearly this difference in ending reveals a different perception of the Psalter, which can also be discerned in the New Testament.[10] And, of course, we have to take account of many developments peculiar to each version. Nevertheless, the degree of similarity is remarkable, and the Greek translation is still rightly regarded as being of the greatest importance for text-critical questions.

The line from the earliest attested versions of the Greek Psalter of the 1st century AD, back to the translation of the so-called Septuagint (=LXX) can only be drawn hypothetically. It is hindered by the continuing discussion of the whole question of the LXX and its origins. Two models are

[10] On Ps. 2 as a Psalm of David, see Acts 2,24f.; 13,33, and their variant readings.

presented for debate: the model 'Greek Targum' – i.e. arising initially from numerous oral translations of individual periscopes, later brought together in writing (P. Kahle); and the model 'authorised norm-translation' – i.e. arising from an original standard translation from which increasingly diffuse variants emerged (A. Rahlfs). The 3rd or 2nd centuries BC seem to be the most likely dates. Generally we think of Alexandria in Egypt as the place of translation. At any rate, the Hebrew text of a Psalter scroll or of various Psalm scrolls must have been available there at that time, and could have served as a source for this epoch-making translation. And this 'source' would no doubt have been connected, in some way no longer discernible, to the texts we know from Qumran.

As for the compiling of the Hebrew Psalter, we may assume that this collection of hymns and prayers belongs to the period of the second Jerusalem temple. But here too, it is difficult to say anything more precise and concrete. We are thrown almost completely onto internal criteria. In order to discover what we can learn here from the 'growth rings' of the book, a number of further considerations are required.

3. The Structure of the Psalter

The Psalter offers us a collection of around 150 separate texts. We now examine how the individual pieces have been marshalled and arrayed in groups, to see if we can gain from the internal patterns any insights into the whole complex, its origins, and its purposes. We begin by looking for any recognisable traces of deliberate structuring and grouping.

(1) The extremities, the beginning and end of the Psalter, are occupied by texts 1 and 150. Ps. 1 receives the reader with a blessing:

'Blessed is the man
   who does not walk
      in the counsel of the godless,
   Nor treads in the way of sinners,
      nor sits in the midst of mockers,
   But who delights in the Law of YHWH
      and meditates on his law day and night.' (1,1f.)

The reader of the Psalter is greeted at the outset as a reader of the Law (the *Torah*), and is admonished. This no doubt presupposes that the book in the hand of this reader already belongs to the Holy Writings, which make up the third part of the Hebrew canon, after the 'Law' and the 'Prophets'. The Law is, like the Psalter, a book upon which one 'meditates', reads with murmuring and pondering, 'day and night', a book for devotion and prayer. At any rate, that is the attitude which Ps. 1 requires of the 'righteous'. Thus this Psalm is a preface, an introduction, even an epigraph for what follows. It opens the gate and leads the way in. Its position of prominence was secured by the designs of the compilers and redactors who wished to give the book a suitable opening. The understanding of the collection which is implied here is quite remarkable.

At the other end, Ps. 150 opens a gate in the other direction. Here we find an appeal to the liturgical choir, 'let everything which has breath praise YHWH' (150,6), a call for cosmic praise from every being gifted with the power of speech. For the writer of this Psalm, the Psalter is only a beginning, an introductory exercise in praise for Hebrew tongues. Now, however, the circle widens, and the whole world is exhorted to take up the *Hallelu-Yah*, without need of text and songbook. The Psalter serves the choir of precentors. The universal congregation sings along in its own fashion. Ps. 150 understands the book which it closes as a primer in worship; the way stands open for every conceivable variation in praise. Here, praise is seen as the Alpha and Omega of the collection, a difference in emphasis from the first Psalm. Do different

15

thinkers and different ideas stand behind this ending, which is really more a colon than a full stop? Do they perhaps stand closer to those who entitled the whole book 'Songs of Praise' (*t^ehillîm*)?

The Septuagint, in common with the Psalm scroll 11QPs^a from Qumran, closes the collection with the so-called Autograph of David, a brief biography composed after the battle with the giant Goliath (Ps.151). This post-script ('outwith the count', the redactors observe), takes account of the fact that almost half of the psalms, seventy-three to be precise, appear to claim David as their author, giving him a certain right to be regarded as the real author of the whole collection. This redaction recognises in the Psalter the Song-book of David, and is accommodated by a series of texts (thirteen in all), which focus on the biography of that king.

It will be seen that the balance between beginning and end, between 1 and 150/151, has not quite been struck. There remain discrepancies, nuances betraying different points of view – signs of a many-phased development, the conclusion of which is still recognisable in the choice of the opening and closing psalms.

(2) The division of the finished Psalter into five books probably also belongs to the last phase of development. 'Moses gave Israel the Five Books, and David gave Israel the five books of Psalms.' (*Midraš Tehillim* on Ps.1,1). The analogy with the Five-Scroll-Book (the Pentateuch) and the parallel Moses-David are extremely significant. The aim is to establish or confirm the status of the book as part of the canon of Scripture. The division is certainly not a result of technical considerations, as is the case with the great scrolls of the Pentateuch. The 150 texts could quite comfortably be accommodated on a single scroll, as the parchments from Qumran show. In the printed editions of the Bible where the psalms are not arranged in stichs, Genesis occupies the same

number of pages as the entire Psalter.[11]

The five-fold division makes use of natural caesurae. The first book adopts the closing doxology from the end of the first David-Psalter, Ps. 41,14:

> 'Praise be to YHWH, the God of Israel,
> from everlasting to everlasting! Amen, Amen!'

The close of the second book is announced at the end of the second David-Psalter with the expanded doxology of Ps. 72,18–20:

> 'Praise be to YHWH, the God of Israel,
> who alone does marvellous deeds!
> And praise be to his glorious name for ever,
> may the whole earth be filled with his glory! Amen! Amen!
> This concludes the prayers of David, son of Jesse.'

The third book reaches to the existing, somewhat older caesura at the end of Ps. 89:

> 'Praise be to YHWH for ever! Amen! Amen!'   (v.52)

The fourth book ends with Ps. 106,48:

> 'Praise be to YHWH, the God of Israel,
> from everlasting to everlasting!
> And let all the people say: Amen!'

In this last case, the positioning of the break is not so obvious. Besides, the general similarly to 41,14 points to a secondary formulation. It may be that the five-fold schema made it necessary to place this last division at a point which was rather less appropriate than the others. A break at the end of Ps. 119 would certainly have been more natural.

---

[11] For example, in the *Qoren* Bible, where the arrangement is not in stichs, Genesis and Psalms both occupy 80 pages.

The books which emerge vary considerably in length:

I   1–41   (41 Psalms)
II 42–72   (31 Psalms)
III 73–89   (17 Psalms)
IV 90–106 (17 Psalms)
V   107–150 (44 Psalms)

The exact correspondence between the third and fourth books is striking, as is the similarity between the first and fifth. However, the significance of this structure is restricted to the *Torah*-analogy, and is therefore merely formal.

An attempt has been made to explain the five-book schema in terms of its use in the synagogue lectionary, whereby sections of the Pentateuch were recited along with the corresponding psalms in a three-year cycle.[12] However, there is no clear evidence for this, and the lack of order in the texts speaks against it. I am of the opinion that the five-fold division occurred at a late stage, at positions which already marked natural breaks, making use of doxologies which were part of the growth-rings of the Psalter, and that it has no deeper reason than to maintain the analogy with the Pentateuch.[13] Nevertheless, this structuring is important, as it is built on older patterns of texts. It provides us with clues to the way the various groups of texts and smaller collections have grown together to form the present collection.

(3) The seventy-three psalms associated with David are not distributed at random throughout the Psalter, but rather they are ordered in groups and cycles:

1. 3–41   (33 is an exception in MT; not in LXX.)   37
2. 51–70   (+ 72: a psalm of Solomon) (exceptions 66; 67)   18
3. 108–110 (+ Hallelu-Yah psalms 111–114; 116–118)   3
4. 138–145 (+ Hallelu-Yah psalms 146–149; 150)   8

[12] A. Arens, 'Die Psalmen im Gottesdienst des Alten Bundes', *Trierer Theol. Studien* 11 (2nd ed. 1968).
[13] But see, G. H. Wilson, *The Editing of the Hebrew Psalter*, 1985.

Two David-psalms (101; 103) – four according to Greek tradition (also 91; 104; cf. 11QPs^a) – are to be found in the complex 90–107, which is introduced by a Moses-psalm (90). Also five stray psalms: Pss. 86; 122; (123 11QPs^a); 124; 131; 133. The Davidic collections, that is, the assembled groups of psalms which mention David in their headings, must be regarded not only numerically but also structurally as the basic material of the Psalter.

(4) We may assume that the group Pss. 3–41, numerically the largest group, forms the basis of the whole collection. This part-collection is for the most part made up of texts which are spoken by, or relate to, indivduals. They therefore belong, like all the David-psalms, to the category 'Psalms of the Individual', as opposed to the other, quite distinct group of psalms with collective subjects. Presumably the group 3–41 once formed an independent unit, although we can say little more about this. Various 'Royal Psalms' (e.g. 18; 20; 21), 'Laments of Ill-Health' (e.g. 6; 38; 41), and in particular 'Psalms of the Unjustly Accused', or 'Psalms of the Enemy' (e.g. 3–13), show clear signs of an origin in the Jerusalem Temple. A precise chronology is not possible, but one tends to think of the post-exilic period. A definite interconnection of the texts (3ff.), together with the formation of sub-groups (e.g. 3–5; 18–21; 26–28; 38–41), gives this part-collection its own distinctive character. The doxology at 41,14 marks the gap which opens up after 41. Its origin is uncertain.

(5) The second Davidic Psalter, 51–72, clearly had a more turbulent history. It grew up independently of the first, and apparently existed separately to begin with. This is seen in the duplication of material: 14 = 53; 40,13–17 = 70. The post-script to 72,70, 'Here end the prayers (t^epillôt) of David son of Jesse', brings out two points: firstly, that the group beginning at 51 came to a definite end at 72; and secondly, that the texts gathered here are to be seen as 'prayers', a definition which is

not confirmed in the Greek tradition, but instead is deliberately corrected to ὕμνοι, 'hymns'.

In the course of time, David's Prayer-book came to be combined with two further collections originating among the singers' guilds and the temple choirs. First it was linked with the so-called Asaph-Psalms (74–82, framed by 73 and 83), community psalms of what is presumably the oldest guild, the Asaphites, which is mentioned a number of times in Chronicles. These two groups of texts were combined in such a way that, after an introductory psalm (50), the prayers of David made up the first section and the Asaph-psalms the second.

50	51–72	73–83

The collection of Korah-Psalms, stemming from the singers of the Korahites, was joined to the David and Asaph texts at a later stage of development:

42/43–49	50	51–72	73–83	

The Korah group (44–48, framed by 42/43 and 49), consisting primarily of collective psalms, was subjected along with the amalgamated David/Asaph group to an extensive re-working. In the majority of places, the Tetragrammaton YHWH was replaced fairly mechanically by the term *ᵉlohim*. This so-called elohistic redaction, which can be observed quite clearly by a comparison of the doublets in the Davidic Psalter (in addition to those already mentioned, compare 57,7–11 + 60,5–12 = 108), does not affect the series beginning at 84. This group must be seen as a kind of appendix. Since this appendix contains Korah-Psalms (84; 85; 87; 88 – Heman; 89 – Ethan; the last two being septs of the Korah guild) along with one David-Psalm (86), it would have had an integrating function. It brings the David/Asaph collections into the middle of the Korah collection:

42/43–49	50	51–72	73–83	84 85	86	87	89

It may even be surmised that the linking of this whole complex with the first David Psalter was part of the same process of integration. It does seem that the same hand which added the supplementary material also joined the two collections, 3–41 and 42–89, which by this time had grown to roughly the same size. And this same hand placed Ps. 2 at the beginning. In this way a kind of symmetry would have been created between the opening psalm (2) and the somewhat similar closing psalm (89), with these two Messianic psalms dictating the tone of the whole collection, and connecting beginning and end, so to speak, as the final links in the chain. It is doubtful whether the minority reading in Acts 13.33, which cites a line from Ps. 2 as belonging to the first psalm, has any relevance here. Nevertheless, Ps. 2 has no heading, and a bracket linking 2 with 89 would certainly make good sense.

(6) The construction of 90–150 is less rigid. More and more we encounter texts without headings, though up to a point these can be arranged in groups according to their contexts. Firmer structures appear again after 119 with the so-called 'Psalms of Ascents' (120–134, with hymnic appendix 135f.) and the last major Davidic Psalter (138–145, with hymnic appendix 146ff). Ps. 137 is a rogue psalm caught between these two groups. Here again we may assume a history charac-terised by successive phases of expansion.

(7) The complex 90–119 is far less clearly structured. Since it closes with the 176-line alphabetical poem which is out of all proportion to the rest of the Psalter, it would be reasonable to assume that the complex should be conceived as a supplement to the Davidic Psalter (2–89). We might think of it as an expanded edition, in which the enormous weight of this 'Golden ABC' produced a new centre of gravity. The basic

21

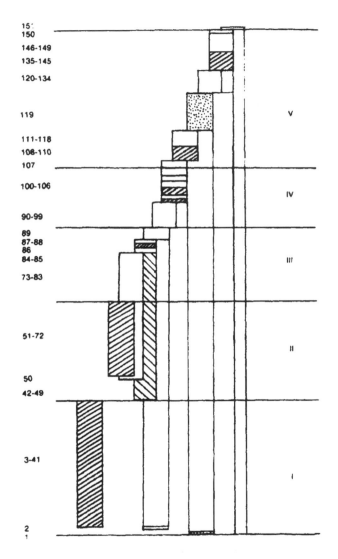

Fig. 4. Growth and structure of the Psalter. Consecutive figures: Pss.1–150(151). I–V: division into books. Rising diagonals: Davidic Psalter. Falling diagonals: Elohistic Psalter.

theme of this anthological poem, which we find in 176 variations, is the Word of God, and in the very first verse those who 'walk in the Law of YHWH' (119,1) are praised. Thus the 'bracket' is now thrown back to Ps. 1, also a wisdom psalm, which places the Torah in the foreground. If 119 is the counterpart to 1, this would explain the incongruity between 1 and 150 which has already been noted. This framework would seek to understand the existing Psalter (1–119) as praise and thanks for the gift of the Law:

> 'May my lips overflow with praise,
>   for you teach me your decrees.' (119,171)

(8) A number of definite groups exist within 90–119:

1. The Royal Hymns of YHWH, once known as Enthronement Songs, which are gathered together without headings, and linked thematically: Pss. 93; (94); 95–99.
2. The hymns connected by Hallelu-Yahs: Pss.(103/104) 105–107.
3. The short series of David-Psalms 108–110 with its associated hymnic appendix: Pss. 111–114; 116–118.

What are left are a number of stray texts which are difficult to fit into the wider structure, like 90, the psalm of Moses; 91 (LXX David); (94); 100; 101 (David); 102; 103 (David); 104; 115 . . . etc. Most of these will have been independent pieces which were accommodated in the last part of the 'Wisdom Psalter' at a fairly late stage.

4. The Purpose of the Collection

Taking an over-view, then, the Psalter is made up of the following parts:

1. the various David-collections, consisting for the most part of texts with a singular subject, so-called 'I-psalms' or 'Psalms of the Individual'. In particular they form the basis of the older forms of the Psalter (2–89; 1–119);

2. the guild collections, mainly texts with a plural subject, so-called 'We-psalms' or 'Psalms of the Community'. In particular they represent a substantial part of the Elohistic Psalter (42–83);

3. various hymnic-liturgical text complexes, consisting of the so-called '*Hallel*' or 'Hallelu-Yah Psalms', some of which are tagged onto the ends of existing groups such as the David-collections, while others make up larger independent units (e.g. 93–99; 111–118). They set the tone of the second half of the Psalter (90–150);

4. the so-called 'Pilgrimage Psalter' or 'Psalms of Ascents' (120–134), similar to the David and Guild collections, and also related to the liturgical texts, yet representing an autonomous part of the whole;

5. a number of independent texts (e.g. 1; 119) which are important because of their position.

If we assume that the Psalter expanded from beginning to end, and that the groupings nearest the beginning are also the oldest, it can easily be seen how the character of the whole collection has changed. If the oldest sections are the most substantial ones, the collections of prayers of David, it would be a mistake to conclude that the meaning and purpose of the compilation was to offer prayers or songs for individual supplicants or worshippers, in order to allow ordinary people to take part in a service of worship using the prescribed formulae. Rather, the character of the various texts as testimonies of faith, the sequence in which some of the individual prayers are placed (e.g. 2ff.), and the attribution of psalms to appropriate situations in the life of David, all suggest that the collections served to focus the mind on the YHWH-faith and rehearse its beliefs through reading and meditating on model texts. The collections are more for teaching than for prayer. They are really 'David's prayers', and are gathered as models or examples for the worshipper.

Some, e.g. the Psalms of Ascents, may have been intended as an aid for pilgrims. Clearly it was not the intention to build a complete collection of David-texts. Were the different groups gathered together at various times or places by particular groups of priests? Is it possible that individual texts or text-documents, somehow thrown together, but not yet written up in continuous columns on scrolls, could have been displayed or distributed separately?

With the addition of the 'choir-books' of the singers' guilds, the picture changed. 'We-Psalms' and choir songs were included. The structure of the Psalter archive received a new emphasis, becoming more like a prayer-book or song-book. At the same time, it must have taken on a more liturgical appearance, as texts were now included which the congregation and the worshipper, hearing them sung or spoken by the choir (and possibly reading along?), would have been able to take up themselves. Yet it is probable that the integration of the song-texts of the guilds marks a thorough-going detachment from the liturgical life of the community. Certainly, the so-called Elohistic Psalter represents a phase where the collection has a documentary-didactic function for the (theological) education of the laity through the texts of prayers and songs. In particular the 'We-Psalms' of the guilds, filled with traditional theology, bring a new element to the growing Psalter. The collection looks more and more like a comprehensive archive, bringing together old and new testimonies to YHWH, and storing them up in a kaleidoscope of faith.

It is difficult to say what might have been the purpose of bringing together the two main collections 3–41 and 42–83. Only in the similarity of proportions and in what are presumed to be the framework psalms, 2 and 89, do we find traces of a tendency to make the material more 'relevant', in the sense that the original text deriving from David or pointing to the anointed king is applied to the individual believer. The legacy of the first temple and its cult, the Zion tradition and the David tradition all gain new influence and importance. Old texts from the royal ritual of the Solomonic temple like 2; 72; 89, come into the limelight and make the Psalter a kind of documentation of the old kingly tradition and of the Zion tradition. In other words, it has become the record of faith of a particular creed, seeking to preserve and restore for each individual the pre-exilic faith in salvation imparted at the sanctuary on Zion. In particular the acknowledgment of the link between salvation and Jerusalem (89), and of the prototype of the God-man, the anointed king (2), must be recognised and taken into consideration. Likewise the idea of the hostile world, an idea which dictates and shapes the image of the enemy in the Psalms of the Individual, gives this religious book more of a tendency towards political topicality:

'Why do the peoples rage,
    and the nations plot in vain?'

This opening verse (2,1) sounds again right at the end (89,50f.):

'Remember, O Lord, how your servant has been mocked,
    how I bear in my breast the scorn of all the nations,
with which your enemies have mocked, O YHWH,
    with which they have mocked the steps of your anointed
    one.'

The didactic trend continues in Ps. 93ff., with the adoption of old, but re-worked cultic texts from the first temple. However, the multifarious nature of these appendices does not allow any reliable conclusion. It is easy to see that the addition of the hymnic-liturgical texts 90–150 brings new emphases to the 'Davidic' Psalter. At the same time, new perspectives provide a certain balance to the Messianic-political demands, and to the all-too strict adherence to the old *Heilsgeschichte* and salvation-experience which characterised the now (semi-)official psalm archives. It almost seems that in the new 'envelope' framework, made up of texts from the Wisdom School (1–119), we can watch as the pendulum swings back. With the new preface (1) and the weight of the reflexive proverbial poem (119), which in terms of its range is effectively a small collection in itself, the existing Psalter now takes on the character of a documentation of divine revelation, to be used in a way analogous to the *Torah*, the first part of the canon, and becomes an instruction manual for the theological study of the divine order of salvation, and for meditation. Is the law-based piety which speaks out of Psalms 1 and 119 intended to embrace and enhance the belief in Messianic salvation, or to abolish and replace it? Certainly, the Widsom Psalter (1–119) seems to have been conceived more for meditative use (1, 2; 119; 147ff.), for private reading, than for liturgical work. Are these signs that the substance of the Psalter, emerging but not yet fully consolidated, was increasingly coming to be regarded as 'Holy Scripture'?

With the final additions (120–150) the centre of gravity of the Psalter archive shifts once again in favour of the hymnic component. Texts of songs and praises outweigh the few prayers of lament from the remaining Davidic collections. Also belonging to this comparatively late phase of the development of the Psalter and of its use – more will be said about this later (IV) – are the musical accents found in the headings of various psalms and psalm-groups (in their new arrangements), which allow the musical performance even of lament texts, quite remote from the liturgy. The conclusion of this phase of expansion is formed by the 'open gate' of Ps. 150, already mentioned, which goes hand in hand with the title of the book, *t^ehillîm* (hymns). The Psalter thus completed, yet proclaimed as incomplete, becomes a musical score of praise,

27

its text now established, destined to be sung for all eternity. As such, it takes its place in the canon. It is likely that its admission to the canon was aided, or even directly caused, by it being declared to be the 'work of David' – a designation preserved in 11QPs^a and LXX. The fully developed Psalter, as a collection of different varieties of testimonies of faith, from various periods and by various people, has the nature of a documentation of the YHWH-faith, and in this respect it is a kind of canon within the canon.

The canonicity of the Psalter, that is, its character as Holy Scripture, seems never to have been disputed. In the Jewish tradition, the book was assigned to the third part of the canon, which in the earliest periods it shaped and coloured. In 2 Macc. 2,13 we find the expression τὰ τοῦ Δ αυίδ (scil. βιβλία) 'the (books) of David', which would have been understood to include the Psalter, mentioned alongside the 'books about kings and prophets'. 1 Macc. 7,16 cites Ps. 79,2f. with the phrase 'according to the words which were written', i.e. cites it as a Word of Scripture, probably the earliest clear evidence (c. 100 BC) of the Psalter as a recognised part of the Holy Scripture. But it is likely that the Greek translation of the book of Ecclesiasticus (Wisdom of ben-Sirach), made in Egypt around 130 BC, which divides the Hebrew canon in three, 'Law', 'Prophets' and 'Other Books of the Fathers', also had in mind the main work of the third section, the Psalter. So by about 100 BC at the latest it had been established that the Psalter, with its 150 or so psalms, was to be reckoned among the Holy Scriptures.

5. On the History of the Text

The history of the Hebrew text of the Psalter unfolded against the same contextual setting which prevailed for the texts of the Hebrew Bible as a whole. Scholarly textual criticism identifies four stages of textual transmission, which are defined roughly as follows:

1. The stage of the composition of the texts, oral or written, in their original form. Literary criticism operates in this stretch of history, using the methods of literary analysis to attempt to reconstruct the original text which in the course of time has often been altered or obscured.

2. The stage of the oldest attested form of the text, that is, the oldest surviving written version. Text criticism in the strict sense strives to identify the oldest surviving forms, by comparing textual variants.

3. The stage of the normative regulation of the consonantal text by Jewish scholars after 70 AD, resulting in the so-called Proto-masoretic Text. Its importance has been impressively demonstrated by comparison with the Qumran texts, some of which are older, and with the Greek tradition. This stage belongs to the field of Historical Jewish Studies.

4. The stage of the Masoretic Text, culminating in the final form of the texts as they appear in the great manuscripts of the Masoretic Schools, particularly that of Tiberias, in the 9th and 10th centuries. These texts, now supplied with punctuation and accentuation, form the basis of the modern printed editions, and are the starting point of scholarly research.[14] Important examples are the *Aleppo Codex* (model copy c. 930 AD) and the *Codex Leningradensis* (c. 1008).

In all, the text experienced four phases of stabilisation, which correspond roughly to these four stages.

In the *first* stage its basic literary structure stabilises, shaped and transmitted by the author and given its first written form. Fed by inspiration and intuition, set down in Old Hebrew or Aramaic characters, a readable text (*textum* = woven fabric) comes into being.

In the *second* phase there occurs a stabilisation of its meaning and use in the eyes of its recipients. After some additional reworking, it is endowed with a definite function, which, being henceforth standard, is widely taken up. The text is copied in Jewish writing, the so-called square script, and is duplicated. It

[14]D. Barthélemy, 'Critique Textuelle de l'AT', *Orbis Biblicus et Orientalis* 50/1 (1982), p.69; 'Histoire du texte hébraique de l'AT', *Orbis Biblicus et Orientalis* 21 (1978), p.350f.

requires a normative text and version. Its 'publication' and public use lend it a certain dignity. By and by there appears a standardised form of the text, usually in the context of an official collection.

In the *third* phase the text is established as Holy Scripture and Word of God, which can only have one form. As one of the foundations of the religious community it requires a canonised text, normalised to the last detail. The result is the established, standardised consonantal text, the *textus receptus*.

In the *last* phase a stable and uniform pronunciation is attempted by the introduction of a system of punctuation. The Masoretic readings consolidate their position. A complicated network of figures and cross-references aim to protect the ideal version from any loss. What results is the Masoretic Text.

With the decline of Hebrew as the vernacular, translations into other languages became necessary. These translations continued to be influenced by developments in the Hebrew text. The Greek translation of the 3rd/2nd century BC, which grew out of the second stage of textual evolution, was from time to time brought into line with the Hebrew version by a series of complicated editing processes. The same applies to the daughter translations into Latin and Syriac, while the Aramaic Targumim seem for the most part not to have come into existence until stage two and three.

Within this history of the development of the Biblical text, however, the text of the Psalms and the Psalter had its own history. A number of developments may be noted here.

1. The fact that each of the psalms was composed in a separate, distinctive process, had the result that their fortunes in the first stage were particularly lively (Chapters II–IV). The individual stories of each, as votive texts, poems, cultic ritual texts, and so forth, made it inevitable from the start that their early phases would run a very complex course, which must have had a significant effect on the condition in which they were preserved. The many phases of transmission and

reworking have left their mark. In the process many texts have been altered, expanded, and corrected, a few damaged and misinterpreted. One need only compare the two versions 14 and 53, which go back to a common original, to appreciate what is possible in this arena. All things considered, given the complicated circumstances of its origins, we must conclude that the text of the Psalter is still in very good condition overall, despite the fact that almost every text has suffered some degree of interference affecting its meaning, and that in some cases the originals can no longer be reconstructed.

2. The Greek translation (3rd/2nd century BC: i.e. 2nd stage of text history) is regarded as one of the worst of its kind because of its slavish adherence to the Hebrew letters. The translators do indeed appear to have taken little trouble over their work. They obviously speak neither good Hebrew nor good Greek, they translate 'literally, and often without being clear themselves what they mean'.[15] Their rate of error is high. Their sins range from a cavalier treatment of the various forms of the Hebrew verb and the functions of the 'waw-consecutive', through ignorance of the meanings of Hebrew words, resulting in the piling up of possible alternative translations in meaningless arrays, to ignorance of the contexts. For example, the words *bny 'lym* in the opening of Ps. 29, have two possible translations: 'sons of God' on the one hand, 'sons of rams' (*'l* = *'yl* = κριός) on the other; but to render them by placing both alternatives side by side is simply absurd. Yet paradoxically, this ugly and inaccurate literalism, which also characterises the many New Testament quotations from the Greek translation, is an excellent tool in the reconstruction of the Hebrew text which the translators had before them. For to date there are no Hebrew manuscripts as early as the 2nd century BC.

[15] F. Delitzsch.

3. Of inestimable help are the fragments discovered in the caves of the Judean desert (1st century BC – 1st century AD), among them the psalm scroll 11QPs^a with canonical and six apocryphal psalms placed in a distinctive order. Unfortunately these finds were not sufficiently well evaluated and utilised in the major edition of the Hebrew Bible (BHS). In these fragments we have before us by far the oldest witnesses to the Hebrew text. They afford us a glimpse of stages two and three; the first stage (the autographs) cannot be documented by textual remains, and is assigned to the disciplines of internal analysis and reconstruction.

4. Particularly influential among the translations, alongside the Aramaic which reflects the view of the Psalms current in the synagogues of the 1st centuries AD, are the translations into Latin, mainly because of the importance which the Psalter came to have in the Latin Church. Typical examples are the three translations completed by Jerome between 383 and 405 AD, which have come to be known as *Psalterium Romanum*, *Psalterium Gallicanum* and *Psalterium juxta Hebraeos*. The first of these was a rushed reworking of the Old Latin Vulgata (Itala) which was current in Rome at the time, under the influence of the contemporary Septuagint tradition. The Gallic Psalter is a new improved edition of the first, influenced by the *Hexapla* of Origen, and his textual work in Palestine. It found wide acceptance in the West, and was ultimately adopted into the Vulgate. The third translation, *juxta Hebraeos*, was neglected, although it was of equivalent standard, no doubt because the *Psalterium Gallicanum* had already become established. This last version, made in Bethlehem around the end of the 4th century AD, is a magnificent translation, which sadly was never given a chance. It rested on the *hebraica veritas*, and therefore was free from errors and weaknesses of the Greek versions which had continued to increase in number and influence.

5. For the Biblical books Psalms, Proverbs and Job (poetic part) the early medieval Masoretes devised a system of accents which differed in various respects from the common prosaic one, probably in order to establish and maintain a standard for musical/rhetorical performance. However, this old metrical modulation is no longer known to us. The system of symbols shows only minor variations (e.g. the precedence of *oleweyored* over *atnach*). F. Delitzsch's verdict holds good: 'For our understanding of the Psalms, a knowledge of the musical values of the accents would solve nothing.'

Chapter II

THE ORIGINS OF THE PSALMS

How did the Psalms come to be written? The history of the Psalter is the history of 150 separate texts. Each text is an individual. Seldom do two or more texts have the same story, and when they do, it is normally only for a short stretch. Even when they share common fortunes in groups and collections, and as part of the canonical writings, this still reflects only one phase in the whole life-history of a psalm. In this our second journey through the garden of the Psalter, we shall deal with questions about the origins of particular psalms. First, we must attempt to gather together the material from which we can glean information about the origins of the psalm texts.

1. *Tradition*

At the first glance it might seem as though, for a good 50 per cent of the psalms, the question of origin is solved by the superscriptions or headings. The opening remarks of these psalms, consisting of various items of data, usually include an intimation which can be construed as a notification of authorship. This intimation, constructed with the so-called *lamed auctoris* (Hebrew *l-* with a personal name), most commonly attested in the form *le Dāwîd*, could mean that the text so headed is attributed to the authorship of the named person. This opinion is re-enforced in the case of a number of David-psalms by precise biographical references which seek to root the text concerned in a particular situation in the eventful life of David, and to explain it on that basis. 'A Psalm of David, when he fled from his son Absalom', reads the heading of Ps. 3. Or: 'A lament of David, which he sang to YHWH because of the Benjaminite Kush' (Ps. 7); 'Of David,

34

when he feigned insanity before Abimilech, who drove him away, and he left' (Ps. 34); 'A song of David, when he was in the cave' (Ps. 142). These biographical references are particularly conspicuous in the second David-Psalter (51–72, eight occurrences): 'A Psalm of David, when Nathan the prophet came to him, after he had gone in to Bath-sheba' (Ps. 51); 'A song of David, when Doeg the Edomite went and reported to Saul, and told him "David has gone to the house of Ahimelech"' (Ps. 52); 'A song of David, when the Ziphites went to Saul and said "Is not David hiding among us?"' (Ps. 54); 'Of David, when the Philistines seized him in Gath' (Ps. 56); 'Of David, when he fled from Saul into the cave' (Ps. 57); 'Of David, when Saul had sent men to watch his house, in order to kill him' (Ps. 59); 'Of David, when he fought Aram Naharaim and Aram Zobah, and when Joab returned and struck down the Edomites in the Valley of Salt, 12000 of them' (Ps. 60); 'A psalm of David, when he was in the Judean desert' (Ps. 63). And finally Ps. 18, which stands alongside 60 as the longest of such biographical descriptions: 'Of David, the servant of YHWH, who sang the words of this song to YHWH on the day YHWH delivered him from the hand of all his enemies, and from the hand of Saul; he said . . .' (Ps. 18). This corresponds almost exactly to the wording of the introduction to the same Psalm in 2 Sam. 22, and this fact gives us a hint of how we might understand these introductory notes.

Right away we notice that the biographical references can easily be identified with passages in the two Books of Samuel, be it that they agree directly with the text found there, or that they encompass the same complex of tradition. Furthermore, they appear to be specifically intended to call attention to the Biblical passage, either to remind the reader of a familiar situation, or to encourage him to read the complete biography found there. One also has the impression that the author of these notes seeks to display his Bible knowledge through all kinds of extraneous details. Be that as it may, the notes certainly presuppose a knowledge of the David traditions of the Books of Samuel, and thus they betray their real purpose, to provide the reader with a setting for the psalm in question, and thus to historicise it. Whether or not the idea of Davidic authorship is in fact correct, it is quite clear that the headings themselves are not from his hand; the form of words displays this quite bluntly. Their various extensions to the proposed name 'David', ('when . . . , when he . . .'), reveal them to have been late scribal supplements, concentrated in the second David-Psalter, which are connected in some way with the (auto-)biographisation of the Psalter, a process which is also reflected in the addition of Psalm 151 (Greek and 11QPs²). In the same context belongs the catalogue of writings given in 11QPs² along with the 'last words of David' from 2 Sam. 23:

'And David the son of Jesse was wise and glowed like the light of the sun, an author,/ and he was intelligent, and irreproachable before God and before mankind in all his ways. And/ YHWH gave him a sharp and clear mind. And he wrote/ 3600[1] Hymns (*thlym*), and also songs (*šyr*) to be sung before the altar at the daily *Tamid*/ sacrifice,[2] for all the days of the year, 364/, for the sacrifices on the Sabbaths, 52 songs, for the sacrifices on the first days of the month/ and for all the festivals and for the day of atonement, 30 songs:/ altogether the songs which he composed came to 446, plus four songs to be played on percussion and stringed instruments.[3] The complete total comes to 4050[4]/ All of these he composed in a prophetic spirit, as it was given to him by the Most High.' (Col. XXVII 2–11)[5]

---

[1] No doubt a symbolic number.

[2] Cf. 2 Chr. 29,25ff.

[3] Inferred from 2 Chr. 29,25ff. (*kly Dwyd* 'David's instruments'), and from the root meanings of *pg*' 'to strike' and *ngn* (*Piel*) 'to pluck strings', 'to make music'.

[4] The Biblical tradition associates seventy-three Psalms with David.

[5] 11QPs².

However, it is by no means established that the formula *l^eDāwîd* was originally intended as an indication of authorship, even if in the course of the development of the Psalter it came to be understood as such. The parallel formula *l^e* with the term 'the Korahites' (plural) (e.g. Pss. 42; 44ff.) seems to have less to do with authorship than with ownership, the property of the singers' guild of that name. Since the formula *l^e'Āsāp* (singular) (50; 73ff.) appears to say the same for the singers' guild of the Asaphites, it would not be unreasonable to assume the same for the *l^eDāwîd*-psalms. Is it not possible that there was a similar, perhaps a larger and dominant group of choral singers at the Jerusalem temple, which, inspired by the picture of David in the Chronicles, saw themselves as his spiritual descendants. Seen in this way, it seems more reasonable to understand the *l^eDāwîd* as being originally an indication and a claim of property. As with the many occurrences of *lmlk* '(belonging) to the king', marked on the handles of jars and pitchers as an ascription of ownership, or the countless inscriptions on seals from Canaan and Israel in which *l^e* is connected with the name of the person the seal belongs to, so it is also in the case of the Psalms.[6] The comment corresponds to a wax seal or stamp with which property rights or guarantees were set down and given force of law. During copying, the 'stamp' would then be included in the heading, and later interpreted biographically in the process of 'Davidisation'.

That, contrary to the later tradition, David, and also Moses (90) and Solomon (72; 127), can hardly even be considered as possible authors of the psalms preserved in the Psalter, has been demonstrated increasingly clearly as exegesis has developed. At the most, it would be possible to speak of traces or fragments. There is not a single psalm which can with any

---

[6] Cf. K. Galling in: *Religion in Geschichte und Gegenwart*, vol. V, col. 690.

probability be said to stem from David. Too many linguistic, cultural and theological difficulties stand in the way. Even if the so-called Lament of the Bow (2 Sam. 1,17ff.) could be proven to be by David, the gulf between this poem and the Psalms shows that a common origin is out of the question. Only with the personalisation of the originally anonymous Holy Scriptures and the distribution of the text-complexes under the names of great authors, Moses, David, Solomon, and the prophets, Ezra, etc., did the Psalms too come to be given an 'author', a simplification which may have had dogmatic advantages, but which in the long run has been at the cost of historical plausibility, and has led to ideological entrenchment.

Rather more reliable than the ambiguous dedicatory formulae are some of the other details passed on in the headings concerning the origins and use of the psalms. The terms by which the psalms are classified, and instructions for their performance will be discussed later (Chapters IV; V). In this present context, however, a number of details are significant. First of all, the unique heading to Ps. 102, which declares the text to be a 'prayer' ($t^e pill\hat{a}$) 'for the afflicted, when he is disheartened, and pours out his complaint before YHWH'. Here we discover something about the use of a psalm as a liturgical formula for a particular type of case, as a 'set-piece' prayer text. There is only the one example of this, but we shall not go far wrong if we extend the remark, applying it to other, if not all, prayers of complaint (lament). It may be mentioned in passing that the word 'complaint' ($si^a h$) refers here to quiet, whispered prayer as opposed to words of reproach cried aloud – a prayer for Hannah, so to speak (cf. 1 Sam. 1,1f.; 1,9ff. note especially 1,13).

Next, the opening line which occurs particularly frequently in the last part of the Psalter, the cry $hall^e l\hat{u}$-$Y\bar{a}h$ ('Praise YH') also seems to have taken on the function of a heading (and a post-script), and thus to have made the texts available for general use in the congregation. Here again we are speaking of liturgical use. However, this does not necessarily tell us anything about origins.

Finally, it is worth considering the details given concerning the origin of two psalms transmitted outwith the Psalter. 'A writing (Heb. *miktāb*, also 'inscription') of Hezekiah, king of Judah, when he had been sick, and recovered from his sickness', reads the introduction to the so-called Psalm of Hezekiah (Isa. 38,9–20). This text is explicitly addressed as an inscription or document of the king. Unfortunately this detail can no more be verified than the introduction to the so-called Psalm of Habakkuk (Hab. 3,1–19): 'A prayer (*tᵉpillâ lᵉ*) of/for the prophet Habakkuk'.

2. *Internal Evidence*

What do the psalms themselves say about their origins? In attempting to answer this question, we shall investigate a number of clues which appear here and there.

1. In Ps. 40 a psalmist tells of a miraculous rescue which he has experienced in answer to prayer, and which he now wishes to proclaim in a psalm:

> 'I waited patiently for YHWH
>   and he turned to me and heard my cry.
> He drew me up out of the pit of desolation,
>   out of the deep mire.
> He set my feet on a rock,
>   and gave me a firm foothold.
> He put a new song in my mouth,
>   a praise-song to our God.
> Many will see, and will hear,
>   and will put their trust in YHWH.' (40,1–3)

For the 'new song', the psalmist may thank this great event. The 'many' hearers may thank the singer. A new psalm has come into being. It is a praise-song, a hymn, a $t^e hill\hat{a}$ 'to our God'. The singer hopes with his new song to bring the congregation from listening to seeing, from seeing to being astounded, and from astonishment to trust; this is brought out in his play on words, see – fear, in Hebrew $y'rw$ – $yy'rw$ (cf. German: *schauen* – *erschauern*). This was probably very effective. But has the 'new song' survived? There is much to be said for the idea that it is the text which we find preserved in the lines which follow (40,5ff.), which begin:

> 'Many, O YHWH my God,
>> are the wonders you have worked,
>> and the things you have planned for us;
> No-one can compare with you!'

It seems as though in the next lines the Psalmist comes back again to the background of the psalm. He lets us into his thoughts. Actually, he had wanted to bring gifts and sacrifices as thanks for his escape to the sanctuary. However, it became clear to him that no burnt offering or sin offering was required of him. He therefore decided to make an offering of a song of praise and thanks. At this point the text of the psalm is a little obscure. Apparently it relates what the psalmist 'then' thought, and at the same time, what he 'now' wishes to say to the community. Perhaps it is easier to follow this if we rearrange the verses in chronological order:

> 7aα 'Then I said (thought):
> 8   I desire to do your will, my God,
>> and your law is within my heart.
>
> 7aβ Look, I have come!
> 7b In the scroll
>> it is written about me:
> 9   I proclaim righteousness
>> in the great assembly . . .'

In particular, the line about the scroll is important in our context. It is unlikely that the scroll is to be identified or connected with the 'Law of God' (*torah*). This 'Law' is probably concerned with the orderly conduct of sacrifices at the sanctuary, perhaps as it has been preserved in the priestly writings in Leviticus. The psalmist knows this Law back to front. He wants to meet its demands at all costs. And yet he chooses the alternative – unlike the psalmist of 66,13–15 – and instead of animals for the burnt offering he brings a scroll written about himself, in order to proclaim salvation[7] in the assembly: sermon instead of sacrifice, psalm of praise in place of cultic animal offering.

Has this 'scroll' been preserved? Presumably, yes. It must have contained the hymn composed for the congregation, the 'new song' that the psalmist wished to present. We may therefore assume that the opening 40,1–4 was either included in the scroll as a kind of preface, or was added later to replace the spoken words of introduction. For indeed there is quite a bit 'written' about the psalmist here.

The problem with Ps. 40 is that it contains in its last section (11–17) a prayer of supplication which fits particularly badly with the praise and thanksgiving context of the opening, but which would have fitted quite well in the earlier unhappy circumstances from which the psalmist has been saved. We may therefore suppose that the prayer too has been recorded on the scroll as a testimony to God's response, and as a description of the background to the act of salvation; and again this is 'written about' the psalmist himself.

At any rate, it is a safe assumption[8] that the scroll mentioned in 40,7 contained parts of Ps. 40 (introduction, praise-song, prayer) perhaps even the text as a whole, which in this way took on its present form and so has been preserved. Since such a hymn or prayer (or combination of

[7] The Greek translation has εὐαγγελίζειν.
[8] Cf. G. Bornkamm, 'Lobpreis, Bekenntnis und Opfer', in: *Festschrift E. Haenchen*, 1964, pp. 46–63.

the two), being contained in the eighteen verses of Ps. 40, must have been fairly short, the scroll-book (*sēper*) could only have been a small scroll consisting of a single sheet of papyrus or parchment, which would usually have had space for about three columns. We may think of the letter-scrolls and legal documents which were found in Egyptian Elephantine, stemming from the 5th century BC. At any rate we are not thinking of the large scrolls (books) made up of many leaves sown together, like the scroll-book on which Baruch wrote down the words of the prophet Jeremiah (Jer. 36).

We conclude:

(i) There was a liturgical-devotional collection of votive texts which served to make individual experiences available for the edification of the whole community. Instead of offering up the usual sacrifices one could produce a personal testimony in the form of a scroll, and give the composition together with a note of its contextual background as documentation of the experience of deliverance, apparently as a substitute for the sacrifice.[9]

(ii) This votive practice was like a collecting bowl which resulted in the rise of 'new songs' and hymns which were gathered together at the place of performance and stored up.

(iii) Since the petition for help in time of crisis was the best documentation of the experience of prayer being answered, it seems to have become the custom to present this along with the 'new song'. This makes some of the many lament-praise combinations more easily understandable (e.g. Pss. 22; 30; 41; 69; etc.), and it also helps explain why prayers spoken in lonely times of need were recorded and passed down. To write them down was to testify that they had been answered.

(iv) Quite a considerable number of the 'I' psalms, whose writers are reporting their own experiences, and also of the hymns, which seek to place such experiences within the sphere of theological reflection, may have arisen in this way. In particular we may think of the many individual and 'bio-

[9] Cf. the worshippers offering their scroll in the bottom corner of Fig. 39.

graphical' testimonies which have been preserved in the David-psalters. Compare in this light Pss. 3; 4; 5; 6; 7; 8; etc.

2. We now follow another line of enquiry, and take as our example the so-called alphabetical psalms, that is, those poems which have a textual structure and sequence of verses based on the *Aleph-Beth*; in the Psalter we are speaking of 9–10; 25; 34; 37; 111; 112; 119; 145. How were these texts written?

It must be assumed that such texts were composed at the writing table. There hardly seems to be any other possbility than to imagine that the author began by setting down on paper the letters of the alphabet, that is, the twenty-two consonants from *Aleph* to *Taw*, in a vertical line. We shall ignore the various irregularities which arise, like missing verses or variations in the sequence, as these are no doubt the results of later interference. Thus far, the process is rather mechanical and formal, and seems to stem from the literacy exercises of the school, where the pupils would write out the *Aleph-Beth* and memorise the sequence of the letters. Next the writer is set, or sets himself, the less mechanical, more demanding task of forming lines and composing verses, using the consonants as the opening letters. Usually he contents himself with one line or verse (as in 25; 34; 111; 112 – short verses; 145), sometimes he leaves himself more room for non-acrostic statements (as with 9–10; 37). The writer of 119 (the Golden ABC) set himself the record-breaking task of writing eight lines beginning with each consonant, giving a total of 176 lines (Fig. 5).

Despite the constraints of the schema, the writer still has enough leeway to let his poetry unfold. Although the opening is predetermined, he can shape the rhythm of the individual verse freely, and there can be no doubt that the strength of these projects lies in the independent single verse. However, the writer can also attempt, in spite of the fixed openings which restrict the development of the poem, to express an

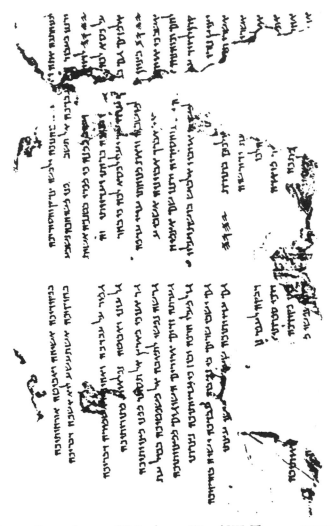

Fig. 5. Ps.119 from 11QPs^a columns VI and VII. The arrangement of the lines makes the alphabetical structure easily recognisable. Column VI contains six lines beginning with *Aleph*, column VII starts with two *Beth*-lines followed by eight *Gimel*-lines and two *Daleth*-lines. Interestingly, Ps.119 is followed by Ps.132 (cf. chaps I.3; V.5).

objective train of thought, and at least to hint at a progression in content from one verse to the next. In general, such lexically arranged sequences of verses seem to make more sense as anthologies and reference collections of proverbs than as the living language of prayer and preaching. Thus, for example, Ps. 119 consists of 176 variations on one and the same theme, namely 'the Word of God'. Seen in this way, it is a Word-of-God theology in proverbial form, arranged alphabetically, comparable with our theological dictionaries and encyclopaedias of technical terms. The rather unimaginative repetition within the groups of eight might support this idea, as in the case of *Teth* or *Daleth* – no less than five occurrences of *derek* (way) – or the piling up of prepositions under *Beth* or *Lamedh*. Yet the verses themselves show that at least in their internal structure they can be called artistic.

The purpose of this kind of poetry has, as far as I can see, not yet been satisfactorily explained. There are no clear examples in the Psalms of the phenomenon known from Accadian hymns and prayers, whereby the opening characters of the lines or strophes, read in sequence, produce a sentence or a name, let alone anything to compare with the almost unique artistic achievement of a double prayer to Marduk and Nabu, in which the first characters of the lines, read from top to bottom, yield the name and occupation of the author (twice), and the last characters give two different dedications (Chapter IX 2.5).

At any rate, such parallels should warn us to concentrate on the schematic, intellectually entertaining side of these poems, and not to attribute too serious a purpose to them. And yet these texts can function as prayers or hymns, despite the artificiality of their construction.

We conclude:

(i) Psalms can be produced at a writing-desk for the amusement of the writer. It is unlikely that the alphabetical psalms are intended as memory aids. Is it really conceivable that such chains of proverbs were ever intended to be committed to memory? Yet the models for such collections of proverbs are likewise rooted in the school.

(ii) It is very possible that non-acrostic psalms may also have been artfully constructed, formed according to self-appointed rules; free productions, subject only to the norms of their poetic form. However, the range of such texts in the Psalter is not great.

3. The opening verse of the forty-fifth psalm takes our enquiry in a new direction. The writer of this psalm, occasioned by the wedding of the king to a foreign princess, begins with a dedication:

'My heart is stirred by good tidings;
  I sing my song to the king,
    my tongue is (like) the pen of a skilful writer!'

The first point of importance is that he calls the psalm 'his work' (here translated 'song'; the plural in the Hebrew text may be the result of an error in pointing). This word is used of every other kind of craftsmanship, be it baking (Gen. 40,17), metal-work (2 Chr. 3,10) or any kind of art-work. The psalm is the work of a 'writer' and singer. Its existence is due to the art of the 'skilful writer'. The poem is presented to the king. The author calls it 'speaking' (here translated by 'sing'), but he surely means the skilled performance of the rhythmic *Sprechgesang*, or speech-song. He is moved emotionally by the experience. And so the lyrics flow, as though by themselves.

The psalm is an occasional poem by a writer and singer of the royal court. It was composed as a work of art, and it is as a work of art that it is to be read and heard. Such art is very close to Wisdom, the culture of speech and thought practised in the courts, which maintained and propagated all the knowledge required for a good education. This psalm, then, has its origins in the king's court, like quite a number of the texts, songs and prayers which collectively are known as Royal Psalms (e.g. Pss.2; 18; 20; 21; 72; 89; 110; 132). A similar background must be assumed for these, although they are more heavily cultic, with a stronger theological orientation than the thoroughly secular wedding psalm. The addressing of the king as 'God' (45,6) reflects the untheological court language of the poem. This psalm has grown up out of the Wisdom tradition, and so comes close to the texts which we call Wisdom Psalms, which include both the alphabetical poems and the problem poems (1; 49; 73; 104; 139). However, it can be demonstrated that the Wisdom Psalms in general, unlike Ps.45, cannot be regarded as pre-exilic. It is of interest in this connection that in the opening of one of these problem poems, namely Ps.49, the writer also speaks briefly about the circumstances behind the composition of his text. He calls his poem a *māšāl*, strictly 'proverb' or 'aphorism', but also 'proverbial poem' or 'solution to a riddle', and with riddles (v.4) the Wisdom genre is brought back into play. We read:

> 'Hear this, all you peoples,
>   listen, all inhabitants of the world
> both low and high,
>   rich and poor alike!
> My mouth will speak words of wisdom,
>   the meditation of my heart will be understanding.
> Incline your ear to the proverb   (emended text)
>   to the music of the lyre I shall solve my riddle.'   (49,1-4)

We conclude that there are in the psalter works of poetic art, composed by writers and singers who wished to be regarded and understood as artists.

4. The quotation from Ps. 49 throws up our last clue, which points to yet another mode of composition. Ps. 78, a long didactic poem – the heading *maśkîl*, 'Wisdom Song', agrees with the contents – is introduced with the words:

'Oh my people, hear my instruction;
    open your ears to the words of my mouth.
I will open my mouth in proverbs,
    and proclaim riddles from of old,
things we have heard and known,
    which our fathers told us . . .' (78,1–3)

There follows a presentation of the history of Israel from which the writer draws his lessons. The Wisdom terms 'proverb', 'riddle' appear again here. But these are made subject to the more general term, 'instruction' (Heb. *tôrâ*). The *Torah*, after all, was first and foremost the priestly instruction and training of the laity in religious questions (cf. Hag. 2), before it acquired a further, expanded sense, becoming a blanket term for the 'Law' as a legal corpus, and finally being extended to cover the whole first section of the canon. In 78,1 this last stage has not been reached. Rather, the word seems to be nearer to its original sense, meaning the instruction given by the scholar of the historical traditions ('which our fathers told us') and the theological teacher of the people ('things we have heard and known'). Poetic art and pedagogical intent come together in this poem, the former being discernible in the strongly proverbial form in which the verses are cloaked, the latter in the narrative style, and the subtle repetition of the moral of the story from section to section. Here speaks the teacher and preacher, admittedly in a set form of speech, but clearly with an admonishing/instructing intention. This teaching was probably spoken rather than sung. It takes its starting point from the records of salvation-history, gathered together in the 'history books' (as the Greek canon calls this part of Scripture), which at that time were probably only accessible to a few experts. It probably goes back to some inspiring event, which is not named, but which will have been similar to those which inspired the great Historical Psalms (eg. 44; 74; 79; 89; 105; 106; 132), at any rate an event giving cause for reflection on history and its lessons for the present.

We conclude and take note that long, didactic, historical texts and moralistic poetry in the style of the sermon have also found their way into the Psalter. In this respect these historical-theological psalms stand together with the theological encyclopedia of the Word-of-God theme in Ps. 119. Both types of poetry owe a great debt to the tradition of theological teaching.

3. Traces of Reworking

There are psalms which come to us straight from the mould. Their texts appear to have been preserved as their writers conceived them. No signs of reworking are to be seen, and no clues to their history either. However, there are also psalms which are not uniform in appearance, which disintegrate in places, and in which the various elements betray the complicated history of their construction. In cases of such complexity it is possible to discover more of their development than in the simpler forms. We shall single out a number of texts as models, in order to see which possibilities we have to take into account.

1. *Ps. 22.* The large text-complex of this psalm, with its thirty-one numbered verses, breaks down on closer inspection into its 'natural' sections. The first is a prayer of lament beginning with the words quoted by Jesus in the Passion Story, 'My God, my God, why have you forsaken me?', and coming to an end in v. 21, despite its moving plaintive tone in

well ordered lines and in clearly defined trains of thought. With v. 22, 'I will declare your name to my brothers', a new section obviously begins, which consists of a song of praise, and which apparently has been conceived so to speak as a prayer of thanksgiving for deliverance, when prayers of supplication have been answered. This section of praise does not reach to the end of the Psalm, but only to the *sursum corda* directed at the 'great assembly' (v. 25): 'May your hearts live forever!' (v.26). This is shown by the completely different style of the last section (vv. 27–31), which is a reflection on the meaning of the experience of salvation for the future of the whole world ('For dominion belongs to YHWH, and he rules over the nations', v. 28).

It is probable that the sequence of these sections ABC represents the chronological arrangement of events. Since the psalm progresses from lament to praise to theological reflection, we must assume that the events which altered its direction occurred between the sections. Whatever these occurrences actually were, whether a word of comfort through the priest (an oracle of salvation), or a development in the author's spiritual awareness (a change in morale), or an actual improvement in the situation, at any rate there must have been some lapse of time involved, and so it follows that the three sections of this Psalm must have been spaced chronologically.

If the psalmist is speaking from his own experience, this would mean that the psalm text first arose as two psalms which were joined together as a single unit against the background of the events experienced. A hint of this join can be seen in the last words of the lament (v. 21) where the Hebrew text contains a phrase which is often ignored: 'You have heard me' (*ᵃnîtānî*). If we may see this statement as a confirmation of the psalmist's answered prayer, perhaps even as a post-script placed under the prayer of lament, then we have in this case a written expression of the intervening event, and evidence that Ps. 22 arose in successive stages, parallel to the experience recorded. This picture of spasmodic growth is not altered significantly if we assume that the final, theological section comes from another hand, and represents an expansion of the psalm complex already hinged at v. 21.

2. *Ps. 19*. This psalm is composed of three parts. A hymn which sings of the glory of God (*kᵉbôd-'ēl*) being proclaimed by the skies and by the sun (vv. 1–6) is followed unexpectedly by a text of a different sort, containing a series of theses on the nature of the Word of God (7–10), to which is attached a more personal conclusion in the manner of a testimony (11–13). Finally, a supplementary verse seems to have been added (14), which appears to have been written by someone who used this psalm in prayer. The thematic unity of this psalm is obvious: it is a patch-work of the various forms of God's revelation, as it is proclaimed in the Heavens, as statutes and precepts, and as a liberating message to the individual. But equally obvious is the literary diversity of the text complex: it is a compilation of a hymn of creation, a series of theological formulae, and a personal prayer (with addendum). Surely the only possible conclusion is that we are dealing here with a textual entity made up of component parts (1–6; 7–10) each of which had its own separate life before they were brought together and provided with a closing prayer (11–13 + 14). At any rate, we will certainly have to reckon with some process of reworking which produced this very complicated psalm text.

3. *Ps. 50*. The text of this psalm is punctuated by the repeated announcement of divine speech. Verse 1 opens with: 'The God of Gods, YHWH, speaks...' This relates to vv. 1–6, which speak of God's coming, and tell how both Heaven and Earth are called to bear witness (esp. v. 5). In v. 7, God begins to speak to his people and to testify against them: 'I am God, your God' (a stray phrase from v. 21b may belong

here: 'I will rebuke you and accuse you to your face').
Curiously, this consists of instructions to bring better and
more fitting offerings of thanks in the form of songs and
prayers instead of animal sacrifices, although according to v. 8,
these do not deserve rebuke or condemnation in themselves.
Verse 16 marks the beginning of another speech of God to the
'wicked' ('But to the wicked God says . . .'), which contains
strong warnings about misdemeanours from which there is no
salvation, because God's Law and God's covenant are being
broken (v. 16b). Verse 23 closes with a promise for those who
make 'sacrifices' of praise.

The balance of this text seems to have been upset, probably
because two forms of speech have been thrown together: the
legal language of accusation, and the language of instruction
and teaching. The former is obviously an old liturgical form
(traditionally called *ríbh*), which brings the people's broken
covenant under God's judgment. The latter is an instruction
and a warning to the individual supplicant and visitor to the
temple to bring offerings of praise instead of animal sacrifices,
for theological reasons, because these bring more honour to
God. The two are connected only in so far as animal sacrifice
in fulfilment of a vow could be misunderstood and misused as
an expiatory sacrifice for the removal of sin, an idea which is
now condemned by the psalm (v. 23). The reference to the
impotence of atonement rites (v. 9?) seems to have been used
as an argument against the fulfilment of vows in the form of
animal sacrifices.

A basic text emerges which should be thought of as an old
liturgical formula, breaking down into the following sections:

vv. 1–6:	accusation
vv. 7(+ 21b)–13 (14–16a addition):	rejection of atonement methods
vv. 16b–22 (without 23):	ultimatum to the whole covenant people

THE ORIGINS OF THE PSALMS

In this way, the witness of Heaven and Earth (v. 4) makes sense.

Stages of reworking become visible, particularly if we assume that the basic text, like the texts of other Asaph-Psalms, is part of the heritage of the former northern Israelite sanctuaries.

4. *Ps. 133*. This short text from the Pilgrimage Psalter consists of an aphorism from the Wisdom tradition about the harmony of brothers and fellows (v. 1), which is underlined by two similies ('like precious oil', v. 2; 'like the dew of Hermon', v. 3). In my opinion, the original maxim was later expanded for use in worship, as part of a general reworking of the song-book. With this reorientation came the two additions to the text which remember the beneficence of the Aaronic blessing in the temple cult. These additions destroy the image of the consecrated oil by linking it with the 'beard of Aaron', that is, of the high priest who gave the blessing, and the image of the dew of Hermon by reading the name of a town near Hermon, *'Iyyôn*(?), as Ṣiyyôn, where YHWH bestows his blessing of 'life for evermore' (v. 3). We must allow for a freer handling of the received texts which led to mismatched forms like this.

5. *Ps. 108*. Ps. 108 is the most obvious example in the Psalter of the secondary construction of a psalm text. Ps. 108 consists, as is well known, of two parts both of which are found elsewhere in the Psalter; Ps. 57,7–11 (= vv. 1–5) and Ps. 60,5–12 (= vv. 6–13). The two parts are fragments from independent texts. Ps. 57,7–11 is the second part of a prayer text structured with a refrain (vv. 5;11). Ps. 60,5–12 is the second part of a text complex, already a compound of various elements, which has at its core (vv. 6–10) a divine utterance from the pre-exilic period: 'God has spoken from his sanctuary'. This core with its surrounding framework was placed on the end of Ps. 108, leaving a gaping hole between the

two borrowed parts, between verses 5 and 6. Here we have an example of secondary, and even of tertiary work, since the restructuring makes free use of texts which were already compilations.

6. *Ps. 136.* Here we have a good example of the growth of a psalm, visible in the 'growth rings' which surround the solid inner text. It opens with the hymnic liturgy of vv. 1–7 + 25–26, a song of praise to the creator, the provider of daily bread (v. 25). The first and last sections correspond: the song opens and closes with 'Give thanks . . .' (vv. 1–3; 26). The references to the *Heilsgeschichte* in vv. 10; 13; 16–17; 21–22 which take us from the Exodus from Egypt to the gift of the promised land, form the first extension. These verses continue the verse-schema of the hymnic style (*lᵉ* + Participle). The second extension may be the result of a scribal reworking which sought to elucidate the hymn by means of additions in narrative prose. These are scattered throughout the existing form: vv. 8–9 (following Gen. 1); vv. 11–12; 14–15 (following Exod. 14); vv. 18–20 (following Num. 21); vv. 23–24. In this last pair of verses, we find the contemporary reason for this second phase of expansion, namely, the desire to express in words a new experience of salvation, and to place it within the context of the whole course of the *Heilsgeschichte*:

> 'The one who remembered us in our low estate,
> and freed us from our enemies . . .'

7. *Ps. 29.* The analysis of this difficult text has not yet reached a definite and final conclusion, but it does appear that a basic text has been subjected to a thorough reworking. One question still under discussion is whether the basic text itself is a modified version of a pre-Israelite or non-Israelite hymn-text. For the basic text we are looking at vv. 1 (without the heading); 3a; 4; 5a; 7; 8a; 9a; 10; 11a (conclusion). In translation, this would read:

'Ascribe to YHWH, you heavenly ones,
  ascribe to YHWH glory and strength!
  Listen, YHWH over the waters!
  Listen, YHWH with power!
  Listen, YHWH with majesty!
  Listen, YHWH breaks the cedars!
  Listen, YHWH strikes with lightning!
  Listen, YHWH shakes the desert!
  Listen, YHWH twists the oaks!
YHWH, enthroned over the flood,
  YHWH, king for ever!
    YHWH give strength to his people!'

The major alterations which now occur produce new
theological emphases. The old litany of the 'seven-thunder
Psalm' (seven times 'Listen', 'Hark', corresponding to seven
blasts of thunder) is interpreted as a didactic poem about the
'voice of YHWH' (Heb. *qôl* can be both an imperative,
'listen', and a noun, 'voice' or 'sound'), in which he reveals
himself powerfully in his theophany of thunder (cf.
1 Kings 19) and proves himself king of the world. Marginal
notes report the occurrence of such a storm in the mountains
of Lebanon ('The God of glory thunders', v. 3), and give the
text a liturgical frame-work ('Worship YHWH in holy
splendour', v. 2; 'In his temple all cry "Glory"', v. 9) and a
cultic meaning ('YHWH blesses his people with peace', v. 11).
The pre-history and history of this psalm is certainly
remarkable, particularly when we think that parts of it were
borrowed into Ps. 96, and in this way found their way into the
liturgy of 1 Chr. 16; and when we remember that Rev. 10,3ff.
speaks of the revelation of the 'seven thunders'.

The fortunes of this text and the others discussed in this
chapter show what possibilities we may have to deal with
when we ask about the origins of the psalms. We must assume
that the majority of the poems presented in the Psalter have a
long road behind them, and have come to be what they are

55

only after various phases of development. The psalm which was able to preserve the form which it received from the hand of its author seems to be the exception among the multitude of texts which went through many hands, and show clear traces of reworking.

4. Concluding Remarks

A number of concluding remarks are required to complete this chapter.

1. The problem of the authorship and origins of texts which, after a long period of development, were finally considered worthy to be taken into the canon of Holy Scripture, raises at the same time the question of their source. So far we have treated these texts as we would any other great works of literature. As monuments of Hebrew poetry, the psalms are literary products of a particular period, created and preserved by particular people. The question of inspiration, that is to say, non-human origin and superhuman influence, is certainly less urgent in the case of the Psalms, being songs, prayers and poems, than it is in other parts of the Holy Writings. Nevertheless, it requires to be mentioned in this context.

Certainly the 'classical' model of inspiration, a simple dictation by the Holy Spirit, together with the instrumental imagery of pencil and mouthpiece, can hardly be considered, or at least not without significant qualification. Psalmists writing according to words with the same first letters or other unpoetic methods can hardly be calling on higher inspiration, any more than the writers of the drastic tirades of curses and hate found in some of the psalms written against enemies. On the other hand, a higher level of authority may be assumed for texts explicitly presented as oracles and utterances of God, such as Ps. 50,7–21; 60,6–8; 91,14–16, and here it is possible to speak of prophetic inspiration and the 'counsel of the Lord'.

At this point, however, another model of inspiration emerges, which L. Alonso Schökel has called 'the model of literary creation',[10] which does justice to the needs of this situation. This model has the advantage that it rests on the idea of linguistic innovation in poetry, always the best analogy for inspired speech. More importantly, it has the advantage that the event of inspiration – which, after all, would presumably defy human categories and images anyway – does not need to be tied down and localised, or even personalised. Anyone who has ever spoken a prayer, composed a song or written a poem will realise that in this process of creation there is room enough for influence and inspiration coming not from within, but from over and above the individual. It will be obvious that this concept of inspiration can be far more difficult to define and to document than the model of authorship by the great authorities (David, Moses). However, it is equally clear that even in the case of a work of great craftsmanship like Ps. 119, or of work of a low literary standard, inspiration need not and may not be denied. The wind blows where it will. The results of human linguisitic effort in no way exclude the impulse or influence of the Spirit. Even a poorly structured poem or a damaged prayer can hold a priceless content. But the contents of the psalm-prayers can only be passed on and received if they are used as they were intended.

2. Thinking of texts generally, their origin, use, development and distribution, leads us finally to take a concluding look at the rise of the individual piece. Only a very few psalms can be dated with any certainty: most precisely, perhaps, 137 ('By the rivers of Babylon', v. 1), and 74 ('They have burned down your sanctuary', v. 7); and also 89, a composition of the exile. The basic texts of the Royal Psalms (2; 18; 72; 110, etc.) must be regarded as pre-exilic. Along with what seem to be

[10] L. Alonso Schökel, *Sprache Gottes und der Menschen*, 1968, esp. pp. 121ff.

archaic fragments in the Zion-Psalter (e.g. 24; 48) and a number of hymns which are admittedly very difficult to classify (93; 89,5–15; 80,2ff.), they are the oldest psalms in the Psalter. The bulk of the collections are not older than the second temple. In the course of collecting the psalms in the post-exilic period, heirlooms from the cultic rituals of the first temple would have been reclaimed and up-dated. In particular in the realm of the so-called 'Royal Hymns of YHWH' (29; 47; 93–99) and of the exilic 'Laments of the Community' (44; 60; 74; 80; 81; 89; 108) we come up against the phenomenon of the re-use of bricks from older buildings (e.g. 98,7–9 in 98, but especially 96 as an anthology of classical quotations, and 60; 108). The new temple accepts the heritage of the old. Presumably the youngest psalms are in the last third of the Psalter. Psalm writing did not stop with the close of the Psalter. The apochryphal psalms and the praise-songs and liturgies from Qumran, the Psalms of Solomon and the psalmody of the New Testament, all bear witness to this. But the creation of new texts out of the existing Psalter material by processes of adaption probably came to an end as the book was increasingly treated with canonical reverence. Here begins the history of the Psalter's reception through the ages (Chapter X).

Chapter III

THE LITERARY FORM OF THE PSALMS

Like all attempts to put ideas into words, the psalms have a definite shape and form. This is true, to varying degrees, of all of the three basic types of text appearing in the Psalter, prayer, poem and song. The prayer, as an example of elementary communication and use of language, with the purpose of self-expression, of being understood and of being persuasive, must present the desired meaning clearly and adequately, and so requires a suitable linguistic medium. This vivid, profound and extremely demanding form of speech must make full use of the available linguistic repertoire, and exploit every possibility for human expression. Poems and songs are *eo ipso* forms of linguistic art which seek the best attainable way to present in structured speech whatever they feel moved to say. Here we will naturally expect to find poetic style, because the optimal text-form is part of the aim of this kind of speech. The beginnings of defined form can already be seen in the spontaneous cries of, for example, a prayer of lament, despite the uncertainty about how far the fully formulated written texts represent the prayer spoken *in actu*. The spoken words of prayer must have been influenced by established standards, conventions and customs which would have given it its particular character. What is certain is that the act of setting the words on paper, with all the modelling which that involved, was the most important single factor in the formation of the existing psalm texts. This stage must be distinguished from the stage at which the prayer was spoken. Whether a prayer was first formulated on paper and then used in worship (generally aloud and in public), or whether a prayer which had been heard and had proved itself effective was then jotted down retrospectively and perhaps dedicated as a votive offering or presented as a model for the 'narrative' psalm of thanks (C. Westermann),[1] either way, the circumstances of writing are different from the circumstances of oral use, and are governed by different factors. Among these factors we would generally count the free development and uninhibited formation of the written piece. And here we find the forces which govern form: here the psalm is adapted and shaped. We shall explore the principles behind this process of formation, and seek out the linguistic/poetic characteristics of these texts.

1. *Patterns of Sound*

By 'sound patterns' we mean that level of textual analysis which deals with sound and tone, that is to say, the vocalic and consonantal structure of words and sentences, as opposed to the rhythmic (musical) structure which we deal with on the level whole lines. Although on both of these levels it is necessary to work with the Hebrew text, this outline will attempt to make allowance for readers without a knowledge of Hebrew, so that they too may gain an impression of the linguistic art of the psalmists.

Let us take as an example a verse from a Royal Hymn of YHWH, Ps.93,3. The characteristic style of this psalm can be seen right at the opening: 'YHWH reigns/clothed in majesty / / YHWH is clothed/girded with might.' Transliterated, v.3 reads:

> *nāśᵉ'û nᵉhārôt YHWH*
> *nāśᵉ'û nᵉhārôt qôlām*
> *yiśᵉ'û nᵉhārôt dokyām*

'The floods have lifted up, O YHWH,
  The floods have lifted up their voice,
    The floods have lifted up their roaring.'

[1] Cf. C. Westermann, *Praise and Lament in the Psalms.*

With careful reading, particularly reading aloud, a number of points emerge:

1. The verse is dominated by 'dark' vowel combinations, *a–u*, *a–o*, *o–a*; exception: *yiš^e'û*. This is called assonance.
2. The second and third lines have an end-rhyme.
3. The first two words of the first two lines give alliteration on *n*.
4. Most of the words have a sonorous *n* or *m* (or *y*).
5. The word *dokyâm* (basic form: *dokî*, the breaking or pounding of waves) has an onomatopoeic character (it imitates the thundering of waves against the shore), as does the verbal form at the beginning of the line (the *š* evokes the crashing and roaring of the surf).
6. The three lines, with their element of repetition, emulate the flow of successive waves upon the beach.

With the exception of (6), these points all relate to the sound-patterns of the text. They demonstrate how consciously and carefully the psalmists places his words and builds his sentences, how he seeks to paint his message in sound-pictures, to highlight related elements by use of related sounds, and to effect special stresses and emphases by the repetition of sound. Once made aware of such intonation and sound-structures, we can make similar discoveries of repetition, assonance and alliteration everywhere in the Psalter. Ps. 93, for example, continues (v. 4):

> *miqqolôt mayim rabbîm*
> *'addîr(y) mimmišb^erê yâm*
> *'addîr bammārôm YHWH*

'Than the thundering of great waters,
    Mightier than the breakers of the sea,
    Mighty on high is YHWH.'

Once again we can observe assonance (*ayim – îm – ām – am*) and alliteration (*m, y*), the sonorous roaring and foaming, faster now, more intensive (doubling of *m, q, b, d*), surging up into the heights. But the heights stand unshakeable.

The waves crash against the last refuge, YHWH, and are destroyed. The firmament of heaven stands victorious over the primordial powers of Chaos.

Ps. 127[2] a text from the pilgrimage collection, which (like Ps. 72) is associated with the name of Solomon because of the allusion to building works, begins with a double wisdom saying:

'*im- YHWH lo'-yibnē bayit šāw'-'āmelû bônâw bô*
'*im-YHWH lo'-yišmor-'îr šāw' šāqad šômēr*

'If YHWH does not build the house,   in vain they labour who build it.
If YHWH does not guard the city,   in vain does the guard keep watch.'

Clearly recognisable are the *b*-alliteration in the first line and the *š*-alliteration in the second. Both represent so to speak the 'key word' (Buber) of the line: *b – bānâ*, 'to build', and *š – šāmar*, 'to guard'. Since they dominate the whole sound-system of the lines, they hammer home the importance of God's building and guarding in the process of erecting a house or protecting a city. At the same time, they underline the warning that the project might easily fail (*š → šāw'*, 'emptiness', 'nothingness'; possibly *b →* an original *bᵉliyya'al [b!]*, 'uselessness', 'destruction'?). Further examples: 22,6; 129,3; 146,2 . . .

2. *Style of language*

If we define style as the selection and construction of words in a sentence, a line or a text, in other words the diction of the author's manuscript which the discipline of stylistic analysis seeks to describe,[3] we will scarcely find two psalms which display the same design. The differences can be large or small

[2] Cf. the translations of Ps. 127 discussed in X.6,7.

[3] B. Spillner, *Linguistik und Literaturwissenschaft. Stilforschung, Rhetorik, Textlinguistik*, 1974.

depending on what type of text we have before us: prayer, song, poem, liturgy, etc. However, all psalm texts are to some extent written in the restricted language of verse, are stamped by the strict formal rules and syntactical principles of poetry, or at least are influenced by conventions forced upon them by the needs of the occasion. Poetic features in the style of the sentences have received attention in the exegesis of the Psalms. It was noticed that:

- the first and last word in a statement carry a particular emphasis (beginning and end stress).

- a particular rule of word-order applies for lists and chains of words whereby they run from shortest to longest (H. Ehelolf),[4] a rule which also applies to whole phrases and longer sections of text: 'YHWH is my light (*'ôr |î*) and my salvation (*wᵉyiš' |î*)' (27,1); 'YHWH is a sun (*šemeš*, or *šelet*, "round shield" – originally one syllable) and a shield (*māgēn*, "long shield" – originally two syllables); he bestows favour (*ḥēn*) and honour (*kābôd*)' (84,11).

- a particular 'theme word' (*Leitwort* – M. Buber)[5] may dominate a piece of text, and can be the key to its exegesis: e.g. *ḥsh* 'to flee to', 'to take refuge in', Ps. 7; 'the (temple) gates', Ps. 24.

- religious language requires the use of metaphors, as in this way the inexpressible can be expressed: 'YHWH is my shepherd', Ps. 23.

- in verse the Scripture sets the three-dimensional scene in which the Word is alive (M. Krieg):[6] 'I will exalt you, O YHWH, for you lifted me (sc. like a bucket of water) out of the depths', Ps. 30,1.

---

[4]H. Ehelolf, 'Ein Wortfolgeprinzip im Assyrisch-Babylonischen', *Leipziger Semitistische Studien* VI/3, 1916 (1968).

[5]M. Buber, 'Zur Verdeutschung der Preisungen', in: *Das Buch der Preisungen*, 1962, pp. 211–219.

[6]M. Krieg, 'Todesbilder im AT', or 'Wie die Alten den Tod gebildet' (*Abhandlungen zur Theologie des Alten und Neuen Testaments* 73, 1988), esp. 2.2 and 2.3.

The linguistic art of the poet and the prayer-writer is creative and begets its own style.

Let us take as an example Ps. 3. The language of this simple prayer smacks of everyday colloquial usage. It is not for nothing that the psalmist, after a straightforward opening calling on the name of YHWH, relates what is worrying him, and blurts out what has frightened him: 'How many are my foes!' However, the conventions of the lament-prayer demand some kind of repetition or underlining of this cry from the heart. So the psalmist continues 'Many rise up against me', which at the same time characterises the foes by their spontaneous hostility. The saying which the psalmist hears from the mouth of the enemy and takes up himself, 'He will get no help from God', again betrays a colloquial use of language. However, this attack on his last hope is also a theological statement which the worshipper refutes with a confession of his own, expressing in picturesque language his trust in God: 'You, O YHWH, are a shield around me (the long-shield, the size of a man), my glory, who lifts up my head' – the latter being obviously a piece of armour, which raises the possibility that instead of 'honour' (*kbwd*) the text may originally have read 'helmet' (*kwb'*). Be that as it may, the image of the armour of God fits very well into this hostile scene, which must be understood as a case of real danger, not as fiction. The simple style of the prayer continues in the second section. It speaks of crying out and being heard, sleeping and waking, and asks for God's intervention and deliverance. However, the outlook on adversaries, on fear and on trust again opens the way for unusual images in the midst of the basic colloquial style. These show what concerned the psalmist: 'I will not fear their "web" (rather than "tens of thousands", "multitudes" – a minimal emmendation)[7] which

---

[7] *m'rbwt*, 'web', instead of *mrbbwt* 'tenthousands'.

they have woven around me' (v. 6). The image is of being trapped in the net of the foes. And again: 'You have struck all my enemies on the jaw, you have broken the teeth of the wicked' (v. 7). The wild beasts have been rendered harmless, a drastic image of the dramatic end of those enemies, bringing liberation to the beleaguered and persecuted supplicant (v. 7f.). The prayer closes in the formulaic language of conventional piety (v. 8).

This style of prayer epitomises the Psalms of the Individual. The degree of set formula varies. It can rise to the alphabetical anthology of Ps. 25. Mostly it sways between traditional verse and spontaneous formulation, much as it does in Ps. 3. As in all cultic language, a general trend towards archaism can be observed. Use is made of words and images, expressions and idioms which, insofar as the comparison is possible, appear to belong to an earlier period. Basically, this has to do with the inertia and immobility of religious language.

What can be established here with respect to the language of prayer is true in various ways for other styles of psalms, such as the hymnic style, whether it be expressed in imperatives or in participles, or the didactic style with its closer relationship to the wisdom forms. To date, research on the styles of these psalm-forms is incomplete. However, it surely goes without saying that analysis of style will be of primary importance for our understanding of any psalm. Since the study of the language of the psalms and of its place within the history of the Hebrew language as a whole is still very much in a state of flux, little more can be said about it. It is certain that the language of the psalms, when they are not playing on older material, belongs to the late phase of Classical Hebrew, but that the influence of Aramaic is very limited (e.g. Ps. 2), and the influence of the Greek is virtually non-existent. This would lead us to guess at dates of origin between the 6th and 3rd centuries BC.

3. *Line Structure*

'Line' or 'verse' are the terms we use to denote the formal poetic unit, sustained by a continuing rhythm, which is the basic element of Hebrew poetry. This basic structural element has its roots in the proverb. Usually a line is divided into two sections, occasionally three or four, called stichs, *stichoi* or cola (singular: stich, *stichos*, colon), short or half-verses. It would, of course, also be possible, and not without certain advantages, to take the stich as the basic unit.

The structure of a line is governed by three factors: (1) the rhythm, the metrical pattern, the foot or bar; (2) the inter-relationships of the stichs within the verse, the so-called *Parallelismus membrorum*; (3) special additional connections and figures of style, within or between lines, which allow a wealth of variations. We might mention:

(a) Chiasmus – diagonal cross-over arrangement

(b) Symmetry – arrangement about an axis

(c) Climax

(d) End-weight

(e) Forked verse

The model can be extended almost without limit.

1. *Rhythm.* The metrical system of Hebrew verse has only ever been very roughly defined. A number of theories have been developed to explain the metre.

(i) The accentuation system: $+--(-)+--$
every independent word contains a major accent.

(ii) The alternating system: $+-+(-)+-$
successive rising and falling (with possible syncopation).

(iii) The stichometric system:
number of syllables (or consonants) restricted to given parameters (e.g. 17, 15, 16 . . . etc.).

While no theory can define the verse-rhythm with certainty, they can between them make a decisive contribution to our understanding of the basic meter, with the result that the regularity of the meter can usually be clearly seen. Taken together and used tentatively, they serve a useful purpose. Since it cannot be assumed that 'the' line in Hebrew poetry had the same rhythmic structure at all periods and in all texts, a number of different standards like those mentioned above are more appropriate than a rigid and normalised schema.

As an example we shall take Ps. 13. After the heading, this psalm begins with five (four?) questions, each introduced by the plaintive cry 'How long . . .?' (We may assume that the phrase has dropped out of the second stich in v. 2.) According to the accentuation system (i), there are therefore five clauses (half-lines, half-verses) each with five accents, two for 'how long' (two separate words, despite the fact that they are hyphenated in the Massoretic Text) and three others ('et–, v. 1, has no accent). The alternating system (ii) again gives us five (or six) feet in each stich. Counting the consonants according to the stichometric system (iii) we get the values: 18, 19 (counting 't), 17, 18, 16 (MT).

Next, according to system (i), we have four stichs each with four accents (grouped 2 + 2), which form two verses each with two stichs in *Parallelismus membrorum*. By system (ii) there are four stichs each with six rising and falling patterns (grouped 3 + 3; a problem arises with the first part of the first stich in v. 4 which only has two such cycles in MT; but a third one may be assumed). Numerical values by system (iii): 9 + 8 / 9 + 10 // 10 + 6 / 8 + 6 (MT).

In the last section, system (i) yields two parallel groups of three (= one line) and finally two twos or a four (five if we count *kî*). System (ii) gives two fives and two threes. System (iii): 14 / 13 // 10 / 8 (MT).

For comparison, the results of the three systems may be laid out in tabular form:

(i)	(ii)	(iii)
5 ‖ 5	5 ‖ 5(6)	18 ‖ 19
5 ‖ [5]	5(6) ‖ 5	17 ‖ 13[+ 5]
5	5	16
4 ‖ 4	6 ‖ 6	17 = 9 + 8 ‖ 9 + 10 = 19
4 ‖ 4	6 ‖ 6	16 = 10 + 6 ‖ 8 + 6 = 14
3 ‖ 3	5 ‖ 5	14 ‖ 13
2 + 2	3 + 3	10 ‖ 8

The 'pyramid structure'[8] which emerges from the decreasing lengths of the stichs is clearest in system (i), obscure in system (ii). It is recognisable in system (iii) if we discount certain consonants, e.g. those which are actually being used to represent vowel-sounds. However, it is system (i) which seems to come closest to representing the rhythm of this psalm:

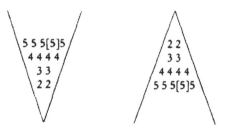

2. *Parallelismus membrorum*, a fundamental and extremely common stylistic device in ancient oriental poetry, rests on the principle of the repetition of certain features of a sentence, both of its form and of its content. The resulting rhyme-effect can be extended to all the elements, yielding a rich variety of possibilities which in the last analysis cannot and should not be distinguished too finely. For these rhyme-relationships

[8] See also p. 77 below.

effect a 'stereophony of thought content' (B. Landsberger), making it possible to re-model one and the same utterance under at least two aspects, to view it from two sides, so to speak, 'in stereo'. The choice of the particular variety of 'form-rhyme' and 'thought-rhyme' lies with the poet, the natural spectrum ranging from identity of thought content (synonymous parallelism) to a contrast of opposites (antithetic parallelism).

Take for example Ps. 6, the prayer of lament and supplication of an individual psalmist. It begins with a call upon the divine Name (*invocatio*, often standing outwith the verse structure): 'YHWH!' This is followed immediately by two negative requests which are parallel down to the last detail of their formulation:

'Do not punish me in your anger,
And do not discipline me in your wrath.'

The verse articulates two different sides of one and the same thing, which it expresses more or less synonymously. The variation is minimal, the elements are interchangeable. In this way it repeats its message in new words, strikes, so to speak, the same chord twice, and increases the force of the request ('please, please don't!'). The verse which follows (v. 2) also has a strongly parallel structure:

'Be merciful to me, YHWH, for I am growing faint,
Heal me, YHWH, for my bones are in agony.'

Only in the next verse (v. 3) does a gap begin to open up between the parallel stichs; and no wonder, for the poet is now contrasting himself and his God:

'(And) my soul is in great agony,
And you, YHWH, how long . . .?'

By means of this parallel, he pre-empts the unspoken possibility that his God might remain unmoved and inactive, and raises the hope that he might react appropriately to the circumstances hinted at in the first part of the verse.

Ps. 104, the so-called 'Biblical Sun-hymn' or 'Akhenaton Psalm' (which actually has no direct relationship with that sun-hymn from the 14th century BC,[9] and indeed only mentions the sun in passing), must be reckoned as poetry of the highest level. Like many hymns, it is based on double triplets brought into parallel (3–3), and the parallelism is aided by the hymnic participle style (English can make similar use of a present participle, or can translate with a relative clause, 'who', 'you who'). After the psalmist's summons to himself 'Praise YHWH, O my soul', and the invocation 'YHWH, my God, you are very great', the parallel verses begin (vv. 1c–5a):

'You have clothed yourself in splendour and majesty,
    Wrapping yourself in light, as in a robe,
Stretching out the heavens like a tent,
    Building your chamber above the waters,
Making the clouds your chariot,
    Riding on the wings of the wind,
Making the winds your messengers,
    Flames and fire your servants,
Setting the earth on its foundations . . .'

The art of the parallel in this instance lies in the fact that, in spite of the static, stereometric frame of reference, there is a conceptual development from one stich to the next, transcending the individual verses. This development is achieved by making the different stichs deal not with the same but with different events. In this way the reader's attention is drawn first to the light, then to the heavens, from the heavens to the firmament, then to the clouds, from the clouds to the wind, then to the storm ('winds', plural), from the storm to the lightning, then to the face of the earth . . . The parallelism is

[9] See p. 202 below.

restricted theologically to the homogeneity of the works of creation. Another point which emerges here is that parallelism can also extend between whole verses (distichoi), and can even bind groups of verses together. There are virtually no limits to the possibilities.[10]

4. *Arrangement of Component Texts*

Lines of sequences of verses can be gathered and combined into larger units in a number of ways. For example, chains of verses can arise rather mechanically by alphabetical structuring. This was discussed in Chapter II. It is easier to see in this a didactic trend or even simple amusement than artistic ability. Yet this pattern is popular in the Old Testament, both within and outwith the psalter (cf. Lam. 1–4; Nahum 1; Prov. 31; also in the apocryphal psalms, e.g. Ps.C (col. XXII]). Occasionally an author or compiler succeeds in producing a fairly reasonable organic whole, as for example in Ps.9f., and also Ps.25. The large project of Ps.119 is unique, and as such it is extremely impressive (Fig.5). Alphabetical psalms, that is, psalms with the verses ordered according to an alphabetical accrostic, are: Pss.9–10; 25; 34; 37; 111; 112; 119; 145.

It is possible to speak of 'strophes' when the sections are clearly differentiated both in form and in content. An example of a text divided both according to rhythm and according to style and diction (however this came about) is Ps.19 which breaks down into parts A (vv. 1–6), B (7–10), C (11–13; 14). An especially effective means of strophic division is of course the refrain or 'chorus', a text which returns at given intervals. A refrain will be formed by a particularly prominent verse which is able at once to separate and to link the different

[10] See W. G. E. Watson, *Classical Hebrew Poetry: a Guide to its Techniques*, 1986.

sections of the poem or song. In Ps. 46, for example, vv. 7 and 11 should be seen as a refrain, made up of triplets, in contrast to the verses of the main corpus of the psalm where the rhythm is in fours:

> 'YHWH of hosts is with us,
> our fortress is the God of Jacob.'

If we insert the refrain after v. 3 where it is missing in the MT, and if we regard v. 9b as a gloss, then the refrain divides the psalm into three equal strophes, each with three verses. However, the strophes are not always so even. Ps. 42/43 breaks down into four unequal sections. The common refrain (42,5.11; 43,5) proves the unity of these texts, erroneously separated in the count. Further examples of strophes separated by refrains are to be found in Pss. 56; (59?); 62; 78(!); 80.

In most psalms, however, the pattern and arrangement of parts can only be seen and classified when we take in view the whole organic unit, and identify its basic textual structure. This will be seen in the next section. In attempting to define the composition we must always be restrained, and we may under no circumstances content ourselves with discovering a symmetrical or concentric or chiastic (cross-shaped) schema. Virtually all texts can be forced into such a structure. Many studies of the Psalter get stuck on the formal-schematic level without making the connection from the formal structure to the semantic structure. The exegetical model developed by M. Krieg, with its four 'poetic criteria',[11] has proved very helpful in the interpretation of the poems in the Psalter. He views the text

  1. as a unit, under the headings: symmetry ('Every poem displays a tectonic symmetry.');

[11] As note 6; (esp. 2.3).

2. as a structure, under the heading: repetition ('The "thought-rhyme" of *Parallelismus membrorum* is only the most conspicuous of a plethera of stylistic figures involving repetition.');

3. as a dimension, under the heading: imagery ('Images give the poetic text its three-dimensionality: they create the poetic dimension, which is distinct and unmistakable in each case.');

4. as language, under the heading: restrictiveness, or conciseness ('Poetic language is restricted and elevated language.').

5. *Text Structure*

The term 'text structure' plays a major role in linguistic and literary scholarship in general, and no less in the exegesis of the Psalms. Various systems have been developed for the structural analysis of the psalm texts, '*analyses structurales*' and '*analyses structurelles*' (M. Girard), and it has to be said that they do not all mean the same thing by the word 'structure'. Obviously we must first clarify on what level of textual analysis the word is to be deployed. It is therefore necessary to offer some indication of what the term 'structure' might mean in our context.

We start with the assumption that texts are construed according to a particular plan which is implemented consciously or unconsciously. The gulf between careful planning and conventional formulation can of course be very great indeed, since it arises out of a difference in form, e.g. prayer or poem. But in every case, it is important for the recipient, and therefore also for the interpreter of a psalm to be aware of the structural intention and achievement of the psalmist, in order to be able to discern his message. It is true of both the simple prayer and the stylised poem that the linguistic architecture of the whole piece expresses its overall meaning. However, we must bear in mind that these architectural metaphors (structure, plan, pattern, etc.) have only a limited application.

In the practical work of exegesis on the Psalms it proves useful to begin by seeing how a psalmist opens his psalm, and how he closes it. In all speech, the first word is of paramount importance, as it marks the speaker's point of attack, where he himself stands or professes to stand, from where he makes himself heard, in which direction he speaks or calls, and where he knows or presumes the listener to be. The pitch and volume of that first word also convey how things stand with the speaker, in what circumstances he finds himself, and how he makes himself heard. And the opening gives the first signal of why he speaks, prays or sings, whom he is addressing and what he hopes to achieve. It expresses aim and intention.

'Blessed is the man . . .' begins Ps. 1 without a heading, and with this greeting opens an admonishing lecture on the two ways of living. 'Why do the nations rage?' askes Ps. 2 from the viewpoint of the ruler of Jerusalem in the political sphere. Ps. 3 begins with the invocation 'O YHWH, how many are my foes!' and in this way introduces a prayer of supplication against personal enemies. 'When I call . . .', begins Ps. 4, with thought to a situation similar to the one in which he finds himself . . .

Like the opening, the close of a text is of particular importance. Where and how the terminal point is positioned is an important question for our overall understanding of a psalm (E. Jenni).[12] The speaker is aware that his last word will linger in the air, shaping the final cadence, imprinted longest in the mind. So he seeks out his most impressive words and phrases, and tries to round his speech off. In looking for these 'last words', however, we must take note that some psalms have a tail-piece as well as a heading, a closing note which is not part of the corpus itself, but rather which goes back to readers and users of the text who have sought in a kind of post-script to add their own prayer requests.

---

[12] E. Jenni, 'Zu den doxologischen Schlußformeln des Psalters', *Theologische Zeitschrift* 40 (1984) pp. 114–120.

Such post-scripts are particularly obvious in the case of the alphabetical psalms in which, after the last *taw*-line, there follows a further closing phrase. An example is Ps. 25,21, where the last line resounds:

'May innocence and integrity protect me
   for I wait on you.'

Then follows a further request, outwith the personal prayer (v. 22):

'O God, redeem Israel
   from all his troubles.'

Similarly in Ps. 34, such a superfluous verse stands at the end of an alphabetical text (v. 22):

'YHWH redeems the life of his servants,
   none who trust in him will be condemned.'

But such post-scripts also appear in other places. For example, we might point to Pss. 2,12b; 14,7; 19,14; ... 104,31ff.; 145,21b (11QPs^a); 148,14b ...

It is not always possible to distinguish with complete certainty between the post-script and the closing line of the psalm text. However, the decisive factor for the function of such terminations is not whether they come to us first or second hand, but how they seek to understand the psalm itself. In this way, it can of course happen that a psalm may have several 'last verses'. On the other hand, one is often left with the impression that a psalm ends abruptly, without any clear signs of a consciously constructed conclusion. This may result from the fact that in the process of editing, texts were often shortened and split; and any rate, the missing conclusion is a factor which will have consequences for the meaning of the whole. E. Jenni's observations on the missing ending, displaced or replaced by doxologies or formulaic expressions of praise or supplication in the future tense (e.g. 'I will praise you for all eternity', Ps. 30,12), his comments on the expanded ending (e.g. 'Hallelu Yah') ('Rejoice and be glad, you righteous' 32,11), and his observations on the abrupt endings of many psalms are particularly englightening and helpful.

The beginning and the ending are the prominent positions, between which the text of the psalm itself is stretched. Recognising its design and pattern remains the highest aim of structural analysis. To this end, it is vital that we take note of the natural division of the text, and regard the components both separately and in relation to one another. Since every psalm has its own distinctive form, a few concluding examples may demonstrate how to identify the unique structural profile of any particular text.

1. Ps. 148, a hymn, very obviously breaks down into two sections (vv. 1–6 and 7–14a) around which the cry 'Hallelu-Yah' ('Praise Yah') lies like a framework at beginning and end. Despite their different lengths, the two sections are parallel in structure. The psalm lists in the form of a litany the great ones who are being exhorted to partake of the hymnic cry of praise, in the first section 'from heaven . . . in the heights above' (v. 1), in the second section 'from earth . . . (in the) depths below' (v. 7). The two sections also end in the same way, namely with the wish that 'they might praise the name of YHWH' (vv. 5a; 13aα), with an added theological basis: 'For he commanded and they were created (the great ones of Heaven!)' (v. 5b); 'For his name alone is sublime' (v. 13aβ). In the face of such parallelism between the two sections, we might wonder whether the second, like the first, was originally formulated as a litany, and now appears in the liturgy in an abbreviated form; it goes without saying that the psalm was performed liturgically. The close of this hymn probably lies in v. 13b, where the two halves of the world, above and below, are again brought together: 'His majesty is

higher than the earth and the heavens.' (Or is this an appendix?) All that remains is a clearly distinguishable post-script consisting firstly of a wish: 'May he raise up his horn for his people' (following LXX), and secondly of a rubric similar to some of the headings: 'A hymn for all his saints, for the Israelites, the people who are near to him.'

2. Ps. 13. The graduated verse-structure of this psalm has already been discussed.[13] If we imagine that a text, like a building, is built from the bottom upwards, the pressing question is whether the figure which emerges might be of importance for the semantic structure and the development of the line of thought. Those who feel inclined to answer this question affirmatively, in terms of a progressively more forceful prayer, will be quick to point to the significance of the fact that in the last line of the poem, the writer promises to sing.

3. Ps. 110, is a pre-exilic text, a fragment of a Royal Psalm with a very succinct style, which frankly presents the interpreter with a problem. The text contains two divine utterances which are introduced and identified as weighty *verba ipssima* by the words 'YHWH says to my lord' (v. 1) and 'YHWH has sworn – he will not change his mind' (v. 4). Despite the obscurity of the archaic and no doubt somewhat distorted text, it is still possible to see that the two parts deal with two different relationships between the king in Jerusalem and his Lord which would have found their ritual expression at the enthronement ceremony: the king's sitting at the right hand of God (v. 1) corresponds to God's being at the king's right hand (v. 5). We might expect that the two sections would go on to develop these two aspects, but the condition of the text does not allow any definite conclusion on this.

4. Ps. 87. It is not difficult for us to convince ourselves that this psalm has not been preserved unaltered. It seems that in

[13] See p. 68 above.

an early stage the text became confused by scribal errors and the re-alignment of verses. However, if we read it in the following order, we can make reasonable sense of it:

2   'YHWH loves the gates of Zion
       more than the dwellings of Jacob.

1   Its foundation stands on the holy mountain,
5b   he himself, the Most High, has established it.

4a   I count Rahab and Babel among my acquaintances,
       also Philistia and Tyre, together with Cush;
5a   But to Zion I say "Mother",[14]
       and "a man is born in her!"

3   Glorious things are said of you, O City of God!   *Selah.*
7   Singers and dancers, all serenade you.
6   YHWH, it will be told among the peoples:
       "This one was born in Zion!"   *Selah.*

A restoration which must be left to speak for itself. This new reconstruction of the Zion psalm, corrected to follow LXX, has a particular beauty of form.

5. Ps. 104. This hymn, which has often been compared to the sun-hymn of Akhenaton, sings of God's creation with particular reference to his nourishing and protecting of the world by water. Appropriately it begins with the motif of the setting up of the Heavens as the upper part of a pile-dwelling in the primeval waters (vv. 1–4), and of the earth as a landscape and seascape in which the mountains hold waters in their places (vv. 5–9. In the process, water supplies are created, in the forms of springs and streams (vv. 10–12) and showers of rain from the upper waters (vv. 13–18), enabling plants and animals to survive. The heavenly bodies ensure that all living things find food, the wild beasts by night, humanity by day (vv. 19–23). Even the remainder of the primeval waters, the oceans, bring forth life, supporting both large and small

---

[14] 'Mother' instead of 'Man', following LXX (dittography).

marine creatures, and also ships. Foremost among the dwellers of the deep is Leviathan, the sea dragon, whom God created for his own amusement, 'to play with him' (vv. 24–26). In this way, everything is meaningfully ordered in the system of creation. 'How many are your works, O YHWH! In wisdom you have created them all!' (v. 24). So the functioning of this system depends on him alone. Therefore the closing prayer (vv. 27–30) is addressed directly to the creator with the plea that life on earth might be preserved. 'All of them look to you to feed them at the proper time . . . (v. 27). Also stemming from this concern are the various post-scripts[15] which testify to the popularity of this psalm (vv. 31–35), and also the framework (v. 1a = v. 35b) which turns the hymn into a devotional text ('Praise YHWH, my soul'). However, the structure of the whole re-enforces the basic concept of the hymn, that in God's creation one thing may be built upon another, but in the end everything depends on God not withdrawing his Spirit which sustains all life. The structure of the text reflects the alignment of ideas.

[15] K. Seybold, 'Psalm 104 im Spiegel seiner Unterschrift', *Theologische Zeitschrift* 40 (1984) pp. 1–11.

Chapter IV

THE PURPOSE OF THE PSALMS

With the term 'purpose' we attempt to grasp the fact that the
psalm texts were composed and formed for particular reasons,
and with particular aims in mind. They are to be pronounced,
cited and recited, practiced and presented, sung and performed, at any rate they are to be heard. They serve a
purpose; they have been created to be used.

Looking again at a number of different cases, we find that
this is certainly true of private prayer. Generally speaking, the
psalm as it is transmitted in writing was first conceived in a
preparatory phase and prepared for performance. In form and
content it takes its orientation from the possibilities and
realities of 'offering'. But this itself, the presentation or
offering up of the prayer, executed as far as possible in
accordance with convention and ritual, is governed by
different rules, the rules of the context in which the action
takes place. It is of course plausible that the phases of
preparation and production more or less coincided with the
phase of performance, for reasons connected with the
situation or person of the supplicant; that is, that the
supplicant simply began to speak *ad hoc*. But even in this case,
where a transcription of the text was made retrospectively for
posterity, it is still better to keep the various aspects separate,
drawing a distinction between the formation of the text and
the offering up of the prayer. On the other side, once the text
has been made freely available, there opens up the endless
chain of recitation and re-use in which much private prayer
becomes stylised and formulaic; for not every personal sigh of
prayer can be adapted for general use.

In the case of hymns and songs it goes without saying that,

while the text may be the medium of expressing the content, it is not the only medium of the performance. Music, dance, gestures and so forth are all part of the production. Although our exegesis runs into difficulties with the musical notation accompanying the song-texts, it must not be forgotten that the manner of the delivery, for the most part unknown, brought out the full effectiveness of the text.

In the case of poems the phase of presentation may be different. It could be, if we think for example of the acrostic poems, that they were not intended for public performance at all, but rather for private readings and meditation. However, this does not exclude the possibility that such psalms could be used in quite different contexts, and the new situation could have given these silent texts a new resonance.

1. *Major Uses*

In this chapter we are concerned in the first place with the primary contexts in which the psalms were used. It has become customary to use the term formulated by H. Gunkel '*Sitz im Leben*' ('setting in life'), more precisely '*Sitz im Volksleben*' ('setting in the life of the people'), or in the case of the Psalms, '*Sitz im kultischen Leben*' ('setting in the life of the cult'). However, in spite of (or perhaps because of) its striking imagery, this phrase conceals a certain ambiguity, particularly when used in the singular (as though a psalm can only have one *Sitz im Leben*!) (Gunkel also thought of the different types of psalms as having a collective *Sitz*.[1]) We are better thinking of situational, cultural or functional contexts. Literary criticism is concerned with the pragmatic approach to a text, that is, the circumstances in which it arose, the non-linguistic framework of the linguistic utterance.

[1] H. Gunkel, *Einleitung in die Psalmen*, 1933 (1966) pp. 1ff.

1.1 *The Prayer*

A prayer is always more than a text. It is spoken. Generally
the psalm-prayers were offered aloud, that is, in public.
Hannah (1 Sam. 1,12ff.) was rebuked by the priest because she
spoke softly and unclearly. One should call out (*qr'*), even
shout in prayer.

'YHWH, I call out to you, hurry to me;
   hear my voice when I call to you.'   (141,1)

'YHWH, my God, I call for help by day,
   and by night I cry out before you.'   (88,1)[2]

'I will cry out to God for help,
   I will cry out to God to hear me.'   (77,1)

Usually the supplicant would stand (1 Sam. 1,26), sit
or kneel (Ps. 95,6), and pray with raised hands (Isa. 1,15;
Pss. 28,2; 141,2). It was possibly a part of the ritual to
prostrate oneself on the ground before beginning to pray, as a
display of worship (*ḥwh*), as some ancient documents testify.[3]
Depending on where the supplicant finds himself, he speaks in
the direction in which he imagines God to be. The 'unjustly
accused' of Ps. 5 expects to be able to enter the House of God
and to throw himself down 'in reverence before you, towards
your holy temple' (5,7). Something similar is found in Ps. 28:

'Hear my loud pleas
   as I cry out to you,
   as I raise up my hands
      towards your most holy place.'   (28,2)

The supplicant in Ps. 42/43 is far from temple and sanctuary. Nevertheless, he directs his attention towards 'your
holy mountain, and your dwelling place' (43,3), and attempts
to adjust himself inwardly to prayer (42,1). There were a

[2] Emended.
[3] Cf. O. Keel, *Die Welt der altorientalischen Bildsymbolik und das AT*, 1984
(3rd ed.), pp. 287ff.

number of possibilities. Accompanying and preparatory rites form the framework and the sounding board for the word of prayer. By these the worshipper, sick, and therefore excluded from the sanctuary, prepares himself with expiatory offerings for his prayer of supplication and confession. The book of Job, for example, speaks of this: 'Then Job stood up and tore his robe and shaved his head; then he fell to the ground and worshipped' (1,20). Understandably the psalmists speak little of such conventional rites, except when they wish to emphasise the orderly execution of the requirements. On these occasions they form part of the 'pictures of misery' evoked in the laments, which seek to motivate divine intervention. In addition to the dramatic gestures described in Job, the tearing of robes and donning of sack-cloth, the cutting of hair and scattering of ashes, all of which belong to the rites of fasting and mourning, ritual silence and weeping also play a role in the gesture system.

> 'I am weary from groaning;
>   all night long I flood my bed,
>   and drench my couch with my tears.
> My eye grows weak with grief . . .'   (Ps. 6,6f.)

Possibly special times were set aside for prayer (55,17; 69,13; 88,13). The attendance of a priest can be inferred in the prayers of lament which presuppose an answering oracle (e.g. 28). However, it is often impossible to discover anything more definite. Investigation has been able to reveal a number of possible situations which may have occasioned some of the prayers of the Psalter. We might mention the liturgies for entering the temple gate (15; 24), asylum offered in the context of legal proceedings with divine judgment (3; 4; 5 etc.), the ceremony of supplication or the ritual of repentance (6; 38; 69; 102 etc.), the teaching of the Torah and other isolated activities of individual worshippers. Special liturgical texts were designed for community occasions (IV.4). In the diaspora, the *Qiblah*, the orientating of prayers towards Jerusalem (1 Kings 8,38; 2 Chr. 6,34; Dan. 6,10), increasingly played a role, as did the custom of praying on the 'balcony', the windowed upper floor of the house (Tobit. 3,11; Jth. 8,5; Dan. 6,10).[4]

The ways of offering up prayers of praise and thanks were every bit as varied as those for prayers of lament. The prayer of thanks of the liberated, made in the context of congregational worship (in the case of the Psalms this meant in the temple), was stronger than the prayer of lament and supplication which of necessity was freer (cf. the background to the prayer in 107,4: desert; 10: imprisonment; 17: illness; 23: storm at sea). However, the writers of the short book of Jonah have clearly paid little heed to this rule. Jonah spoke his prayer (it is a prayer of thanks) in the belly of the fish (Jon. 2). The prayer of thanks, and often the lament cited or recited with it, belongs in the ceremony of the thank-offering, an act of worship which made room for the laity and their own initiatives. It was conceived either as part of a service of community worship or as an independent event, as the liturgies of Pss. 66 and 107 reveal. At any rate, this was an opportunity for the supplicant to fulfil vows and comply with sacrificial requirements. This event, known as the *tōdā*, provides the framework for the 'narrative song of praise' (C. Westermann), the testimonies, reports and contributions of visitors and pilgrims, some of which have come into the substance of the Psalter. In the presence of the 'brothers', 'in the midst of the congregation' the psalmist 'declares' and 'praises' (22,22). Some bring 'a new song', others content themselves with a few words of thanks (66), others still offer written texts. The didactic style is present in almost all texts. This hints at the transition to the 'pure doctrine' of Wisdom.

[4] E. Peterson, 'Die geschichtliche Bedeutung der jüdischen Gebetsrichtung', *Theologische Zeitschrift* 3 (1947), pp. 1–15.

The observation that a psalm-prayer may accompany or even replace an animal sacrifice is interesting.

'Shall I eat the flesh of bulls
　　and drink the blood of goats?
Bring a song of thanks as a sacrifice to God
　　and so fulfil your vow to the most high'. (50,13f.)
'Sacrifice and offering you do not desire . . .
　　burnt offerings and sin offerings you do not require.
Then I said: look, here I am,
　　in the scroll it is written about me.' (40,6f.)
'I will praise God's name in Song,
　　I will magnify him with songs of gratitude.
That will please YHWH more than an ox,
　　more than a bull with horns and hoofs.' (69,30f.)

In the word-play *šîr* – *šôr* ('song' – 'ox') the psalmist illustrates the interchangability of the sacrificial animal and the offering of a song of thanks. Small wonder that the language of cultic activity is carried over to the offering of prayers and songs, in order to explain their function.

'May my prayer be counted as incense before you,
　　the raising of my hands as an evening sacrifice.' (141,2)

The community of Qumran, which distanced itself from the contemporary temple cult, was particularly fond of these transferred formulations. For them, prayer was 'a pleasing sacrificial meal' (CD11,21), 'the scent of an offering of righteousness' (1QS9,5), 'the heave offering of the lips' (9,4; 10,6), and 'the flute music of the lips' (1QS10,9).

1.2 *The Song*

A song is also more than its text. It is sung and accompanied musically. It is of course conceivable that prayers were also sung, or spoken in a kind of *Sprechgesang* with rhythmic clapping, or performed with a wail of lament. In the ceremony of thank-offerings at least, prayer and song are very close to one another, and are mostly identical. However, we know only very little about the nature of the performance, especially about the musical forms, and what little we do know rests on the data of the psalms themselves.

(*a*) Since the psalmists occasionally announce their performance, or are called upon to perform, with the words 'sing' or 'play', or with the term *zmr* (noun *mizmôr*) which refers to instrumental accompaniment, we may assume that in these cases the psalm was sung and accompanied musically.

(*b*) The most likely instruments are not the signal instruments which were reserved for official events: the horn, the trumpet, or the orchestral instruments which are mentioned in Chronicles (1 Chr. 13,8; 15,19ff.; 25,1; 2 Chr. 4,12f.; or looking at the 'heathen' ceremonial music of Babylon, Dan. 3,5ff. etc.).[5] Rather, the typical instruments for accompanying song were the harp (*nebel*) and the lyre (*kinnôr*),[6] the hand-drum (*tōp* – more for procession and dance) and the long-flute ('*ûgāb*). Compare, for example, Ps. 150 with its list of instruments. Both the stringed instruments, be they plucked or struck, and the wind instruments are suited to the accompanying of melodies and melodic sequences. The stringed instruments could be used together with the percussion instruments (timpani, drums, wood blocks, sistrum, etc.) for the rhythmic structuring of a song. A number of references in the headings, mostly secondary, provide a later confirmation of such use of accompaniment: 'with stringed instruments' (e.g. Ps. 4); 'for flutes' (e.g. Ps. 5); 'on/according to the *gittith*' – either an instrument or a key (e.g. Ps. 8); 'for the director of music'.[7]

[5] P. Grelot, 'L'orchestre de Daniel III,5,7,10,15', *Vetus Testamentum* 29 (1979), pp. 23-38.

[6] On the meaning of this word, see the article in the *Theological Dictionary of the OT*, IV.

[7] Cf. the register of David's works, p. 36 above.

(c) The titles of the melodies to certain psalms are known from the headings. Examples are Ps. 22: 'to (the tune) "hind of dawn"'; Ps. 45: 'to "lilies"' (or better, 'lotus buds'); Ps. 56: 'to "a dove on the distant terebinths"' (?); and others. Since, however, we know nothing of these, the references only lead to the conclusion that there was at a relatively late date a repertoire of tunes and melodies from which certain ones could be recommended for the performance of particular psalms.

There is still no conclusive answer to the question of the meaning and function of the ominous *Selah* (*selâ*) which appears seventy-one times in the Psalter, in thirty-nine different psalms. We may think with the LXX (διάψαλμα) of an instrumental interlude (an intermezzo), or a pause for prayer, or a response. However, the reasons for placing it in the given positions are unknown and unfathomable.

(d) Attempts, supposedly on analogy with ancient or modern oriental music, to recreate the original tunes to which psalms might have been sung at the time of their writing, or at least to bring them within reach of the imagination, are interesting, but all lack the necessary historical basis. We must regard such euphoric modern compositions based on putative ancient tone-systems with some scepticism.

(e) It must of course be assumed that the temple music as a whole developed in a much more colourful way than we can now recognise from the few remaining references. In particular, the great community events of the post-exilic period were structured musically around the orchestras and choirs of the temple. In the description of the dedication of the temple by Solomon in 2 Chr. 5–7, where the pattern of a contemporary ceremonial act of worship from the 3rd century BC shines through, we read with respect to the musical structure of the festival:

'And the Levitical singers – Asaph, Heman, Jeduthun and their sons and brothers – all stood on the east side of the altar dressed in byssus, and playing cymbals, harps and lyres. With them were 120 priests blowing on trumpets. And when they played and blew together, it sounded like a voice of praise and thanks to YHWH. And as they struck up with trumpets, cymbals and accompanying instruments, and with the words of praise for YHWH: "for he is good, his love endures for ever!" – then the temple was filled with a cloud. And because of the cloud, the priests were not able to enter to perform their duty; for the glory of YHWH filled the temple.' (2 Chr. 5,12–14; cf. also 7,6 and 1 Chr. 16,4–43)

From the text we conclude that, besides the singers' guilds and choirs with their instrumentalists ('instruments for sacred songs', 1 Chr. 16,42), there was also the priestly group of trumpeters. The trumpet had obviously displaced the ancient horn as the signal instrument. From the psalm-text in 1 Chr. 16 and its context we also discover how a hymnic text from the Psalter (Pss. 105,1–15; 96,1–13; 106,1.47–48) might have been presented liturgically, and we are given a tiny glimpse of what was possible in the Jerusalem temple at that time (cf, also Ps. 150).

(f) Since dances, circuits of the sanctuary and of the city, and processions are also all mentioned, it must be assumed that some psalms-texts have their roots in these contexts. All access to this musical culture, once lively at the Jerusalem temple and in Israel, is now denied us. But this much is certain: the hymnic texts in the Psalter are only models for celebrations and festivals, or excerpts from a rich liturgical repertoire, which the compilers later found worthy to serve for posterity. It seems that they have omitted a certain amount. It also seems that they were well aware that a recitation or repeat performance can never be the same as the unique original presentation. And naturally we may wonder what was said about the aim and purpose of the Psalter collection (I.4). These texts were clearly selected from the abundance of cultic texts available, to serve the individual not in the official worship of the temple but for his personal prayer-life (Ps. 1), and for this, the instruments for performance were not always identified, and indeed were not always necessary.

(g) While we remain in the dark about a great deal, we may nevertheless conclude:

> 'that the hand-drum or tambourine had its place in particular in processions, and in the songs of victory sung by the women (68,25). The ram's horn was more a signal than a musical instrument; it announced the sacred times and seasons (81,3), and the coming of Yahweh (47,5). In the post-exilic period it was replaced by the trumpet. Songs of thanks were accompanied by the lyre (43,4; 57,8; 71,22). All these instruments were combined, with the addition of the flute, to accompany a loud and many-voiced choir, on occasions of worship before Yahweh and of ceremonial offerings (81,1–3; 98,4–6; 150,3–5). Here, the clashing cymbals ousted the duller hand-drum in the post-exilic period.' (O. Keel)[8]

Musical Instruments

1. in the Psalter:

lyre	(*kinnôr*)	33,2; 49,4; 137,2
harp	(*nebel*)	33,2; 57,8; 81,2; 150,3
strings (general terms)	(*nᵉginâ*)	4,h; 6,h; 54,h; 55,h; 67,h; 76,h; 77,6
	(*mēn*)	45,8; 150,4; cf. Sir. 39,15
	(*gittît*)?	8,h; 81,h; 84,h
hand-drum	(*tōp̄*)	81,2; 149,3; 150,4
cymbals	(*ṣilṣᵉlîm*)	150,5
long-flute	(*'ûgāb*)	150,4
horn	(*šōp̄ār*)	47,5; 81,3; 98,6; 150,3
trumpet	(*ḥᵃṣôṣᵉrâ*)	98,6

[8]Op. cit., p. 326.

2. outwith the Psalter:

small harp	(śabkā' = Gk. σαμβύκη)	Dan. 3,5ff.
psaltery	(pᶜsantērîn = Gk. ψαλτήριον)	Dan. 3,5ff.
lute	(śālîš)?	1 Sam. 18,6
sistrum	(mᶜna'anîm)	2 Sam. 6,5; Job. 21,12
cymbals	(mᶜṣiltayîm)	1 Chr. 13,8; 15,16ff.
flute	(ḥālîl)	1 Sam. 10,5; Isa. 5,12.
double flute	(sûmponya = Gk. συμφωνια)	Dan. 3,5ff.
pan-pipes	(maśrôqiyā')	Dan. 3,5ff.

3. instrumental groups:

Ps. 33,2:	(vocal) + lyre + ten-stringed harp
Ps. 81,2f:	(vocal) + hand-drum + lyre + harp / horn
Ps. 150,3–5	horn / lyre + harp / hand-drum (+ dance) / stringed instrument + long-flute / cymbals
2 Sam. 6,5	(vocal) + lyres + harps + hand-drums + sistra + cymbals
Job. 21,12	(vocal) + hand-drum + lyre + long-flute (music in the home)
1 Chr. 25,1ff.; 2 Chr. 5,12f.	the temple orchestra Levites: lyres + harps + cymbals Priests: trumpets
Dan. 3,5ff.	the court orchestra of the Babylonian king

1.3 The Didactic Poem

In the category of poems, to which we reckon all texts other than prayers, songs and cultic texts, very little can be said about purpose and use. In general they show a didactic trend. They seek to inform, to instruct, to teach. A likely setting in worship would be the *tōdā*-testimony, the proclamation at the festival of thank-offerings, as we can see from a number of

Fig. 6.   Egyptian curved harp.

Fig. 7.   Egyptian triangular harp from Thebes, 14th–11th century.

Fig. 8.   Egyptian portable harp.

Fig. 9.   Lyrists on an Old Syrian cylindrical seal, 19th century.

10

11

12

13

14

Fig. 10. Blind lyrist (woman); ivory figurine from Kumidi, 14th–13th century.

Fig. 11. Court scene with lyrists; ivory handle from Megiddo, 13th century.

Fig. 12. Lyrists on a Philistine jug from Megiddo, 12th–11th century.

Fig. 13. Prisoners playing lyres on an Assyrian relief from Nineveh, 8th century.

Fig. 14. Lyrist (woman) on a storage jar from Kuntillet Adshrud, 8th century.

15

16

17

18

Fig. 15. Scarab, 7th century (Jerusalem?). Under the lyre, which is decorated with a rosette, is written in Old Hebrew script: 'For Ma'*dānāh*, the king's daughter.'

Fig. 16. Egyptian standing lyre.

Fig. 17. Lyres on coins, 1st century AD.

Fig. 18. Nymph depicted as kithara player, accompanying dance. Relief, Sidon.

Fig. 19. Woman with hand-drum (tambourine); clay figure from Tell Farah.

19

93

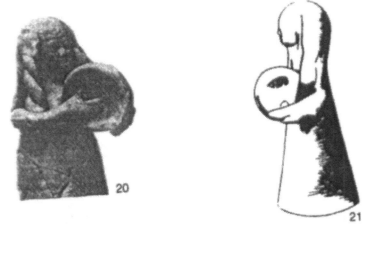

Fig. 20.   Terracotta figure from Tell Shiqmona, 9th–8th century.

Fig. 21.   Girl with hand-drum; 8th-century clay figure.

Fig. 22.   Terracotta figure, woman with tambourine; Phoenician.

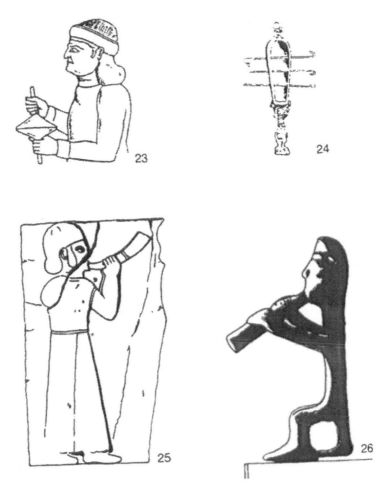

Fig. 23. Cymbals, from a relief from Nineveh, 7th century.

Fig. 24. Sistrum; Egyptian illustration.

Fig. 25. Horn (shophar) player; bas-relief from Carchemish.

Fig. 26. Flautist from Ashdod, 10th century.

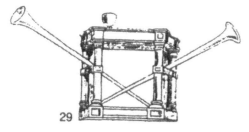

Fig. 27.   Egyptian long flute, Old
Kingdom.

Fig. 28.   Double-flute; clay figure
from Tell Farah.

Fig. 29.   Jewish trumpets,
represented on the Titus Arch in
Rome, 1st century AD.

Fig. 30.   Double-flute, lute and
curved harp; Egyptian illustration
from Thebes, 14th century.

Fig. 31. Military band with tambourine, cymbals and lyres; Assyrian relief from Nineveh, 7th century.

Fig. 32.. Group of women, warbling and clapping; Assyrian illustration, 7th century.

Fig. 33. Double-flute, lyre and tambourine; Phoenician illustration from Cyprus.

97

34

Fig. 34. Lyre, tambourine and
double-flute; illustration from a
Phoenician bowl from Olympia,
6th century.

Fig. 35. Double-flute and
portable harp; wall painting from
Maresa. Hellenistic period.

35

98

texts which make the transition from testimony to teaching. Ps. 32, for example, is a song of thanks with strongly pedagogical elements. From painful experience it warns against having to be brought to one's senses and led by force, like the horse and the mule by the 'bridle', that is, by the forces of one's fate (32,9): 'The godless has many woes, but the goodness of YHWH surrounds the one who trusts in him' (v. 10). Such testimonies as Pss. 127; 133; 131, or even the problem psalms 14; 49; 73 could have found their place here. At any rate, we may assume that such poems came into the collections of the sanctuary as intellectual and spiritual votive offerings, without having been intended or used for public performance. Occasional traces of reworking – we shall return to this – indicate that they were placed on a par with, or were brought into line with, the liturgical texts. The alphabetical poems seem to have come into the collections in a similar way, as scholarly studies of proverbs, and as school exercises. It seems unlikely that they were ever presented aloud. However, as texts for meditation and reflection, rather like a chain of prayer in which one meditates one's way through from A to Z (or from *Aleph* to *Taw*), they may have enjoyed considerable popularity.

1.4 *The Liturgical Psalm*

In the case of liturgical texts, the primary purpose is obvious. They serve to regulate and to order the course of a service of worship intelligently and in accordance with ritual. Here a remarkable phenomenon can be observed, which allows us some insight into the history of worship and liturgy in ancient Israel.

Possibly the oldest texts of this type, which are to be found in the so-called Royal Psalms (parts of Pss. 2; 18; 20; 21; (45); 72; 89; 101; 110), relate directly or indirectly to the ancient ritual of the Jerusalem state-sanctuary, which probably stemmed from the time of the early kings. They reflect different phases of the coronation ritual, which bring together in the anointing and enthronement of the newly inaugurated ruler various elements of tradition such as the Rights of Kings, the Covenant of David, his adoption as a Son of God, Title, Sovereignty, and the Proclamation of Peace, all of which belong to the complex of the so-called 'Messianic ideology of Kingship'. A very few texts are rooted directly in this ground (perhaps 2; 110?), others relate to it from a greater distance (89). The distance becomes most obvious when a text once anchored in the pre-exilic cult receives an exilic or post-exilic edition, with all the reworking which this involves (e.g. 18; 132).

The Zion Psalms had a similar history, being rooted in the pre-exilic temple cult, but now being altered and restructured for other purposes. We think of the words of Ps. 137:

'There (sc. in Babylon) our captors asked us for songs,
    our tormentors asked us to be joyful:
"Sing us one of the songs of Zion!"
How can we sing YHWH's song in a foreign land?'

(137,3f.)

The same thing happened to the old Theophany Psalms. What seems once to have been part of a dramatic cultic festival liturgy, now appears as text fragments in a new context which for its part reflects the forms of worship of the (late) post-exilic temple community. At this point we may take up what has been said elsewhere about Pss. 50 and 69.[9] The exilic Feast of Lamentation, well known from the Old Testament, has been recognised as the original *Sitz im Leben* of the whole series of collective Psalms of Lament, such as Pss. 44; 50; 74; 79; 80; 81; 89 (also Isa. 63,7 – 64,12 and Mic. 7,8–20). This was a gathering for worship and fasting, either on the site of the old temple, or at Mizpah (Jer. 41), or at Bethel (Zech. 7; 8), at

[9] See p. 51 above.

which the people remembered the destruction of Judah and Jerusalem, lamented the present hopeless situation, and struggled with the catastrophe theologically, attempting to reconcile it with their faith. Little wonder that in these psalms the mot diverse elements come together: salvaged heirlooms from the temple cult (cf. the many quotations), reflections on history based on the available written tradition (esp. Pss. 78; 89), but most importantly that theological movement which was decisive in shaping the history of the faith of Israel for about a century, and which, for want of a better term, is called the deuteronomistic movement after its central work, the Book of Deuteronomy. This deuteronomistic theology expounded the Word of God as history, promise and law, made concrete in narration, oracle and prayer. It sought a dialogue of prayer and revelation, based on a relationship with God which was understood as a 'covenant' in the sense of a legal contract, and attempted to understand the new situation in the context of a great divine judgment against God's people on account of their breaking of the covenant. This determined the style of the liturgical texts. Pss. 50 and 81 reflect the struggle with the concept of a broken covenant, as in the other direction does the indictment against God in Ps. 89. The liturgy of these festivals of lamentation and ceremonies of atonement – with which the Book of Lamentations (*Threni*) and the prophecy of Deutero–Isaiah are also connected – can be discerned from the psalms which have been mentioned, and from the exilic middle section of the great 'Temple dedication prayer of Solomon' (1 Kings 8,31–51).[10]

The same is probably also true of the older creation texts which may have belonged to the cultic festivals of the pre-exilic temple. We might think particularly of Ps. 74, a psalm of lament about the destruction of the temple, which can be dated to the exile, with its quotation from a hymn of creation

[10] T. Veijola, *Verheißung in der Krise*, 1982.

(vv. 12–17), or Ps. 102, which cites a hymn at vv. 25ff. And this may also be assumed for the group of so-called 'Royal Hymns of Yahweh' (once also known as 'Enthronement Psalms') which are gathered together without headings in Pss. 29; 47; 93–99 (not 98?). Literary analysis of these texts, which S. Mowinckel[11] once identified along with many other texts as coming from what he postulated to be an Enthronement Festival and its cultic legend, yields the same picture in every case: old cult-lyrical and hymnic fragments have been brought together in a new form, making it possible to sing these old sacral cultic texts as a 'new song' (96,1). What had once been the privilege of the priests now became the common right of the worshipping community. Part of the most treasured inheritance was the central tenet to be confessed and proclaimed, that it is YHWH who reigns as king of the world, who rules and judges as king, and who is to be praised as king. This symbolic title, cultivated in the first temple, became the central *theologumenon* of the post-exilic community, a development which Ps. 29 illustrates most vividly.[12]

Examples for consideration:

Ps. 24: An old hymnic portal liturgy (vv. 1–2; 7–10) has been enriched with an entry Torah (a discussion in the gateway) directed towards the individual (vv. 3–6).

Ps. 2: A royal psalm becomes a document of a politically active faith, through theological additions (2b; 7a; 12b), particularly through the maxim at the end: 'Blessed are all who (thus) take refuge in him', and especially in the context of Pss. 3ff.

Ps. 47: Old hymnic verses of the kingship of God in 1; 2; 5; 8; (9) are briefly discussed and adapted by a congregation speaking in the plural: 3; 4; 6; 7; 9.

[11] S. Mowinckel, *Das Thronbesteigungsfest Jahwäs und der Ursprung der Eschatologie*, 'Psalmenstudien II', 1922.
[12] K. Seybold, 'Die Geschichte des 29. Psalms und ihre theologische Bedeutung', *Theologische Zeitschrift* 36 (1980), pp. 208–219.

Ps. 89: A quoted fragment of a hymn forms the first of the two pillars (vv. 5–15) on which the exilic liturgy builds its provocative lament and accusation, the second being the recapitulation of the covenant of David (19–37).

Ps. 93: (see III. 1) A hymnic piece with a poetic character about the magnificent victory of YHWH over the waters of Chaos (vv. 1–4) is expanded by sentences reminiscent of a credo concerning the statutes and the house of YHWH (v. 5).

Ps. 96: A conglomeration of older hymnic citations, some of which are attested in other psalms (29; 98; 145).

Ps. 98: A fragment of an old myth-hymn (vv. 7–9a) is framed by a new chorale (vv. 1–6; 9b).

Ps. 101: An old royal text, a kind of manifesto of the king (vv. 2a; 3; 4; 5; 6a; 7; 8), is transformed into a 'song of virtue and justice' for everyone by a new opening (1) and additions (2b; 6b).

In this way the liturgical heritage of the first temple seems to have been adopted by the psalmists of the second temple, recited, but also re-interpreted. The results we have, preserved for us in the compositions in the collections of the Psalter.

2. Reworking and Re-use

In addition to this reception of the cultic inheritance from the surviving corpus of the temple archive, an extensive process of textual revision, we must take account of the fact that the psalms conceived after the exile, that is to say, as good as all Psalms of the Individual, have been subject to re-use, and often they still show signs of the reworking which has taken placed in this context. Here we take up what was said in Chapters II and III about the many layers of a psalm text, and its successive development. Only rarely can a redaction be recognised which transcends the separate psalms, as possibly in the Asaph and Korah collections, and the Psalms of

Ascents. And yet it is precisely these Psalms of Ascents which furnish us with our best example of the re-use of psalm texts.

Stemming mainly from individual authors, the texts of this collection (120–134) appear to have been subjected to an official temple and priestly/theological revision. In this way, statements, experiences and professions of faith which are extremely personal were opened up and made accessible for general use. Let Ps. 129 serve as an example. This psalm is, if I understand it correctly, the poem of a man tested by suffering, who expresses in words an experience of lifelong oppression:

> 'They have oppressed me greatly from my youth onwards,
>   but they have not subdued me.
> Ploughmen have ploughed on my back,
>   and have made their furrows long.
> YHWH is righteous,
>   he has cut the cords of the wicked.
> Let them become like the grass on the housetops
>   which withers before it grows up,
> With which the reaper does not fill his hand,
>   nor the sheaf-binder his arm.
> We greet you in the name of YHWH.'   (vv. 2–4; 6–7; 8b)

A simple testament of faith, which is credible even in its curse against the unnamed evil-doers. The imagery and the rather awkward style make us think of a person from a rural area, who with a heavy hand sets down words born of long reflection and profound experience. The testimony, obviously left at the sanctuary as a votive offering, found its way as such into the collections of prayers and songs, as happened also with Pss. 120; 126 and others. A closing greeting was easily added.

The redactors, however, saw it differently. They clearly thought that such extreme experiences of suffering (lifelong bondage?) were not so common, and so were less convenient for transmission and appropriation to a new situation. So they took 'Israel', i.e. the congregation, the temple community, as the subject of the experience of faith expressed in the text, by giving the poem a new opening, which in its formulation follows the existing text:

'They have oppressed me greatly from my youth onwards
– let Israel say –
They have oppressed me greatly . . .'   (v. 1)

and by identifying the evildoers as enemies and 'haters of Zion', that is, anti-Zionist political powers (v. 5). Less skillful, indeed almost superficial and thoughtless, is the expansion at the end which explains the image of drought in terms of the absence of the 'blessing of YHWH' (v. 8a). The addition is unsuccessful because it elevates the metaphorical imagery ('like the grass') to the level of reality (greeting the harvesting reapers) and wishes on the enemies of Zion a failed harvest. Since it presupposes that the evil-doers were able to understand and receive the blessing of the passers-by, it presumably sees the 'Zion-haters' springing up in the home or neighbouring populations. Both of these trends, the orientation towards Zion and the spiritualisation involved in the concept of blessing, reveal the activity of the redactor of the Psalms of Ascents. I have attempted to demonstrate this elsewhere.[13]

The same and similar processes of revision must be assumed for many other individual psalms, where reception and recitation has been made possible in this way. Traces of re-use are to be found particularly at the beginning and end of the texts. We shall come back to the headings in the final section of this chapter. The endings or post-scripts of certain psalms still show the fingerprints of the worshippers and singers who handled these texts, from the earliest times, and as long as notes could still be added.

These post-scripts can best be seen in the alphabetical

[13] K. Seybold, 'Die Wallfahrtspsalmen. Sudien zur Entstehungsgeschichte von Ps 120–134', *Biblisch-Theologische Studien* 3, 1982.

psalms which are 'closed' texts. In Ps. 25, for example the *Taw* strophe (v. 21) is followed by a prose addition

'O God, redeem Israel from all his troubles.' (v. 22)

The sigh of a worried supplicant and reader of the cycle of proverbs. In Ps. 145, after the last line, stands a 'for ever and ever', usually explained as an *additum*. A number of Hebrew manuscripts continue at this point:

'And let us praise YH henceforth and in eternity.
Hallelu-YH!'

The Psalter manuscript from the 11th cave at Qumran attests instead a text which is to be translated roughly as follows:

'May YHWH be praised, and may his name be praised in eternity and [. . .] This as a memorial offering [. . .]'

'A subscription on the use of the psalm?' asks the editor. At any rate, a post-script to the poem in the form of an ascription of praise.

Ps. 34 is subscribed with the words:

'YHWH redeems his servants,
Those who take refuge in him will not be condemned.' (v. 22)

A whole series of additions appear to come together at the end of Ps. 104. From v. 31 the structure becomes loose; isolated requests pile up. Do they stem from worshippers and singers who have used the text gratefully?

'May the glory of YHWH last for ever!
May YHWH rejoice in his work!
He looks at the earth and it trembles!
He touches the mountains and they smoke! –
I shall sing to YHWH my whole life long
I shall sing praise to my God as long as I live! –
May my life be pleasing to him!
I rejoice in YHWH! –

> May the sinners vanish from the earth
>   and the godless be no more! –
> Bless YHWH, my soul! –
> Praise YH!'   (vv. 31–35)[*]

Re-use, in French '*relecture*', is a familiar phenomenon in the Psalms. Much evidence of the activity of worshippers and readers has still to be discovered.

3. *Functional Remarks in the Headings*

Finally, on the question of the purpose and use of the psalms, we must take account of the headings or superscriptions which are placed at the beginning of most psalms. We deal with them here in the closing part of this chapter because they clearly reflect the latest and last stage of use.

The importance of the headings for the exegesis of the psalms has not always been correctly assessed. Here we take up again what has already been said on the subject with respect to the questions of authorship and of the manner of performance.

It is fundamental to bear five things in mind with respect to the so-called psalm headings:

1. They are not titles, although in English they are sometimes loosely referred to as titles, but rather, they are ascriptions, indicating to which collection the psalm belongs, what type of psalm it is, how it is to be performed musically, and occasionally other details (e.g. biographical references).

2. They are not written by the author himself, and probably do not even originate with the editors and compilers. They probably represent a very late phase of the collection. They often seem to have arisen quite arbitrarily; why do Pss. 18 and 60 have such extended rubrics, why are they missing in Pss. 33; 71; 93ff.? In the last third of the Psalter they are conspicuously less frequent.

---

[*] See above, P. 79, note 15.

3. They record remarks which appear unrelated to any context within the heading. Only the very common *lamm'nasse*ᵃ*h* (55 references in psalm headings) always appear in first place, and never alone, leading us to think of a technical musical term; it is often followed by the name of a melody. Usually it is translated 'for the director of music', or similar. As early as the LXX, the meaning of the term must have been obscure, for there it is translated 'to the end', εἰς τὸ τέλος, derived from *nṣḥ*, 'eternal'.

4. Only very few of the headings offer functional information. Ps. 102 is the exception here, especially as this text really is suited to the 'pouring out' of the afflicted soul. Ps. 92 is intended 'for the Sabbath day', Ps. 100 for thanks-giving, Ps. 30 for the dedication of the temple (*ḥᵃnukkâ*). According to the Greek tradition, Ps. 29 was intended for the feast of tabernacles, although it is difficult to see the reason for this. We might wonder why so few texts were assigned to specific festivals. The allocation of texts to days of the week is reflected in the early translation and exegesis of Ps. 24 (Sunday), Ps. 48 (Monday), Ps. 94 (Wednesday), Ps. 81 (Thursday – Old Latin and Aramaic traditions), Ps. 93 (Friday – LXX). The Talmud reserved Ps. 82 for Tuesday. The headings to Pss. 38; 70 and 145 (11Q) call to mind the burnt offering to which this text might have been sung. Ps. 100 may be thought of as a song of profession of faith for use with a thanks offering.

5. When giving a classification of genre or type (hymn, song, prayer, poem) they seldom seem to relate closely to the content of the texts. For example, two almost identical psalm texts (14 and 53) are given different headings. Very little can be deduced from these concerning the actual possibilities for use and performance.

Chapter V

THE CLASSIFICATION OF THE PSALMS

'The . . . task is now to bring *order* to these multifarious texts, which span so many centuries. The scholar should be attempting to discern the inherent natural structure of the whole: he should make a number of reliable basic observations whereby it falls almost by itself into an ordered system.'[1]

The task, as H. Gunkel describes it here, of 'bringing order' to the whole body of material, can be approached from a number of different starting points. Starting with the received form of the present Psalter in its given order of texts, we can ask about the lines of division which have been carved into the corpus and transmitted with it, in order to examine the contexts of the resulting groups. Gunkel clearly saw this method as unpromising. He was concerned to pursue the 'inner order of the individual psalms', and for him that meant ordering together homogenous texts which had arisen in the same way, so that the 'natural' order of families should emerge 'almost by itself', called forth by their 'inherent' relationships.

For, as he writes in his classic work *Einleitung in die Psalmen* (1933), it is:

'an unbreakable principle of scholarship that nothing can be understood without its context. Consequently, *the real task of research on the Psalms will be to rediscover the connections between the individual songs*, which are not offered to us by the tradition, or at any rate not to any great extent. Once we are in a position to bring together the psalms which innately belong together, we may hope to be able to gain a sure understanding of the poems by means of thoroughgoing comparative studies, and

[1] H. Gunkel in: *Religion in Geschichte und Gegenwart*, vol. IV col. 1611.

thus with the help of clear counter-examples to solve many individual difficulties.'[2]

This is the epoch-making programme of the science of form criticism, which suggests a re-ordering of the Psalms. It has been formative for our understanding of the Psalms to this day.

In order to do justice to Gunkel's achievement, it is necessary to consider some of the earlier attempts to bring order to the material. We shall restrict ourselves to two typical systems of classification.

1. *The Headings*

One method of gaining an ordered perspective is to take note of the introductory remarks, the headings, titles or superscriptions, paying of course particular attention to the terms relating to type. The most common terms are the following:

> *mizmôr*, song with background music; occurs fifty-seven times in the Hebrew text, in thirty-five of which it is connected with David. Consequently it dominates the Davidic collections, and is the preferred term for the Psalms of the Individual (with a few exceptions, e.g. 47; 67; 80; 100).
>
> *šîr*, cultic song, or temple song; occurs twenty-nine times, including thirteen cases where it is combined with *mizmôr*. The most striking usage is the combination with *ma'ǎlôt* in the Psalms of Ascents (120–134). The remaining distribution is of little significance; but it is notably rarer in the Davidic collections (only 30; 65–68; 108).[3]
>
> *maskîl*, aesthetic or didactic poem; occurs thirteen times in the headings, a number of them in the Korah collection (42; 44; 54; 88; 89) and in the second Davidic collection (52–55).

The remaining terms are so uncommon that they can hardly have been suitable for classification:

[2] *Einleitung in die Psalmen*, p. 3.
[3] Cf. 11QPsª; also p. 36 above.

110

t^epillâ	prayer	five occurrences (cf. 72,20)
t^ehillâ	hymn	one occurrence (145)
šiggāyôn	?	one occurrence (7)
miktām	LXX: stele inscription	six occurrences (16; 56–60)

The headings present a problem, still not completely resolved, which hinders us from gaining any greater clarity about the system of identification. At any rate, they have only a very limited suitability for group classification.[4]

2. Classification by Content

This inadequate system has had the result that readers and exegetes of the Psalms have always been looking around for better possibilities for finding their bearings in this large body of texts. An obvious method, which has been attempted since ancient times, is the grouping together of material which is the same or similar in particular aspects of subject matter. The Early Church knew the group of the seven Psalms of Atonement (6; 32; 38; 51; 102; 130; 143), which were frequently expounded together. It is, however, only a small step further to speak of Royal-Psalms and Enemy-Psalms, of Psalms of Ill-health or Creation or History, of I-Psalms and We-Psalms, in which, following the Biblical model of the Psalms of Ascents, Zion-Psalms, and David-Psalms, the key-word is the common factor marking off the group. Inevitably, they overlap.

The correctness and usefulness of this kind of grouping is disputed. And yet, in this system of classification, the central aspect of textual ordering had not yet been brought into play, namely the literary form. It was in this area that Gunkel pioneered important new developments.

[4] Cf. G. H. Wilson, *The editing of the Hebrew Psalter*, 1985.

3. Classification by Type

For Gunkel, three conditions must be fulfilled before individual psalms can be put together into a common group:

1. There must be a 'particular *basis in worship*' in which the texts are all rooted, a uniform setting in cultic life.
2. There must be a 'common treasury of *thought and feeling*', a uniformity of meaning and of mood.
3. There must be a 'shared *diction*', a uniformity of style and structure.

Psalm-texts selected and compiled according to these three criteria comprise, or belong to, a '*Gattung*' or 'type'.[5] This *Gattung* is for Gunkel something like a literary model, a mould which shapes in content and in form the words and expressions required for a particular sphere of worship, a strict convention of rules for the fashioning of style and text, a convention which epitomises the linguistic requirements of a given situation. The individual psalms are therefore mainly non-cultic imitations and reflections of cultic models. No single psalm represents the ideal of its 'type' completely. They stand at varying distances from the reconstructed prototype.

At this point the workers then engaged in this field of research began their critique. In particular, S. Mowinckel represented the view that the individual psalms themselves, and not just their prototypes and structural models, are connected with real cultic situations, such as festivals, rituals and the like, and are to be understood as part of such general contexts; and indeed that this applies to almost all psalms, with few exceptions.[6] Here it will be necessary to decide each case on its merits.

However, the principles of classification, developed from

---

[5] *Einleitung in die Psalmen*, p. 22f.

[6] S. Mowinckel, *Psalmenstudien* I–VI, 1966; *The Psalms in Israel's Worship* I–II, 1962.

Gunkel's criteria of *Gattung*, remain generally valid to this day, albeit with various improvements and refinements which have altered the schema here and there, bringing the literary aspect of textual structure into the foreground. We now sketch the psalm-types, following the pattern as it is commonly understood today.[7] Following Gunkel, eight major types are recognised:

1. Hymns
2. Songs of Yahweh's Enthronement
3. Laments of the Nation
4. Royal Psalms
5. Laments of the Individual
6. Thanksgiving of the Individual
7. Prophesy in the Psalms
8. Wisdom in the Psalms

Then also 'minor types', such as:

- Blessings and Curses
- The Song of Ascents
- The Song of Victory
- Thanksgiving of Israel
- The Legend
- The Torah

And also 'mixed types', 'type changes', 'liturgies'.

This analysis can for the most part be adopted without the use of the problematic titles 'Enthronement Songs', 'Prophetic Psalms', 'Songs of Victory' and 'Thanksgiving of Israel'.

3.1 *Hymns*

This group embraces texts which are generally regarded as hymnic, i.e. which combine song, profession of faith, and prayer, and which had their fixed place in the public worship

[7] As note 1, p. 109 above: cols. 1609–1630.

of both the first and the second temple. We assign to this group Pss. 8; 19; 29; 33; 100; 103; 104; 105; 111; 113; 114; 135; 145; 146; 148; 149; 150. In addition, as sub-groups, we count the Royal Hymns of YHWH (Enthronement songs) 47; 93; 95–99, and the Zion-Psalms 46; 48; 76; 84; 87; 122. Since some texts have hymnic sections of varying lengths, the overall size of the group is difficult to determine. The border lines with pure poetry on the one hand and liturgical compositions on the other are flexible. There is little to be said about structure. Often commentators content themselves with the rather feeble division:

A Introduction (Theme)
B Main Section (Exposition)
C Conclusion (Coda)

But there is scarcely a text which exactly follows this basic pattern.

An important development is F. Crüsemann's suggested sub-division of the group into 'imperative' and 'participial hymns'.[8] In this distinction, the characteristic features are identified as, in the former case, the exhortation ('sing!', 'play!', 'praise!'), and the ensuing recitation of praise (Heb. *kî*, 'for': 'for his love endures', Ps. 136, etc.), and in the latter, the chain of participles ('wrapping yourself in light . . . stretching out the heavens . . . building . . . making . . . riding . . .', Ps. 104). The two have different functions. The imperative introduces songs for public worship, cries of joy (*t^erû'á*),[9] and musical productions. It serves a liturgical-dramaturgical purpose. The participial description aims at an objective representation of theological contexts. It lists articles of faith, and presents for view the entire history of divine deliverance.

[8] F. Crüsemann, *Studien zur Formgeschichte von Hymnus und Danklied in Israel*, Wissenschaftliche Monographien zum Alten und Neuen Testament 32, 1969.
[9] P. Humbert, *La 'TEROU'A'. Analyse d'un rite biblique*, 1946.

Compare, for example, Ps. 100 with Ps. 104. Although the term 'hymn' is now being stretched, these two basic forms have a recognisable shape. The problem of complex structures, e.g. the Royal Hymns of YHWH, has already been discussed.

3.2 Royal Psalms

The ten so-called Royal Psalms (2; 18; 20; 21; 45; 72; 89; 101; 110; 132; Nordic scholars set the figure higher)[10] only form a 'Gattung' or 'type' insofar as they relate to the so-called 'Ritual of the King', and the royal cult at the state sanctuary. Since they stem from the heritage of the first temple, we must apply to them the liturgical categories of pre-exilic period (as indeed to the other older hymns). They therefore defy any classification which is mainly derived from post-exilic times. Their group identity bears the stamp of the pre-exilic tradition. Sample text: Ps. 2.[11]

3.3 Laments of the Community

To this group we generally count Pss. 44; 60; 74; 79; 80; 83; 85; 89; 90; 137. They are prayers of the 'people', or better, of the community, in a time of trial. For the most part, they would have found their setting in an act of worship dedicated to lamentation and atonement. We are thinking here of the exilic 'popular festivals of lamentation' (Zach. 7,12; 8,18), or ad hoc services of worship. Probably at these services, God's answer would have been given in the form of oracles of salvation, delivered by the prophets (cf. Ps. 60,6–8). The liturgical texts built on lament and supplication commonly open with an invocation, and close with a promise of praise. Expressions of confidence and trust are also connected with

[10] E.g. J. H. Eaton, Kingship and the Psalms, 1976.
[11] III.5.3 above.

this. A characteristic feature is the argumentative style, recalling promises of the past, pointing out contradictions in the present, suggesting conclusions, offering motives, all in order to win God's intervention. It is questionable whether there was ever a *Gattung* 'thanksgiving of Israel' to correspond to the individual psalm of thanks. Clear evidence is lacking. Sample texts: Pss. 44; 85.

3.4 *Laments of the Individual*

The fact that the Psalter arose in the (late) post-exilic years may well explain why the group most strongly represented in it are the 'Psalms of the Individual'. H.-J. Kraus includes under this type: Pss. 3; 5; 6; 7; 13; 17; 22; 25; 26; 27; 28; 35; 38; 39; 41; 42–43; 51; 54; 55; 56; 57; 59; 61; 63; 64; 69; 71; 86; 88; 102; 109; 130; 140; 141; 143;[12] – thirty-five texts in all, almost a quarter of the psalms. To this we can add the Psalms of Confidence (4; 11; 16; 23; 27; 62). In actual fact, we are dealing with prayers of supplication (and in this respect, Gunkel's term is unsatisfactory) of a single person in unfortunate circumstances. Among the components of these prayers are the invocation, the representation of self (depiction of misery), requests, combined with expressions of confidence, arguments to motivate God's intervention, declarations, and vows of thanks and praise. The main element of structure is disputed: the oracle of salvation, or affirmation of answered prayer causing the worshipper's sudden change of mood in the middle of the psalm-prayer (cf. Ps. 22). The number of possible combinations of these elements is inevitably large, since in the majority of cases it is not a question of stereotyped prayer formulae, but of biographical (i.e. contemporary) testimonies.

The question of assignment to a particular *Sitz im Leben* in

---

[12] H.-J. Kraus.

the form of institutional prerequisites has proved to be fruitful for the division of the group. These have made it possible to combine the individual character of the prayer with the situational context. Consequently there is a rather large sub-group of 'Prayers of the Accused', the prayers of those who are awaiting God's judgment in a case in the temple court (Pss. 3; 4; 5; 7; 11; 17; 23 etc.). There is a group of Psalms of Atonement, or Psalms of Ill-health, offered by those who are far from sanctuary and cult but who wish to adhere to the rites, in effect prayers of expiation (Pss. 6; 13; 38; 39; 41; 51; 69; 102; 130 etc.). And there are borderline cases (e.g. Pss. 35; 109), and of course individual prayers which cannot be classified, presumably because they have a distinctive history of their own. The variety in this group is enormous.

3.5 *Thanksgiving of the Individual*

'Approximately twenty complete *Songs of Thanks* have been preserved for us.'[13] This includes from the Psalter Pss. 30; 32; 34; 40; 41; 66; 92; 116; 118; 138. The ancient term for these texts, whether they were presented as song or as instruction, was *tôdâ*. This seems to have been derived from the Festival of Thank-Offerings, in which the sacrifice, also called *tôdâ*, was occasionally replaced by the performance of a psalm. It was this liturgical event, this festival for the fulfilment of oaths (cf. Pss. 66; 107; 118) which gave these psalms their shape. Their purpose was thanks for an experience of deliverance, and praise for the deliverer in the presence of the community. *Tôdâ* can mean both. Both can be a lesson for all who hear, and this is why the element of reporting plays such an important role. Since the psalmist occasionally quotes the prayer which he spoke in his time of need, proclaims that it has been heard, and offers it with the Song of Thanks as a

---

[13] *Einleitung in die Psalmen*, p. 265.

votive gift to the sanctuary, we may conclude that the Prayers of Lament transmitted without a section of thanksgiving also had the same history. In these cases, the required thanks-offering would have been satisfied in the form of an animal sacrifice, or of a 'live' performance.

Strictly speaking, the so-called Psalms of Confidence do not form a *Gattung* as such, since it is not possible to assign them to a shared cultic setting and origin (Pss. 4; 16; 23; 62 etc.).[14]

3.6 *Wisdom Poems*

To this open-ended group belong the Alphabetical Psalms (Pss. 9–10; 25; 34 etc.), being psalms with a fixed formal structure, and also the free didactic poems which have a variety of objectives (Pss. 1; 19; 49; 73).

3.7 *Psalms of Ascents*

The collection and fixed group of Psalms 120–134, which seems partly to have sprung from the circles of pilgrims, and to be intended to serve them as a song and prayer book, is made up of texts of various types (*Gattungen*). Compare 120 with 122, or 132 with 134. Here, group identity is in part determined by secondary use. In this respect we could also include Pss. 48 and 84; indeed, the group is open in principle to include all the Zion Psalms.

3.8 *Historical Psalms*

Referred to by Gunkel and Begrich as 'Legends' because the 'narration' stands in the central position (Pss. 78; 105; 106), they do not form a type in the strictest sense, unless of course we were to go back to the basic meaning of the proclamation of salvation-history (*Heilsgeschichte*) and its place in worship, which is the context in which these texts are to be set.

[14] Ibid. pp. 254 ff.

3.9 Liturgies

Ps. 15 and Ps. 24,3–6 are ascribed to the category of 'Entrance Liturgies' or 'Portal Liturgies', also known in the Old Testament from Isa. 33. This is a kind of 'catechism' (K. Galling)[15] which was set before the pilgrim on his entry to the sanctuary, or which unfolded as a kind of dialogue between the gate-keeper and the pilgrim in the temple gateway. It is difficult to say to what extent we can refer to other texts like Pss. 100 and 118, and particularly mixed texts like Pss. 92 and 102 etc. as liturgies, firstly because the term liturgy is by no means unambiguous, and secondly because too little is known about the forms of worship in ancient Israel, only a few glimpses and some general assumptions.

3.10 Assessment

Gunkel's triangular schema:

$$\text{Setting} \qquad \text{Content}$$
$$\text{Form}$$

has proved itself methodologically, and can be used as a rule of thumb for all texts orientated towards actual use. Improvements and refinements are possible both in the three points of the triangle and in the relationships between them. The fact that the results are not always satisfactory is to be attributed mainly to irregularities and gaps in the tradition. However, in terms of the aims of type-classification in Gunkel's sense, it must be stressed that each psalm-text has its own individual character, and must therefore be understood and treated as an independent organism. In this way, the allocation of type-categories ultimately helps us to an understanding of the development of the individual psalms, the real aim of all Psalm research.

[15] K. Galling, 'Der Beichtspiegel', Zeitschrift für die atl. Wissenschaft 47 (1929), pp. 125–130.

We can now attempt to simplify the system of psalm types even further, and to set it on a few basic principles. For example, C. Westermann has suggested the division of the tableau of types into the two basic forms of all religious language, namely the expression of need (the lament) and the expression of praise. What underlies these two main types (*'Hauptgattungen'*) are the two things which '. . . move people most, suffering and joy. The Psalms of Lament are pain put into words before God, the Psalms of Praise are the putting into words of joy. They belong together, in a polar relationship; in their polarity they show what it is to be completely human . . .' Alongside these, the other psalm types have only a subordinate and derived importance. 'Within the main types, various groups can be distinguished (i.e. Gunkel's types); in all these groups, however, the main distinction between praise and lament remains recognisable.' The praise-type breaks down into reportorial and descriptive psalms, which are more or less covered by the traditional classes of Psalms of Thanksgiving and Hymns. The lament-type has three aspects, namely God, the enemy, and self. Classification is possible according to where the centre of gravity lies.[16]

One consequence of this is that the terms 'lament' and 'praise' have been badly overstretched, and as new *termini technici* have been robbed of their original meaning. Like all attempts at schematic structuring, this can lead to misunderstandings. For this reason, it might be sensible and prudent to leave room for the traditional and comprehensible basic cateogries, prayer, song, poem. Not least because these terms correspond more or less to the Hebrew equivalents, and because they, along with others, represent the most

---

[16] C. Westermann, *Theologie des ATs in Grundzügen*, Grundrisse zum AT 6, 1978, pp. 134ff. (137; 138; 149).

elementary expression of human religion.[17] At any rate, to conclude our assessment of Westermann, it remains a desideratum to read and consider in this light the headings over the psalms in our Bible editions.

Gunkel was well aware that the Psalter, as a many-faceted collection evolved over a period of centuries, could in the last analysis not be dealt with in such a simple schema of literary types. Perhaps he over-estimated the scope of his own 'basic observations'. In any case he is quite clear about where he himself sees the inadequacies of the system.

It was his opinion that the majority of psalms were to be assigned to a major type, the setting of which lay in the cult. Yet he believed that only a minority of psalms were directly related to the cult, and therefore genuine examples of a cultic type. Rather he saw them as texts which could only indirectly be said still to be connected with cultic procedures. The degree to which they were distanced from the formative rites varied, but in most cases it was considerable. Nevertheless he held firmly to the idea that even the 'Spiritual Poems', to which the 'Cultic Songs' had been added, remained subject to the original cultically-conditioned types and to the influence they had on form. Although he recognised that religion had 'thrown off the mantle of sacred usage, in which it had previously thrived', that it had become 'free of the piety of all ceremonial' – 'a religion of the heart', he did not see the texts as being free of the form-shaping influence of the cultic *Sitz im Leben*, or at least not in any large measure. And yet at the same time he did see a free spiritual poetry beginning to arise. In view of this distance from the cult of most of the available psalm-texts, or at any rate in view of the large proportion of

[17] N. K. Gottwald, *The Hebrew Bible: A Socio-Literary Introduction*, 1985, suggests the following grouping of Psalm types: In the Psalms as a whole he detects a threefold pattern which highlights the individual and social functions of the texts: 1. 'orientation', 2. 'disorientation, destabilisation', 3. 'relocation, reorientation' (pp. 525–541).

free spiritual songs in the Psalter, we might ask whether it is acceptable or appropriate to use the cultic schema in the attempt to bring order to the material. The cultic type-schemata apply to texts which have only to a small degree been preserved, and the spiritual poems partly follow laws which are remote from, or at best derived from the cult, and partly they are quite subjectively individual. In other words, Gunkel's schema only applies to parts of the psalm texts, and only partially achieves its self-appointed goals. It is a model for the growth of cultic texts, but is less suited to the ordering of the material in the Psalter.

It seems that, in the spirit of Gunkel, other 'basic observations' are required with respect to the mixed collection of cultic and spiritual poetry, if the 'natural divisions' of the Psalter are to be seen more clearly. The scholarly battle over the traditional principles, the order of the texts and the type-characteristics of the Psalter collections, must be fought anew.

4. *Analysis by collections*

The transmission of the individual psalms in Psalter collections makes it possible to see 'natural' divisions in these conglomerations of texts, which have an advantage over the 'types' in that they have been passed down to us in their present form; they were acknowledged and used at the time when the Psalter was being formed. So far, very few results have been produced in this field (I. 3.4). We can, however, put together a number of observations.

1. The collections of the Psalter vary considerably in character. The *Davidic Psalters* offer principally texts relating to individual worshippers, including the received Royal Psalms. They tend to achieve a harmony of ideas and a uniform theology by establishing David as an idealised author who on various occasions (sometimes as part of a narrative) 'sang' the words (Ps. 18,h). Their aim is not so much to

encourage the messianic expectation as to built up faith in YHWH in every possible situation. Their theological key-word is *ḥsh*, 'trust', 'believe', 'have faith'. They are collections of exemplary testimonies of faith (also the introductory Ps. 2) rather than 'prayer or song books'. Notice 72,20 where these collections are termed 'prayers of David'. The growth of the Davidic Psalter has already been discussed (I. 4). 11QPs^a represents the end of an abandoned rival line of development.

The special character of the *Asaph Collection* lies firstly in the fact that it primarily contains collective poetry ('Laments of the Nation') and secondly in the fact that the Asaph psalms are almost without exception drawn from the heritage of the Northern Kingdom. It is a collecting-bowl for old (even ancient) tribal traditions.

Less clear-cut, but nevertheless distinctive, is the 'Zion theology' of the *Korah Psalms* (42–49; 84–85; 87–88).

The *Psalms of Ascents* (120–134) are characterised quite explicitly by their headings. The so-called *Enthronement Psalms* have no headings, and so are not clearly marked off. They stand for the most part together: 93–99 (– 94 + 29; 47). The same is true of the *Hallel Collections*, which mainly present hymnic texts.

All these collections have already been discussed (I), so these few pointers should suffice here. It is too early to risk a classification according to form. However, it cannot be overlooked that Gunkel's principles could also be applied to these collections.

2. The gatherings of separate texts into the different psalters has left here and there a collocation or grouping which can still be recognised, and which can be traced back to a type-controlled origin with a common setting in cultic life. We may think of the Prayers of the Accused (3–7), Prayers of the Sick (38–41), the Liturgies of Thanksgiving (65–67), the Royal Hymns of YHWH (93–99) and other groups of more

than two consecutive texts which also belong together in terms of their *Gattung*. They have remained together as the Psalter developed because they had the same origin.

On the other hand, more extensive goups and sequences linked associatively, such as Pss. 3ff., probably go back to the redactional processes which produced the collections. It is the possibilities for (re-)use which dictate the presentation. Didactic and theological considerations are also at work, at the latest when the Psalter collections were exposed to the influence of Wisdom and a series of newly written poems were added (1; 119; the dispersed alphabetical poems).

The last stage in the ordering process was the ultimate division of the material into five (unequal) books, making use of older caesurae. From the different varieties of group formations, it will at the very least be recognised that, depending on the phase of transmission, a variety of different ordering principles were in use.

5. *The Sequence of Texts*

1. It would seem that the Jewish scribes left the part-collections of the Psalter as they found them. We must assume that these were already ordered into groups, perhaps stored up in special jars or tied in bundles. The concern of the scribes must have been to take the Psalter collection, which had grown to a considerable size, and render it comprehensible and manageable. The settling of the sequence of individual texts would have been their first tool. This was only possible by numbering the pieces, and/or by writing them con-secutively on a large scroll.

Judging from 11QPs[a], the sequence appears only gradually to have become established. The connecting of psalms seems (even in the part-collections?) in many cases to operate according to subject matter, in others according to key-word relationships, but also often according to origin. Pss. 5–7;

20–21; 40–41; 46–48; 54–57; 61–64; 65–66; 69–71; 79–80; 93–100; 103–105; 105–106; 111–112; 120–134; 135–136; 140–143; 145–150 all form subject-groupings (following Gunkel), which, however, only relate to neighbouring groups in a few cases. Key-word relationships join texts and text-groups in longer chains.[18]

2. From 3 to 89, the vast majority of psalms are provided with a heading. The few exceptions (33; 71) carry little weight. From 90, many more texts carry no heading other than the Hallelu-Yah doxology (28 of them; LXX 24: about half). The principle of arrangement is not the same in every case. And, of course, we do not know whether the last third was decorated with empty lines, red blocks (rubriks in red ink, such as are attested in manuscripts from Qumran)[19] or similar. The psalms are numbered in the Greek manuscripts; in Hebrew the earliest evidence for this is in the medieval period.[20]

3. There was a tendency to group together psalms with the same heading, or with the same opening lines: e.g. Pss. 3–6; 19–24; 29–31; 38–41; 47–51; 62–68; 75–77; 82–85; 108–110; 139–141. Or Pss. 56–60; 42–45; 52–55; 88–89, etc. so that bunches or clusters are formed.

4. In each case, *Hallelu-Yah* Psalms form end-groups to larger complexes, e.g. 104–106 to 90–106; 111–117 to 107–117; 146–150 to the whole Psalter. *Hôdû* groups form openings, e.g. 105–107; 118; 136.

In order to conclude with a more concrete picture, let us make a preliminary excavation, and examine the chain of psalms 1–10. It is immediately clear that 1 stands by itself. It is a special case. Without a heading, this text or an early form of

---

[18] Cf. Chr.Barth, 'Concatenatio im ersten Buch des Psalters', in: *Festschrift E. L. Rapp*, 1967, pp. 30–40.

[19] Cf. M. Baillet, J. T. Milik, R. de Vaux, 'Les "petites grottes" de Qumran', *Discoveries of the Judaean Desert* III, 1962, pp. 79ff.

[20] But cf. the numbering in the Bodmer Papyrus XXIC, p. 9 above.

it is (like Ps. 112) a greeting to the reader, and so forms a kind of preface to the whole Psalter, or at least to the edition which stretches from 1 to 119. It addresses the God-fearing reader who meditates on the Scripture day and night. It speaks of the Torah, yet it may be assumed that it also regards the texts which follow it as being like the Torah, or at least consistent with it. It sets the reader at the crossroads, forcing him to a self-examination before he begins to read the texts.

Between 1 and 2 the Hebrew textual tradition has no caesura. For 2 has no heading, either because this gave way to 1, or because 2 itself was intended as a kind of heading for what followed. The attempt to take 1 and 2 together as a single psalm-text has no other basis than the presence of similar beatitudes at 1,1 and 2,12, a very formal argument which is insufficient for the purpose; on the contrary, the texts are so different in style, form and message that we cannot pursue this idea. 1 is a didactic Wisdom Poem of late post-exilic origin, 2 an old royal text from the pre-exilic epoch. In this sense, the gap between 1 and 2 may be seen to be considerable. 1 provides a framework for 2ff., and 2 is precursory to the series 3–72 (89): both have an introductory function, and yet they stand quite separate from one another (like the prefaces at the beginning of this book).

The connection between 9 and 10, on the other hand, is relatively clear. 9 as an alphabetical poem which, despite a disturbance at the point of transition, is continued in 10. They are *one* psalm, and the Septuagint numbers them accordingly. In this case, the absence of a heading in 10 confirms that the two texts belong together.

The link with 11 is of a similar sort to that between 2–3–4–6–7–8–9/10 . . . Between these texts, the connections are fairly tight. After 2, the texts follow one another spaced, so to speak, at regular intervals, and in each case they are both joined and separated by new headings. 2 leads the way, a

Royal Psalm from the Jewish temple ritual, revised with a post-script at 2,12 which applies the text to the reader, and turns the psalm, like those which follow it, into 'David's' testimony of faith. It's exemplary nature is given *eo ipso*.

The rest follow, with only the apparent exception of 8. Ps. 8 is also an I-Psalm, and knows the oppression of hostile powers. In form it is a prayer of the individual worshipper, or more precisely, a Prayer of the Accused, a type to which 6 (atonement Psalm of Ill-health, with threat of enemies also present) and 9/10 (free alphabetical poem) also belong with certain modifications. In short, these are all Individual Psalms of the Enemy, including in a sense 8 (enemies of God) and 2 (enemies of the king).

It will be seen, then, that the links in the chain are by no means thrown together capriciously. They are arranged with care. This impression becomes even stronger when we take account of the progression of shared ideas. 3–8 are largely characterised by the motif of the night. 3 has always been regarded as a morning prayer, 4 and 5 as evening prayers. But 6 is also spoken 'in the night' (6,6) as indeed might 7 be. 8 looks up to the night sky. 3; 5; 7 have the shield metaphor in common. In 5; 7; 8; 9/10 the concept of the name of God plays a role. But most importantly, the whole series, starting from 2, traces in many aspects and variants the shared attitude which is expressed in the verb *ḥsh*, 'trust', 'have faith': taking refuge under the protection of the gracious God. We encounter *ḥsh* in 2,12; 5,11; 7,1; (11,1 . . .), and its counter-part[21] *bṭḥ* in 4,5; 9,10. In addition, words for hope are found in 5,3; 9,18. However, this proof is unnecessary, for it is quite obvious that the motif of trust is dominant in all of these texts, which build a chain of assorted credal statements. In this way, the wider context dictates the character of the individual

[21] See the appropriate articles in the *Theologisches Handwörterbuch zum AT*, I 1971, II 1976.

testimonies. Yet Gunkel regarded only 4 (and 11) as suitable for allocation to a 'type' . . .

Chapter VI

PERCEPTION OF FAITH

The experience of faith which speaks out of the Psalms is of inexhaustible richness. In the present chapter we can only attempt to offer an impression of this abundance, and to indicate ways of finding one's bearings in this lush and blooming garden. A few preliminary considerations are required.

We use the term 'experience' for the difficult process of the assimilation of observations and insights which, to be quite vague and neutral, can be classed as 'religious', and which are already present or come into play when one devotes oneself to the questions of the nature of life, the fundamental principles of the world, and the ultimate meaning of human existence. Such insights exist as the collective experience of tradition. Depending on culture and lifestyle they are brought into systems of symbols, which preserve the new-found understanding of life, and make it available for others. Such systems of symbol and meaning can be called religions. The individual is restricted to expressing his unique (but for social reasons rarely original and independent) experiences in terms of the received system of thought, combining them with the symbols he has learned, and thus adding to the conceptual reservoir of the tradition. It is this very complicated process of acquiring, transmitting, revising, enriching and impoverishing which makes up religious life. In this process, and from it, faith can live. Faith is conscious of encountering truth in this process, insofar as the insights have brought conviction of truth; and it is conscious of encountering revelation, insofar as the insights did not spring from human endeavour. However, in this encounter, truth shows its human face, and experience is kindled in the concrete world of everyday life.

1. The Currents of Tradition

Israel too, had developed its system of thought. While this system has its own clear identity among other historically comparable systems, the rules governing the process of discovery and growth are valid here as in other religions. One of its characteristics is the fact that in the process of discovery it has adopted certain themes, and the continued development took place in such a way that a number of persistent basic themes were explored, expanded, corrected, reformulated, and selected. In the world of scholarship, this process is known as 'the tradition', and the themes thus fashioned are known as 'traditions'. So, for example, in the last few centuries, as people have become more aware of these processes, and have begun to apply historical-critical analysis methodically, it has become apparent that on the whole a very few themes have overwhelming importance in the Psalms. We call them the Zion, David, theophany traditions, the traditions of the kingship of Yahweh, the creation, the *Heilsgeschichte*, the cult, and others, according to the central concept around which the minor elements are ordered. Most importantly, the comprehensive nature of these theme-traditions, which transcend the individual psalm, is ideally suited to drawing together the texts into complexes, in order in this way to open up wider intellectual (and that means theological) contexts. With this observation of theological themes comes the discovery of a literary principle of some importance. The sections of text in which the various theme-traditions are presented are often of a cultic-hymnic nature, and in many cases give the impression – we have mentioned this repeatedly – of being the heritage of a very early period. It may be assumed that we are often confronted by old archive material, particularly in the blocks of tradition in which a credal theme of this kind is presented. In not a few cases this undoubtedly goes back to the pre-exilic period and to the pre-exilic temple. Although all this is relatively valid, with qualifications and applied to specific cases, we can nevertheless attempt, by assembling the different theme-traditions, to produce something in the nature of a cross-section through the history of the religious belief, or at least what remains of it, from the end of the pre-exilic period. This attempt requires methodical ground-work in each individual case. Only a very rough sketch can be offered here.

1. In my opinion, the so-called Royal Psalms (2; 18; 110 etc.) must surely be among the oldest. Their common theological theme is the *Königsheil*, that is, divine salvation mediated through the king on *David's throne*. One prerequisite for this tradition is the concept of the sacred dignity of the institution of monarchical kingship in the ancient orient, which found its expression in the god-like and sacrosanct person of the king. The Davidic king was regarded as 'the son of God' (2,7), he sat 'on the right hand of God' (110,1). He was the anointed one (= Messiah) (2,6), i.e. God's vassal, his representative on earth, who was appointed to preserve law and order, and in this way to guarantee the divine blessing of prosperity and fertility (72). His foremost duty was to ensure social and spiritual peace – strikingly portrayed in Isa. 11,1ff. – and above all, political peace.[1] No wonder the expectations placed on the reigning king, officially nourished and propagated in the kingship ritual, were extremely high, indeed immense, especially at times when the realisation of these hopes ran against the trends in Middle-Eastern power politics. Meanwhile the ancient picture of David, which served as the basic model for all such ideals, was held higher and higher, eventually becoming an antetype of the expected king who would restore the majesty of Israel. In the kingless post-exilic era, the texts relating to royal prayers

[1] Cf. O. H. Steck, 'Friedensvorstellungen im alten Jerusalem', *Theologische Studien* 111, 1972.

and royal rituals were presumably read as promises (2; 110), or as lessons of history (18) showing how God's gracious works (*ḥasdê YHWH* 89,1) were once made manifest in his dealings to and through David and his successors (*ḥasdê Dāwîd* Isa. 55,3), for the salvation of Israel.

2. The *Election of Zion* and of the Jerusalem Temple as residence and site of the divine presence is another theme which no doubt released strong emotions, and had far-reaching consequences as a faith-tradition in Israel. This tradition builds on very early material, going back to the Jerusalem of the Jebusites, i.e. pre-monarchical and early monarchical, borrowing images of the 'Most High God' ('*el* *ᶜlyôn*) who dwells in his earthly palace (temple) on Mount Zion, establishes justice among his people, and helps them to victory over raging enemies. It builds on the imagery of the sacred ark, the ancient tribal palladium which David reputedly brought to Jerusalem and Solomon set in the temple, in the Holy of Holies, as a symbol of his kingship. The oldest section of Ps. 24 (vv. 7–10) is probably connected with temple and ark; this is the impression given by the honorary title 'YHWH of Hosts' (*YHWH ṣᵉbā'ôt*). Perhaps it is connected with some kind of parade or procession. Also relevant alongside 24 are the so-called Psalms of Zion, 46; 48; 87, which adopt older themes, combining in their own way the images of the Mountain of God, the River of God, the City of God. Fixed elements are 'the City of YHWH', 'the City of the Great King' (46,4; 48,2), 'the Holy Dwelling Place' on 'the Holy Mountain' (46,4; 48,1; 87,1), 'the River of God' (46,4; cf. 87,7; 65,9), that mythical place where God lives. 'The entire Zion tradition in its oldest form was for the Israel of the day nothing other than a contemporary exegesis of the ark and its tradition, accomplished with the help of

Canaanite motifs' (J. Jeremias).[2] Its place was the temple, and it remained there until it could be preserved for posterity in the prophetic and psalm-like writings (Isa. 6; Mic. 4,11ff.; Ezek. 38f; Zech. 13,1). As a theology of divine presence and audience, the Zion tradition had created something lasting, also for those times when people would worship God in Spirit and in Truth.

Thematically, the Zion tradition hangs together with the tradition of the Theophany of God, which describes under what cirumstances and with what concomitants the advent of God in the cult takes place. It is the tradition of an event experienced and passed on in worship which the relevant sections of psalms reproduce in powerful colours (18,7–15; 68,1ff; 97,3–6). The oldest of these texts (Pss. 18; 68; 97) record the pre-exilic existence of such liturgical traditions, as do the references outwith the Psalter (such as Isa. 6; Judges 5; Deut. 33 etc.). 'The hymnic representations of the Theophany in the Psalms are therefore to be understood as reflections of an event transmitted in the cult, an event which they presuppose, and which they mirror to varying degrees in their words . . .' 'In terms of the history of form, they are to be classed as Credos or Hymns, in which the community reacts to the appearance of God and of his salvation, and visualises and communicates in profession and in worship that which has been experienced in the cultic act' (A. Weiser).[3] How that happened in practice can be deduced from a number of references, but on the whole we are still in the dark about this. Generally it is supposed that the events were passed on liturgically, perhaps by the recitation of the festival pericope, or by dramatic cultic symbols like the cloud of smoke

---

[2] J. Jeremias, 'Lade und Zion. Zur Entstehung der Ziontradition', in: *Probleme biblischer Theologie, Festschrift G. von Rad.* 1971, pp. 183–198.

[3] A. Weiser, 'Zur Frage nach den Beziehungen der Psalmen im Kult', in: *Festschrift A. Bertholet*, 1950, pp. 513ff.

(Isa. 6,4; 1 Kings 8,10f.), the blast of trumpets (Ps. 47,5) and the festive cry (*t^erû'â*) (Ps. 47,5; 68,11, etc.), which causes the earth to shake in a joyful echo of the coming of YHWH. A. Weiser even asserted: 'The Sinai theophany took place in the temple of Jerusalem (Ps. 50,2), so that in Ps. 68,17 it can be said quite candidly "Sinai is in the Sanctuary".'[4] In addition to the old royal songs like Ps. 18, such advent celebrations, offering their glimpse of the presence of God, have also left traces in individual prayers, probably of post-exilic origin. (Services of worship of this kind were also celebrated in the second temple, as the Priestly Work [in Lev. 9] proves with the theological key-word *kābôd* [= δόξα] 'light of Glory'.) Ps. 63 might be mentioned, where the worshipper declares: 'I have seen you in the sanctuary, and beheld your power and glory' (v. 2), but also Ps. 17 where the psalmist prays for this: 'But in justice I shall see your face, when I awake I shall be satsified, when I see your form' (v. 15). It is uncertain to which festive cultic rituals such verses relate, but it cannot be disputed that they do relate to cultic procedures. The idea of the advent of God remained a permanent item in the liturgical tradition, even after the accompanying rites ceased to be performed dramatically, and were re-interpreted as symbols of the divine being (compare 1 Kings 19 with Ps. 29).

3. It is becoming more and more clear that the classical themes of *salvation-history* from the Pentateuchal tradition, the promises to the patriarchs, the exodus, the Sinai covenant, the wilderness wanderings, and the '*Landnahme*' (conquest/settlement of the promised land), all have their place in the Psalter. They appear remarkably concentrated in the Asaph Psalms (50; 73–78), a series of texts which for the most part are to be reckoned to the collective, liturgical psalm-type. Here we find text fragments, probably of pre-exilic origin, which come from the geographical area of the former

[4] Ibid., p. 520.

northern kingdom of Israel (as a comparative study will show). The obvious conclusion is therefore that this group brings us samples of the theological and literary heritage of the northern territory, where, as scholars have always recognised, the classical traditions of salvation-history were fostered with particular care. The ancient sanctuaries of Gilgal, Bethel, Shiloh, Shechem, etc., are the most likely. However, we may assume that an influx of the ancient Israel-'Jacob' traditions into the wider collection of the complete Psalter occurred through the influence of the Asaph guild. If this is true, we are dealing with a successive reception of ancient Israelite material (after the fall of the northern kingdom 722/1) and a lengthy process of revision in the thinking of the post-exilic temple community, which indeed can be demonstrated in a number of texts (e.g. 80[5]; 50; 83).

The background traditions of the Asaph Psalms can be seen in a number of old theological and liturgical structural elements. Clearly we are looking at the whole ideological complex of God as Deliverer and as Judge, as this is presented in covenant theology. The 'shepherd of Israel' (80,1), the 'God of Jacob' has brought the vine up out of Egypt and planted it in 'his inheritance' (*naḥʰlâ*); he has 'established in Joseph a statute, when he went out against (LXX: from) Egypt' – the great statute, the first commandment of the decalogue:

'I am YHWH your God, who brought you up out of Egypt: you shall have no other god among you, and you shall worship no other god.' (81,10).

He has grounds, before the witnesses of Heaven and Earth (50,1ff.; 81,1ff.) to summon his people to judgment, and to demand an accounting from his covenant partner 'who made a

[5] Cf. W. Beyerlin, 'Schichten im 80. Psalm', in: *Das Wort und die Wörter, Festschrift G. Friedrich*, 1973, pp. 9–24.

covenant with me over a sacrificial meal' (50,5). He appears as judge against the 'gods' 'in the assembly of El' (82,1), against the nations, and enemies (76; 79; 83) and against the wicked (75). Even the great didactic poem Ps.78 thrives on this tradition. Its Deuteronomic/Deuteronomistic heritage, and consequently its possible origin in the northern kingdom has been well established (and a reworking from the standpoint of the Zion tradition in vv. 65ff, is extremely probable). It reveals the great current of tradition in the Asaph group, and points towards its estuary, where it flows together with the traditions of the Southern Kingdom.

4. The idea of the *Kingship of God* seems to have had its roots outwith Israel.[6] In Jerusalem it was integrated with the themes of Zion, the ark and the theophany, as can be seen from Isa.6; Pss.24; 29; 47 etc.: 'I saw the Lord seated on a high and exalted throne, and the hems of his robe filled the temple' (Isa.6,1). YHWH adopted the title 'King of the Gods' from the Canaanite high god El. This image, firmly anchored in the pre-exilic temple cult, becomes in the exilic/post-exilic period the basis of a likely development, which can be traced in the writings of the prophet of the exile, Deutero-Isaiah, and also in the poems known as the Royal Hymns of the YHWH (Pss.29; 47; 93–99). Each of these psalms makes reference to this *theologumenon*, expressing it in different variations on the key phrase 'YHWH is king' (*mālak YHWH*), and each expounds it in its own terms for the benefit of the post-exilic worshipping community. The fact that other pieces from the earliest temple tradition were taken up and used in the process is illustrated by the re-use of established credal statements. The expansion of the image into the universal is already present in the root concept: YHWH is praised as 'King above all gods' (95,3), i.e. as ruler of the world (47,2). Later the title

[6]Cf. W. H. Schmidt, *Königtum Gottes in Ugarit und Israel*, Beihefte zur Zeitschrift für die atl Wissenschaft 80, 1966 (2nd ed.).

became part of the repertoire of hymnic doxologies (e.g. 22,28; 146,10 etc.).

5. 'The testimony to the Creator in the Psalms' (L. Vosberg)[7] makes up another similarly structured complex of ideas. It can be found in around twenty psalms, but only in a few does it become an explicit theme (74; 89; 104; 148; also 33; 95; 135; 136; 147). Often the talk of *Creator* and *Creation* is connected with talk of God's victory over the powers of Chaos in the primeval sea (e.g. 65; 74; 93; 98; 104; probably also 24). Since this theme for its part has a connection with the themes of Theophany, Kingship of God, and Zion, a wider context emerges which is suited to the language of mythology. We shall come back to this. The creation theme appears also to have a Canaanite, or perhaps (from Gen. 14,18–20) Jebusite origin, and was applied to YHWH along with other titles. The oldest texts, on the other hand (89; 74), make it clear that the hymnic sections contained and used in them which speak of the creation (89,9–14; 74,12–17) are pre-exilic. 89 is a Royal Psalm which relates to the time of the monarchy; 74 is a Lament on the destruction of the temple (probably 586 BC) and makes reference to the old order. For both of these the testament of creation is a valid strand of tradition which sets faith on a firm foundation, even when the temple lies in ruins and the crown of David has been trampled underfoot. Two basic theological statements are intensified in this tradition to statements of faith. Firstly, Heaven and Earth are God's own personal handiwork. They are therefore 'ordered', conceived intelligently, designed purposefully, and formed deliberately:

'YHWH, how many are your works.
– in wisdom you have made them all –
The earth is full of your creatures.' (104,24)

[7] L. Vosberg, 'Studien zum Reden vom Schöpfer in den Psalmen', *Beiträge zur Evang. Theologie 69, 1975*.

Secondly, this order can be sustained as long as the creator acts as its guarantor, protecting it against the powers of destruction. This is the setting of the motif of the dragon fight, as a mythical/symbolic expression of the fragile state of this world:

'You have set a boundary which they cannot cross;
never again shall they cover the Earth.' (104,9)

From these two *theologumena* we discover the purpose for which the world and its creatures were made. This now becomes the subject of later hymns, such as 8 with regard to the purpose of humanity, 104 with regard to God's provision, 19 with regard to a cosmological revelation, and 147 with regard to the meaningfulness of the world order.

Into these five theme-traditions, David's throne, Zion, Salvation History, Kingship of God and Creation, centuries of religious experience have been compressed. They can be linked together in a number of ways. Since all of them are open to other images, since, so to speak, they only have an inner nucleus which can be combined with other nuclei, there must surely have been attempts as early as the Solomonic temple to establish a wider system of relationship. The scholarship of the last century saw the festival calendar as the ribbon woven through all the independent themes. Some saw the different themes distributed among the various major festivals like the great historical traditions of the Old Testament, others ascribed them to one particular festival (e.g. the Festival of YHWH's Enthronement, P. Volz, H. Schmidt; the Royal Enthronement Festival, S. Mowinckel; the Royal Festival of Zion, H.-J. Kraus), still others saw them rooted in the Jerusalem festival cult itself (Cultic Covenant Festival, A. Weiser).[8] Since very little is known about the festival forms

[8] H. Volz, *Das Neujahrfest Jahwes (Laubhüttenfest)* 1912: S. Mowinckel, *Das Thronbesteigungsfest Jahwäs*, 1922: H. Schmidt, *Die Thronfahrt Jahves*, 1927: H.-J. Kraus, *Die Königsherrschaft Gottes im AT*, 1951: A. Weiser, *The Psalms*, pp. 23ff.

of the monarchical period – with the exception of the royal ritual of Judah for the enthronement of the Davidic kings – we must content ourselves with the more general assumption that the majority of themes had their setting in the temple cult, that they were fostered there and performed liturgically until some of them found a new usage in the repertoire of post-exilic psalmody. This is the natural assumption from the literary data of the psalms in question.

If we bring together the southern themes into a consecutive 'history', such as: YHWH comes, conquers, creates, rules, chooses Zion and David, establishes a residence . . . , then in my opinion two things follow. Firstly, the similarity to myth is conspicuous, particularly to the Canaanite Baal-myth as this is known to us from the late bronze age texts (13th century) from the ancient city of Ugarit. The obvious question is whether there were other 'myths' (in the technical sense of the word: primeval 'history', which seeks to explain that which exists by reference to its primeval origins) which in the cult of the monarchical state-sanctuary in Jerusalem provided a framework or basis or pattern for the theme-traditions which have come down to us. Were they, we must ask, part of an extensive Jerusalem 'sanctuary legend', a *hieros logos* which upheld and proclaimed the importance of the temple?

It must be admitted that a number of points speak for such an assumption, not least the cult-myth relationship, and the significant fact that in the catalogue of themes the classical traditions of salvation history are missing: patriarchs, exodus, Moses-Sinai, wilderness wanderings, settlement of the land, history of the judges.

Against this, we must consider that historical traditions are by no means absent from the Psalms; we should not forget the great historical psalms such as 44; 78; 80; 105; 106; 132, or the hymns 135; 136, which even attempt to link the historical traditions with the southern traditions. However, the nature of this linking shows that what we are dealing with here is the secondary addition and integration of theme-traditions which have separate origins. The fact remains that among the psalm-texts or fragments which are demonstrably pre-exilic, the southern themes stand alone. Nor would it be the first time that the old pre-exilic Jerusalem has appeared with its own principle of tradition; there was too strong a claim on it as the state capital of the Davidic monarchy for that to be so. The fact that a certain leveling out of the whole body of theological themes in the Psalter was then achieved in the post-exilic period is attested by the historical psalms mentioned above, which needless to say pursue contemporary aims of their own, and have little interest in a salvation-historical creed as such.

This is the other thing which strikes anyone who seeks a broad and ordered view along the lines of a 'Theology of the Psalms', the ultimate lack of any real interest in a systematisation of the traditions into a symbolic credal schema. The authors and copyists of the psalm-texts have done little to produce such an ordered schema. We could, of course, point to the (albeit not very consistent) substitution of the name 'YHWH' by the term 'God' (*lōhîm*) in the so-called Elohistic Psalter (42–83) as an attempt to produce a uniformity of theological thinking, but characteristically this was in an area where the pillars of the Korah and Asaph groups 42–49,50 and 73–83(ff.) announce a different theological orientation anyway. Perhaps it is a mistake to look for such a schema. Diversity is better than uniformity.

2. *Individual Experiences*

Individual experience is dependent on the collective systems of symbols in which it occurs, and is interpreted and communicated, particularly on the social level, since 'religion' is particularly a concern of the group, tribe, clan or family, or in larger institutions, of the city, state, or kingdom. This only changes when the conventions and traditions lose their importance, when for example radical social change causes a breakdown of group identity, and the individual is forced to stand by himself, thus becoming independent and self-sufficient. However, these developments do not usually run directly and steadily.

There are very few religious texts from Israel's pre-exilic period in which individual writers communicate individual material. We could think of a number of prophets, Isaiah, then Jeremiah and Exekiel. But these last two both point to the opening up of a new era. There is no other Old Testament character about whom we have so much personal data as about these prophets from the end of the 7th and beginning of the 6th centuries. In particular, Jeremiah's lamenting tone reveals moods, emotions and frustrations. His 'confessions' are, at the core, poems of individual lament which have been turned into psalms of lament by later redactionary work.[9] Obviously, the phase of the genuine individual testimony is just beginning at this point. The oldest I-Psalms in the Psalter are the Royal Psalms, but in these the king does not in fact speak as an individual, but rather as the incumbent on the throne and the crowned head, the nameless 'anointed one'. We must therefore assume that, for the most part, the I-Psalms will stem from the post-exilic period. Their experience of faith is therefore experience which stems from those relatively late centuries. In this respect they stand in a long chain of tradition, and are dependent, both in the structure of their experience and in the format in which it is expressed, on established forms which had grown over a period of centuries.

[9] Cf. J. Schreiner, *Jeremia, Die Neue Echter Bibel*, I II, 1981, 1984.

They fit in with the available linguistic culture, particularly with the linguistic repertoire shaped by the cult. Nevertheless, these psalm-texts, growing out of personal experience but expressed in accordance with convention, are testimonies *sui generis*. What we find among the rich variety of these testimonies are experiences which belong for the most part to the piety of the laity and of the people. In addition, there are the larger liturgical compositions and the reflective wisdom poems, but these remain a minority.

(1) In his examination of the Israelite personal names (1928), M. Noth placed particular value on the religious aspect.[10] In both of his main sections, headed I. 'Theophoric elements in the Israelite personal names' and II. 'The Israelite personal names as expressions of piety', he is constantly drawing parallels with the piety attested in the Psalms. The second section in particular shows even in its chapter headings the interweaving of proper names and psalms (names expressing belief, trust, thanks, petitions). The continued research into personal names by J. J. Stamm,[11] and research into inscriptions from ancient Israel, has confirmed that the piety of the ordinary people was the common soil nourishing the three different forms of expression which provide documentary records of individual people. Each therefore complements and interprets the others.

The name *Zephaniah*, for example, was very common in the 7th/6th centuries. The Old Testament knows several people who went by this name, and the inscriptions add a number more. Among them is the prophet so named, a contemporary of Jeremiah. The name consists of a sentence which can be translated 'YH has hidden' (*spn YH*), hidden in the sense of protecting. A name expressing thanks, this could even be

[10] M. Noth, *Die israelitischen Personennamen*, (1928) 1966.
[11] J. J. Stamm, 'Beiträge zur hebräischen und altorientalischen Namenkunde', *Orbis Biblicus et Orientalis* 30, 1980.

regarded as a credal name. The parents who first formed this name and gave it to their child wanted to express their thanks or their faith. (Later others followed them, and the name may have become fashionable, in which case the motives become less clear.) The occasion of this thanksgiving or declaration of faith was surely the birth of the child, or another deliverance experienced by the parents coinciding with the birth, which in the best Israelite manner they ascribed to the personal intervention of their God YH (shortened form of YHWH). Two Psalmists do the same thing in their own way. Pss. 27 and 31, both Laments, acknowledge the same hiding, protecting deliverance of God, and use the verb with the divine subject in an analoguous way:

'For he hides me in his shelter
in the day of trouble.' (27,5)
'In your shelter you hide them (scil. the faithful)
from the strife of tongues.' (31,20)

The contexts make it clear that this 'hiding' can and preferably should be experienced 'in the shelter of his presence', 'in the shelter of his tabernacle', i.e. in the house of YHWH. This would indicate that the same might be assumed of the author of the sentence-name. At any rate we see how the individual experience and its expression are dependent on the tradition of public worship.

'Ruth' is one of the very few exclusively female names in the Bible. (Out of a total of about 1400 personal names in the Bible, ninety-two are used of females; but only a very few of these are genuine female names, i.e. only ever given to girls.)[12] It is a descriptive name, which sums up the experience of the parents at, or in connection with the birth. After long discussion, it seems now to be agreed that 'Ruth' (from the Hebrew rwh, 'to drink one's fill') means 'drink', 'refresh-

[12] Ibid, pp. 97ff. (121f.).

ment', 'beverage', and records the atmosphere of the occasion at the birth of the child.[13] Possibly the name takes a common mood in the oriental heat and transfers it to the particular circumstances of the parents. But the reason for this transference from the Nomadic sphere could be the unspoken thought that this 'refreshment' is a kindness for which the deity should be thanked. At any rate, the psalm-texts which use the same word for particular experiences speak in this way: 'my cup *overflows*' (23,5) says the psalmist, looking back at all he has come through. Similar images of drinking and refreshment, even of drunkenness, are found frequently in the Psalms in the context of the experience of worship:

'They feast (*rwh*) on the fat of your house,
    you give them to drink from your river of delight' (36,8)

Cf. 91,16 as it is rendered in the *New English Bible* (reading *rwh* 'to satisfy' for *r'h* 'to see'). Cf. also 16,5; 17,15.

Nevertheless, we must be clear that a secular interpretation of 'Ruth' is also possible.

(2) Most of all, it is in the *expressions of trust*, both in the names and in the Psalms, that religious experience finds its voice. There would be little point in exploring all the possibilities here. We shall limit ourselves to a few observations which can serve as a basis from which further discoveries may be made.

1. The two most important verbs which worshippers used to express their belief and trust in God are the Hebrew *ḥsh* and *bṭḥ*.[14]

The first of these, *ḥsh*, expresses a process, an act, which could be represented by the phrase 'to flee into the protection of . . .' A number of components appear with varying degrees

[13] H. Bruppacher, 'Die Bedeutung des Namens Ruth', *Theologische Zeitschrift* 22 (1966), pp. 12–18.
[14] Cf. the articles in the theological dictionaries of the Old Testament.

of prominence: crisis, decision, flight, safety. The source and model for the imagery connected with this seems to have been the cultic experience of refuge in the sanctuary. How far this shines out through the use of the root-word must be decided in each separate case. In particular, the first-person statement 'I place my trust in you' has become a standard expression of personal trust, and appears in the Psalms in prominent positions (7,1; 11,1; 16,1; 18,2; 31,1; 57,1; 71,1; 144,2: each time at the beginning of a psalm), as does the participle, which acts as a generalising label, 'those who trust' (2,12; 34,22; [37,40]; [64,10]: in each case at the end). The vigour with which this expression is used betrays a credal intention: the psalmist confesses his faith in God in circumstances and surroundings where his belief and trust must be decisive. The fact that he does this mainly in prayer indicates that he feels and knows that it is trust which his God expects from him, trust on his part corresponding to any kindness on God's.

bth, the second verb, is less dynamic, less active than *hsh*. It expresses a state. It is a trust in which one can rest, in which one can feel secure, because one can rely on the object of that trust. As a psychological statement it has wide usage, both secular and religious. The proportion of theological texts is smaller than with *hsh*, where secular usage is the exception. Nor does *bth* have the credal tone which is characteristic of certain uses of *hsh*. Rather, it is used to indicate a fixed and definite attitude, something quite undramatic, although this does not mean that the dramatic is never implicitly understood.

Both images, the dramatic fleeing to the object of trust and the static abiding in a deep-seated confidence, are clearly seen by the Psalmists as the basic forms of individual religious experience. At any rate there is a marked correspondence between these two main verbs and the I-Psalms of the individual psalmist, a correspondence which is certainly not limited to the so-called Psalms of Confidence, the group to which Gunkel ascribes Pss. 4; 11; 16; 23; 27A; 62; 131.[15] This fact is so striking that it gives rise to a number of considerations.

The verb *ḥsh* appears for the first time in the Psalter in the last line of Ps. 2, in a beatitude which praises all the blessed ones who 'trust in him' (2,12b). There is no doubt that the reference is to YHWH; the question is, who are the 'blessed ones'? Since from 2,10 the king directs his words to the world of people, exhorting them to subject themselves to YHWH's world order ('Serve YHWH with fear, "kiss his feet" with trembling, lest . . .') the closing line is also counted as part of this proclamation. However, this conclusion is brought into question when we consider the origin and meaning of the verb, and its context. Are the subjugated peoples expected to have faith in the same way that a worshipper of YHWH can have faith in the God he knows? Or might an ancient political meaning shine through, as in Jotham's fable (Jud. 9,15) or in Isaiah's words to the Egyptians (Isa. 28,17; 30,2f.): refuge in the shade of the mighty one? That is surely to overlook the force of the distributive words 'all who', by which a blessing in the context of a royal speech can take on the threatening tone of an ultimatum, and thus be transformed virtually into the opposite of what its form implies. What seems more likely is that in the closing beatitude the writer is praising all the worshippers, readers and singers who are able to find their way to the kind of faith which is demonstrated by the king who speaks in Ps. 2,1–12a. Speaking words in critical situations which, according to Isa. 7, King Ahaz was unable to find (Isaiah speaks of 'unbelief'), claiming divine promises, citing scripture and drawing conclusions from it, he is a model of faith, at any rate for the post-exilic redactor of the old Royal Psalms. And it is not for nothing that the shining example of

[15] *Einleitung in die Psalmen*, pp. 254ff.

the king (David?) stands at the opening of the Davidic Psalter (3–41, or even of the complex 3–72). Not for nothing is it followed by Pss. 3ff., psalm texts which are implicitly or explicitly testimonies to faith: explicitly in that the majority of texts in the Davidic Psalter, with the main exceptions of the hymns (8; 24; 29; 65–68; also 23), place the two principal verbs in prominent positions; implicitly insofar as the so-called Psalms of Lament and Thanksgiving are already testimonies in the theological sense, anyway. Our tentative conclusion might be posed as a question: could the Davidic Psalter have been conceived and constructed first and foremost as a collection of testimonies, drawing together selected individual experiences to a complete picture of faith?

The element of hope does not emerge in such a clearly structured way in the statements of faith in the Psalms. For the most part, it is implied by the verbs of trust without a separate verbal expression. Both the process of 'seeking refuge' and the state of 'resting in trust' contain the time-related idea of 'waiting for', which need not be made explicit. Hope appears as a component of faith. However, there are psalms in which the time aspect is given particular prominence. In such cases the verb *qwh*, which is very obviously connected with *qaw* 'line, cord', is often used, whereby in the factitive *piel* it may carry with it the image of the excited watching, lurking, waiting of the hunter at the net (cf. 56,6; 119,95). The writer of Ps. 130 prefers to compare himself to a watchman waiting for the morning (Ps. 130,5f; cf. 5,3). He is waiting for God's word – something which Ps. 119, incidentally, expresses with *yhl*. The writers of the Laments speak more generally. They wait for the Lord; their souls wait (Ps. 42, refrain; cf. 62,5). Here, too, the verbs 'wait' and 'be still' play a role; but like *qwh*, they are not able to become a fixed and valid technical term. So we are left with attempts at a *theologoumenon*. Nevertheless, a number of closing phrases show that the writers are ready and willing to give this aspect particular attention (27,14; 31,24; 33,22; 52,9; 130,7; 131,3).

2. Alongside the many narrative testimonies to individual deliverance and liberation in the past tense ('You have raised me up out of the depths', 30,1; 'He has heard my weeping', 6,8), we should pay particular attention to the psalmists' *metaphors*. For metaphor, which places one word alongside another and so releases a new understanding of the first, is a figure of speech particularly suited to the spontaneous expression of new experience. 'YHWH is my shepherd' (23,1). The '*is*-phrase' sums up the different aspects of the worshipper's experience; guidance, protection, providence, deliverance: God has shown himself to be a shepherd; *his* shepherd. 23,1–4 expands on what that means. At the same time the metaphor, which does not (yet) have the clarity of the original concept, contains within it a symbol which speaks to the emotions because it has grown out of the emotions and derives much of its content from them. The words about the shepherd say more to the suffering person than any theological definition of God's justice. This is because the metaphor presents a value familiar from the reader's own world (the shepherd). Extended to the new experience (YHWH), the familiar serves the as-yet unfamiliar, for in this way a new intimacy can develop. We could gather many metaphors of this type. For example, 'my rock' (28,1), which can be compared with 'he has set me high upon a rock' (27,5; 61,2), and many other instances: 18,2.46; 19,14; 62,2.6; 78,35; 92,15; 144,1; also 'rock of my refuge' (94,22); 'my mighty rock' (62,7); 'rock of my salvation' (89,26; 95,1); 'rock of my heart' (73,26), to give only a selection. Here we see a favourite metaphor, well on the way to becoming an accepted term. One might wonder whether the wide distribution of this metaphor has anything to do with the Rock of Zion on which

the temple was built (under the modern Dome of the Rock). Others are 'my light', 'my fortress', 'sun(?) and shield', 'spring of life', 'my inheritance', 'my refuge', 'my shelter' . . .

3. Another medium for collected experiences is the *maxim*, the poetic proverb. Its origin is in Wisdom, but it was also popular for religious experience. Ps. 32 demonstrates how such a dictum can arise out of a song of thanksgiving (vv. 9 and 10). However, a liturgical *Sitz im Leben* can by no means be assumed for all such maxims. Ps. 133 and its maxim extolling the joy of peaceful co-existence with 'brothers' has been discussed elsewhere.[16] Ps. 127 is a further example of the experiential proverb:

> 'Unless YHWH builds the house
>   the builders labour in vain.
> Unless YHWH guards the city
>   the guard keeps watch in vain.
> In vain you rise early
>   and stay up late
>   and eat your food with toil;
> He gives it freely to his own.' (127,1–2)
> (Older translation: 'he gives it . . . while they sleep')

This proverb reflects on the relationship of act and consequence, a variation on the traditional Wisdom theme of cause and effect, and comes to the conclusion that there is no automatic connection between an action and its result, this connection only being established with the co-operation of God. All forethought, care and effort is 'in vain' (Heb. 3 × 'empty') unless it is 'filled', so to speak, with a success guaranteed and gifted by God. Three attempts are made to approach a crucial question (act and consequence), using three examples (construction, civil defence, agriculture), and the question is brought into the theological sphere.

It has occasionally been argued that the author of Ps. 131

[16] II.3 above.

may have been female.[17] The literal translation of v. 2b points
to this: 'as the child to his mother, as the child to me, (so is)
my soul'. This psalm recounts an experience connected with
self-denial.

'I do not concern myself with things
    which are too high and wonderful for me.
But I have stilled and quietened my soul.' (vv. 1b-2a)

An experience with oneself, then, in the form of a new self-
awareness and a personal decision, apparently made as a result
of contact with the 'high' and the 'wonderful' (v. 1). It is not
by chance that we find such experiences related among the
Psalms of Ascents, that collection of 'popular poetry'
(B. Duhm) which sets particular store by individual religious
experience (cf. also 125,2; 126,5–6; 127,3–5; 128,3; 130,4).

4. From the proverb to the *poem*, which presents religious
experience in verse, is a short step, a step already taken in
Pss. 127; 131; and 133. The most impressive are in my opinion
psalms 23 and 91, which have an unparalleled history of use.

'YHWH is my shepherd, I shall lack nothing.
He makes me lie down in green pastures,
He leads me to a resting place by the waters:
He calms my desire.
He guides me in the right paths, for his name's sake.
Even though I walk through the darkest valley,
I fear no misfortune, for you are with me.
Your rod and your staff, they comfort me.' (23,1–4)

Ps. 23 speaks of a discovery which the psalmist made on
being acquitted of all charges in the divine court of law.
Seeking God's judgment was part of the system of justice, a
method used in otherwise insoluble cases. 'You have set my
table in the presence of my opponent; you have anointed my

[17] E.g. G. Quell, 'Struktur und Sinn des Ps 131', in: *Das ferne und das nahe
Wort. Festschrift L. Rost, Beihefte zur Zeitschrift für die atl Wissenschaft* 105,
1967, pp. 173–185.

head with oil, and have filled my cup to the brim . . .' (v. 5) –
these are the rites of acquittal. At once the psalmist speaks of
his hope: 'Goodness and love will follow me all my days, and
I shall return to the house of YHWH all my life long' (v. 6).

Ps.91, a didactic poem about divine protection in life,
echoing the old words of blessing and consecration, begins
with the lines:

'He may dwell in the protection of the Most High,
He may rest in the shadow of the Almighty,
Who says to YHWH:
   "My refuge (and my stronghold),
   My God in whom I trust."' (91,1–2)

This theme undergoes a fourfold development, each stage
containing a word of encouragement: (1) vv. 3–4 makes use of
two images from the world of birds (hunting and defending a
nest); (2) vv. 5–8 names two dangers (plague and warfare)
from which YHWH's faithfulness protects; (3) vv. 9–10
encapsulates the experience in a credal statement: 'your refuge
is YHWH'; (4) vv. 11–13 extends this protection to all the
paths upon which the faithful are sustained by angels and kept
from the fangs of snakes. The result of all the psalmist's
experience and meditation is summed up at the end in words
from the mouth of God himself (vv. 14–16), 'a miniature of
Old Testament religion' (P. Hugger):[18]

'Because he loves me (says YHWH) I will rescue him.
  I will protect him, for he knows my name.
He calls to me, and I answer him
  I am with him in trouble
  I deliver him and bring him to a place of honour.
  I satisfy him with long life and show him my salvation.
                        (91,14–16

---

[18] P. Hugger, *Jahwe meine Zuflucht*, 1971, pp. 257ff.

3. *Theological Models*

In a number of psalms we find attempts at the formation of a system built on abstract thought and concepts, which is comparable with what we might call doctrine or theory. To this extent it is possible to speak of 'theology' in the sense of a systematically structured presentation of the insights which have been amassed. True, such theology must be related primarily to the individual text, or to groups and complexes of homogenous, or at least affinitive texts. A theology of the Psalter would be a most confused affair; at best it could be constructed as a framework into which the whole collective witness of the psalms could be fitted.

These attempts at a systematic theology can best be classified according to the didactic and literary forms on which they draw. And here again, with reference to what has been said about the formation of proverbial units as expressions of personal insights, we come again to discuss the psalms containing acrostics:

1. *Alphabetical Poems.* While these psalms certainly have something stiff and mechanical about them, and are rightly identified as the product of the writing desk or of the school room, their relevance to systematic doctrine and theory is indisputable. The individual proverbs are devised as pronouncements on a given theme. They start with a prescribed opening letter, but the theme can be freely developed. Assuming that the surrounding format of the Aleph-Beth expresses something like wholeness, comprehensiveness, and that the cycle of teaching or meditation serves in the manner of a medieval prayer-chain (with complicated modifications on the theme for sake of variety), then such a text would be making a claim to completeness, whether or not this claim was actually substantiated. In the case of Ps. 119 it is possible to detect such a claim to a comprehensive theology of

the Word of God; however it must be seen as a weakness in this theory that the chain of $22 \times 8 = 176$ verses achieves a systematic exploration only by 'addition', the gathering of material. And yet, the amassing of insights and testimonies does correspond to the general principle of the canon far more than 'abstraction', analysis and evaluation.

2. Then we can point to the group of texts most commonly categorised as *hymns*, which seek, using nominal clauses and an argumentative style, to depict theological ideas objectively in 'descriptive praise'), identifying them and giving them a precise definition. Since they generally deal with basic themes (creation, humanity, history, revelation), they are the medium of real theological work with a doxological character, a form of work which has become the pattern for all theological work (cf. Paul's letter to the Romans). In this way Psalms 8; 19; 33; 90; 104; 136 all play a substantial role in the developing of theological models, because they offer this kind of approach to the material. Ps. 8, for example:

'What is man, that you are mindful of him,
    and the son of a man, that you should accept him?
You have made him a little lower than the gods (or: than God),
    you have crowned him with glory and honour.
You have set him up as ruler over the works of your hands,
    you have laid everything under his feet.' (8,4ff.)

After the *Imago-Dei* text of Gen. 1,26f. and the Yahwistic cornerstone, Gen. 2,7, Ps. 8 is the most important statement in the Old Testament on the position of humanity within the created order.

Nowhere, with the possible exception of Eccles. 1–3, do we find such deep reflection on time and eternity, and indeed on all the aspects of the problem of time, as in Ps. 90.

'Before the mountains were born,
  before the earth and the world were created,
    you are, O God (*'El*), from everlasting to everlasting!
You let men return to dust,
  you say "Return, you sons of men!"
Indeed, a thousand years before your eyes
  are like the day that has just gone,
    or like a watch in the night . . .
Yes, all our days disappear before your anger,
  our years pass away like a sigh.
Our life will last just seventy years,
  eighty at the most,
    and those, at best, are trouble and misfortune.
Yes, quickly they pass, and then we fly away . . .' (90,2ff.; 9ff.)

Ps. 104 pursues the system of the cosmic economy of water as the divine provision for life; Ps. 19 explores the solar system and its testimony to the creator, which in the scale of revelation is placed alongside that of the Law (*tôrâ*).

3. Psalms 49 and 73 (also 1) are *Wisdom Psalms* both in origin and in type, and they must be counted as 'problem literature' in the most general sense.[19] Their *problem* is the question of the justice of God in the face of the very obvious injustice and inconsistency of human life, which seemed to mock the reigning doctrine of the correlation of action and reward. (This is also the problem of the Job poem, with particular regard to the suffering of the righteous.) Pss. 49 and 73 formulate the problem along very similar lines:

'Why must I see the day of the wicked?' (49,6

'For I was seized with rage against the arrogant,
  when I saw the prosperity of the godless.' (73,3)

Since, for both of them, the action–reward equation must stand beyond question, but the facts of earthly life do not seem to support such an equation, they seek the solution in

---

[19] F. Stolz, *Psalmen im nachkultischen Raum*, 1983.

the final accounting at the end of life. Ps. 73 speaks of the 'end' which corrects all things, and in particular it speaks of the conviction that the proximity of God solves all problems:

'If I am with you, I desire nothing on earth.' (73,25)

Ps. 49 also uses death as an argument:

'Do not be troubled when someone becomes rich,
    and the splendour of his house increases,
For he will take nothing with him when he dies.' (16–17)

It is questionable whether the much discussed verse 15, which seems to speak of the redemption of the soul from the Underworld and of some kind of deliverance, belonged to the original psalm. It is even more questionable whether it is really speaking about a life *after* death. It would be better to understand the statement as a reference to deliverance *from* death, as in the line from Ps. 73 which uses the same word (Heb. *lqḥ*) to speak of God's 'taking into glory' (v. 24). At any rate, the psalms do not know an 'eternal life' in the normal sense.

Ps. 1, a wisdom piece, presents as its solution the doctrine of the two types of person and their 'ways'. It draws together the results of the discussion, and offers the simple rational denominator to which the ethical question is to be reduced. One may well wonder whether this really deals with the question at all.

In the context of rational theological modes of thought, we should also mention in passing those psalms which have as their theme the mocking of other gods. They are marked by a strongly apologetic interest and a propagandistic effect, which should be considered along with texts from the Books of Deutero-Isaiah and Jeremiah (82; 115; 135).

4. Alongside Wisdom Theology, we find in the Psalms a *Theology of the Heilsgeschichte (Salvation-History).*

The great *Histories* of Psalms 78; 105; 106 (also 135; 136) are off-shoots from the great body of tradition which seeks to record and pass on the stories of YHWH's dealings with his people. The centrepiece of this tradition is the historical collection which now forms the first part of the Old Testament canon. Research into this tradition has made a lasting impact on our understanding of the Old Testament, and led to Gerhard von Rad's great framework for a theology orientated around the *Heilsgeschichte* (end of the 1950s, beginning of the 1960s).[20]

The historical Psalms succeed the earlier historical traditions (J, E, D, P, dtrG), which they evaluate from a didactic point of view. They are completely topical, being aimed at their own contemporary situation, to which they present the events of the past as in a picture book, with encouraging and comforting words. Only the complex hymn-text 136 attempts a comprehensive re-telling of all 'great wonders' (136,4), but it too stops with the last uncompleted or questioned wonder of the gift of the land 'as an inheritance to Israel' (vv. 21–22). For that is the problem of its time.

Ps.78, a didactic piece in extended poetic form (72 verses make it the longest psalm after 119), surveys the history of Israel from the Exodus to David, and finds evidence for the faithfulness and goodness of God, and for the unfaithfulness and rebelliousness of the people leading inevitably to punishment.

In a kind of refrain it varies the 'same old song':

'They did not keep God's covenant,
    they refused to live by his laws.' (78,10: cf. vv. 17.22.32.56)

The lesson of history is that guilt hinders the completion of God's plans, a pessimistic conclusion in the light of the contemporary situation. The 'teaching' (*tôrâ*, v. 1) of the

[20] G. von Rad, *Old Testament Theology* vol. I, 1957. (Eng.tr.1975).

psalmist does not end with a full stop, but rather with a question mark: Will God's 'wonders' (v. 4) continue?

The twin psalms 105 and 106 each draw different conclusions from their observation of history. Ps. 105 recognises in the events from Abraham to Moses and to the occupation of the land, which it illustrates quite freely, the history of the fulfilment of a promise, namely the promise which God once made to Abraham in covenant and vow, and which has been valid as a 'decree' (*ḥoq*) and an 'everlasting covenant' (*bᵉrît*) for Israel ever since (vv. 8–10):

This 'word' (v. 8):

> 'I will give you the land of Canaan
> as your inherited portion.' (v. 11)

has been fulfilled, and remains the basis of all hope, and the reason to sing, play, and meditate on 'all his wonders' (vv. 1f).

For Ps. 106, on the other hand, the history from the Exodus out of Egypt to the entry into Canaan is the occasion for a confession of guilt:

> 'We have sinned, along with our fathers,
> we have been wicked and iniquitous.' (v. 6)

It is a history of divine anger and well-deserved punishment, right up to the present day. And yet at the same time, it is the history of the 'mighty deeds of YHWH' (v. 2), the praise of which is linked with the confession of sin. This kind of praise on the part of the guilty is known as a 'judgment doxology'.[21] Its purpose is to bring to an end a chapter of history, and to set one's sights on a new beginning. So the psalm ends with a plea:

> 'Help us, O YHWH our God,
> and gather us from the nations,
> That we may give thanks to your holy name,
> and glory in your praise.' (106,47)

[21] G. von Rad, *Wisdom in Israel*, 1970, (Eng.tr.1972).

And so we see again, here at the close of our discussion, how the psalmists sift tradition and experience, gain knowledge and understanding, and, as in every theological endeavour, end in praise.

Chapter VII

OUTLOOK ON LIFE

'I am of the opinion that the whole of human life, both the basic spiritual position and the prevailing "movements" and thinking, are contained within the words of this book. There is nothing which remains to be said about humanity.' (Athanasius)[1]

1. *The 'I' of the Psalms*

The 'I' in the Psalms is in the majority of cases an individual person, in the sense that a single person drafted the prayer, song or poem for his own use. This does not exclude the possibility that such a psalm-text might find its way into the collection and then be used by others, who might make the 'I' apply to themselves. It is, however, less common for a text fashioned with an individual 'I' to be re-worked into a collective 'I' (Israel, Zion; cf. Ps. 129). Of course, it is quite conceivable that certain psalms which were originally designed as psalms of the individual underwent a secondary adaptation involving a communal or community 'I'. But the idea of an extended process of collectivisation, posited by earlier scholars, should be treated with some scepticism.

Only in relatively few cases is it possible to detect who it is who says 'I' in the Psalms. Since as a rule the details of authorship are not reliable, we are thrown back on the evidence of the texts themselves. It now emerges that in a very few cases it is the king of Judah-Jerusalem who speaks the words of Pss. 2; 18; 101; 110, while for other Royal Psalms which are clearly pre-exilic texts, a court poet (45, cf. v. 2), a

[1] Athanasius, *Ad Marcellinum*, J. P. Migne, *Patrologia gr.*, XXVII 41C.

priest or a precentor (20; 21; 72; 89) would come into consideration. In the bulk of the Psalms of the Individual, the 'I' relates to persons unknown to us from the period and the vicinity of the second temple, the time and place in which the psalm collections arose; so, roughly speaking, the Palestine of the 6th–3rd centuries BC. Here we find a reflection of the life of that time, if only in glimpses, without the possibility of arranging them biographically, or even of creating a panorama of the general conditions of life. If we reckon with around eighty psalms in which an individual 'I' is uttered, it would seem possible to gain some insight into the course of individual lives, and thus into the conditions of life and the attitude to life. Such insights would be of inestimable value for our understanding not only of the Psalms, but of the whole of the Old Testament. However, we must begin to limit our scope right away. Only a very few of the eighty people involved (mostly men; only in a very few cases do women come into the question, as in 123; 131; cf. 1 Sam. 2) rise above typical and general statements to the concrete, biographical level. Then we must remember that the more concrete the words of the psalmist, the harder it becomes for the interpreter to decipher the references and reconstruct the situation. And we must be very careful to resist the temptation to construct a totally imaginative scenario.

Our problems begin with the basic geographical data. In Ps. 42/43, for example, it is made clear that this is a psalm spoken far from the 'holy mountain' and the 'house of God'. Its location is made concrete by the words 'from the land of the Jordan and of Hermon, from Mount Mizar' (42,6). Only the first two references can be located. Taken together, they point to the area of the source of the Jordan, at the foot of the Hermon mountain range (the mountain *Miṣ'ār* may be a part of this), a conclusion supported by the next verse which speaks of 'waves and breakers' (42,7), and alludes to the

waterfalls of that region (near Tel Dan). But here the
questions begin. What hindered the worshipper from making
the pilgrimage to Jerusalem? Is he injured or unwell (the
decisive word in v. 10 is unclear), or is he a prisoner, prevented
by force from making the journey (42,3; 43,1), or is the truth a
combination of both? It is impossible to say.

Ps. 120 is spoken by an exiled worshipper:

> 'Woe to me, that I dwell in Meshech,
>> That I live among the tents of Kedar.' (v. 5)

Qēdār was the name of a Bedouin tribe which used to camp
in the northern parts of the Syro-Arabian desert (Isa. 21,16f;
Jer. 2,10; 49,28f.), so presumably the uncertain *Mešek* was also
there (cf. Gen. 25,13f.). At any rate, the psalmist is beset by a
hostile foreign environment. Here again, further questions
would be redundant.

Many I-Psalms originate with people living in the general
vicinity of Jerusalem, or at least able to make a pilgrimage
there (cf. 121; 122; 125). But not all of them could proudly
boast with the writer of 87: 'To Zion he says: Mother! The
man was born there!' (v. 5 emended; cf. v. 4).

When it comes to *social conditions*, the psalmists are more
vocal. These were reasons for lamenting in circumstances in
which prayer was the only way out, i.e. in illness or in legal
proceedings. Let us consider a number of examples. Firstly,
Ps. 41. The psalmist is looking back on the crisis of his 'sick-
bed':

> 'I said, "YHWH have mercy on me, heal me,
>> for I have sinned against you."
> My enemies speak evil against me:
>> "When will he die, and his name pass away?"
> And when one comes to visit (me)
>> his heart speaks falsely;
> He gathers misinformation,
>> then goes out and spreads it.

All of them whisper against me;
    all who hate me imagine the worst for me:
"Something evil has come upon him",
    and: "Once you've lain down you can never get up".
Yes, even my friend whom I trusted,
    the one who shared my bread,
        has lifted his heel against me.' (41,4–9)

This is quite clear, and is reminiscent of the picture given in Job. 19: Experiences from a sick-bed! The psalmist names three groups of people who prove hostile in the critical situation:

(*a*) His old *enemies*. They see their advantage in the demise of the sick man and of his 'name', i.e. his family, his fortune, etc. The economic hardships of widows and orphans are a constant theme in the Old Testament.

(*b*) The curious *visitors*. They judge the case. (At this social level there was as good as no medical care. Indeed there was very little in ancient Israel at all. Only later, with some misgivings, were 'doctors' permitted; cf. Sir. 38.) The visitors come to the conclusion that something must be wrong in the life of the sick man. Sickness is 'something evil' (= devilish, demonic, literally 'a thing of *b*ᶜ*liyya'al*'); 'poured out' upon the afflicted one, it brings its own stigma. Suspicion arises, intensified by emotion ('hate') and nourished by primitive convention, and assumptions are expressed aloud. Popular wisdom is cited, as in the saying about lying down and getting up.

(*c*) The *friend* (literally 'man of my peace [–covenant]'). Bitter experience: he 'lifts his heel', i.e. takes his leave, not without causing pain.

It is a sobering picture of life which is drawn here. And yet, as the Book of Job shows, no isolated case. No wonder that there is so much talk of 'enemies' in the Psalms. In a crisis situation, the psalmist feels himself surrounded by countless enemies, as the example from 41 makes clear: enemies of all kinds; old adversaries, opportunists, and former friends.

The picture in Ps. 109 of a man falsely accused is no less

dismal. Ps. 109 used to be discredited, quite wrongly, as a psalm of curses and revenge. The psalmist is in fact citing the words of the 'lying tongues':

> 'Appoint an evil man against him,
>> let an accuser (*śāṭān*) stand to his right.
> When he comes to court, let him be found guilty,
>> and let the verdict result in punishment.
> May his days be few,
>> may another take his place.
> May his children be orphans
>> and his wife a widow.
> May his children wander and beg,
>> and be driven from the ruins of their home (? or: community).
> May the creditor seize all his goods,
>> and strangers rob the fruits of his labour.
> Let there be no-one to show him kindness,
>> and no-one to have mercy on his orphans.
> Let his descendants face destruction,
>> in the next generation let his name be snuffed out.
> May his father's iniquity be remembered,
>> and his mother's sin never wiped away;
> May their sins ever be in the eyes of YHWH,
>> that he may purge their name from the face of the earth.'
>
> (6–15)

In the case of this psalmist, the threat lies in a complaint or charge in the law-court, which in his eyes is groundless calumny (vv. 3.7.31). Since he has reason to fear the worst, and sees prayer as his last hope of deliverance, we may assume as in analogous cases that he is awaiting a decision in the temple court proceedings, and can only hope for a favourable divine verdict. The verses quoted described in the starkest terms what it would mean to be found guilty. There are various clues which hint that the opponents (v. 29) are people from the psalmist's own circles. We can only guess why they should have an interest in the total annihilation not only of the writer

163

but of his family, his descendants, even his 'name'. We can only see the case from the standpoint of the psalmist. But the fact that this document was preserved as an example of answered prayer would indicate that he was in fact acquitted of all charges.

But this was no isolated case. The Prayers of the Accused in the Psalter prove that. They trust in the justice of their God, and with much protestation they rely on the judgment which he will pronounce upon them. 'Flee to the mountains like a bird', advise good friends. 'I place my trust in YHWH', the psalmist responds, 'YHWH is just, and he loves justice' (Ps. 11). Others have no choice. For them, as for the sick, prayer is their last chance.

Each case is different. It is necessary to seek in each psalm clues to its background, and it is not always possible to achieve the degree of clarity we might desire. The cases of the following sick and/or accused are particularly impressive: 5; 6; 7; 16; 26; 27; 30; 35; 69.

It is the *descriptions of suffering* which occupy the greatest amount of space in the I-Psalms. The depiction of misery belongs to the basic substance of the prayer of lament/supplication, a prayer which has as its purpose the presentation of the supplicant and his need. It may be that in this way the situation is shown to be worthy of pity. On the other hand, the formulation makes it clear that convention is also playing a part. The language of suffering also lives by tradition. The striking thing is that in many of the descriptions of suffering, the reasons for the suffering remains unclear. It is understandable that no diagnosis can be made on the basis of the psalms; this also has a great deal to do with the lack of anatomical and medical data. However, the fact that it is often not even possible to tell whether the suffering victim is ill, oppressed, imprisoned, under attack or threat of attack, may disturb the reader. What we must take into account here is that a stylised and generalised description increases the usability of the texts as prayers. Consequently it was precisely such simple and non-concrete psalms as 130 ('I cry from the depths') which enjoyed wide popularity. As a general rule, it is the imagery, and atmosphere abstracted from the concrete crisis experience which makes it possible for the text to survive in the tradition. In this respect, Ps. 22 is inexhaustible. Here we find the full richness of the language of suffering. Not without reason did the early Christian communities interpret the story of the passion of Jesus in terms of this psalm. It may not be obvious from the history of the psalm that this was originally a personal prayer, and not a formula for prayer. What is the nature of the suffering of this person?

> 'But I am a worm, and not a man,
>> a mockery before men and despised by the people.
> All who see me, mock me,
>> they draw back their lips and shake their heads:
> "He trusted in YHWH that he might help him;
>> So let him help him, since he delights in him." . . .'
> 'I am surrounded by mighty bulls,
>> the buffalo of Bashan encircle me . . .
> They open their jaws against me –
>> a ravening and roaring lion (. . .)
> My heart has become like wax,
>> it has melted away within me.
> Dry as a potsherd are my gums,
>> and my tongue sticks in my gullet;
> I have been poured out like water,
>> you have laid me in the dust of death.
> Yes, dogs have surrounded me,
>> and the band of evil-doers encircle me.
> They bind me hand and foot . . .
> I can count all my bones,
>> but they stare and gloat over me.
> They divide my clothes among themselves,
>> and cast lots for my robe.'
>
> (22,6–8.12–18; emended in 13–15)

Is it possible from this slightly damaged text to reconstruct the situation in which the worshipper found himself? At best we can think of a person who is awaiting his execution, for which the preparations have already begun (16–18). One might ask whether the dogs (v. 16) are the half-wild curs which make oriental cities so unsafe. But certainly the bulls, buffalo and lions belong to the metaphor. The description of fear is of particular interest: the heart becomes soft 'like wax' and melts; the limbs become paralysed, they seem to dissolve; the gums (Heb. 'strength' is probably a copyist's error) and mouth are dry 'like a potsherd' (a fragment of earthenware); the tongue is unable to move, and cleaves to the inside of the mouth; in short, he feels himself and his life poured out 'like water' which cannot be gathered up again, thrown like a (broken?) pot into 'the dust of death'. Is it possible to give a better description of the fear of death? The many similes and metaphors allow us to experience with the writer how he struggles with suffering and seeks an appropriate mode of expression.

Alongside Ps. 22 we may place Pss. 69 and 102 – all three, incidentally, are compositions with complex structures. Ps. 69, the psalm of a man both ill and condemned ('what I did not rob, I must repay' – v. 4) is distinctive for its swamp metaphor:

'Help me, for the waters have reached my soul (or: throat).
I have sunk in deep mud, where there is no firm ground;
I have landed in deep waters, and the floods swirl over me.'

(69,1–2)

Ps. 102, obviously also prayed by a sick man, is distinguished by its colourful nature imagery, particularly its animal similes:

'For my organs (days?) have vanished in smoke,
    and my bones glow like a hearth,

My heart is scorched like grass, and withered;
  I even forget to eat my bread.
Through loud groans and sighs.
  my bones cleave to my flesh (?).
I am like an owl in the desert.
  like the howlet among the ruins.
I remain awake and grieve
  like a lonely bird on the rooftop.' (102,3–7)

Similar images of lamentation: 38; 39; 55; 59; 77; 88. Only once is it explicitly stated that the suffering has to do with the age of the writer, Ps. 71, insofar as it is possible to relate the plea:

'Do not cast me away in the days of old age;
Do not forskae me when my strength disappears!' (v. 9)

to the present situation of the supplicant. But here again, the immediate occasion of the prayer is the threat of enemies (v. 10f.).

There are a wide range of different points of view. We can only do justice to the Psalms of the Individual and the situations described in them if we examine each one of them separately. The examples which have been given can serve only to point out a few of the possiblities.

2. Life and Death

What outlook on life is reflected in the descriptions of the I-Psalms? We should now be speaking of particular background concepts which are embraced by these personal testimonies, in order to give precise definition to a particular person's attitude to life. We are speaking of the concepts of the basic questions and the marginal questions of life, of its beginning and end, of the ultimate meaning of existence.

Very little is said in the Psalms of the beginning of life. Only in critical situations does a writer remind himself and his God of his birth: 'It was you who drew me from my mother's womb, and kept me safe at my mother's breast' (22,9). And the writer of Ps. 139 praises God that he was created so wonderfully and formed so perfectly, so that nothing fallible can have any place in him:

> 'You yourself created my kidneys,
>   you knit me together in my mother's womb.
> You knew my soul long ago,
> My bones were not hidden from you,
>   when I was formed in the darkness,
>   skilfully in the depths of the earth.
> Your eyes have seen all my days,
>   all of them are written in your book.
> My days were all counted
>   before any of them had come.' (139,13–17)

Here we see images of how a person becomes a person, of his formation 'in the depths of the earth' (cf. Job. 1,21), and the idea that longevity is predestined ('The Book of Life', Ps. 69,28). It is difficult to say how widely these ideas were distributed, but a number of parallels show that they were by no means unique.

We know somewhat more about the concepts of death and of life after death. According to the usual Oriental concept, prevalent in ancient Israel as elsewhere, death is merely a development of human life, albeit one with particularly severe consequences. For in death, a person would enter the shadowy realm of the Underworld (Heb. Sheol, $š^e$'ôl = Hades) the 'land of no return'. There, according to the common view, the life of the 'souls of the dead' continued, but in a much restricted manner. Each person would retain the status he had at the moment of his death, which is why those who had been executed and discredited (even those who 'died by the sword') had a particularly lamentable fate. According to Isa. 14, the World of the Dead was in turmoil when the King of Babylon appeared, and all the princes rose from their thrones in a mock greeting to the new arrival. This poetic fiction rests on existing widely-held ideas. But the shadow existence is dismal; eternal silence and darkness surrounds the disembodied shadows, whose presence there can only be recognised so long as their names are remembered in the Land of the Living. The Underworld lay in the furthest depths; in the Israelite understanding there could be no line of communication with the world above, far less with the realm of God. And so we hear the common complaint:

'What will it profit you if I die,
    if I go to the grave?
Can the dust praise you?
Can it proclaim your faithfulness?' (30,9; cf. 88,10–12)

Ever more urgent is the Psalm of Hezekiah (Isa. 38):

'For the Underworld does not praise you,
    death does not worship you;
They who go down to the grave
    cannot trust in your faithfulness.
The living, only the living praise you,
    as I do today.' (Isa. 38,18f.)

In some Laments, the writer imagines himself already to be in the Underworld. 'From the depths of Sheol I cry'; 'I had gone down into the earth, she had closed her bars behind me' (Jon. 2,2.6). In the case of the Psalm of Jonah, this may be understood in context: Jonah is, after all, in the belly of the fish, at the 'roots of the mountains'. However, in other Laments, it is expressed in exactly the same way, so that we have to ask whether we are dealing with a conventional form of expression. Chr.Barth[2] has pursued this question and come to the conclusion that an established image does indeed lie behind it, whereby the sick, the imprisoned, the threatened

[2] Chr.Barth, *Die Errettung vom Tode in den individuellen Klage- und Dankliedern des ATs*, 1947.

are seen as being already in the power of the Underworld, and in the sphere of death. The Underworld, the sphere of a reduced and declining life-force, reaches far into the sphere of life itself, extending its dominion even to the living. One consequence of this insight is that all those Psalm-texts which speak of salvation from death or from the Underworld may have to be understood as testimonies of the experience of the living, of deliverance from the threat of death, back into life. This means ·that the Psalms make no clear and unambiguous statement concerning a life *on the other side* after death. The much discussed texts 16,10; 49,15; and 73,24 do not demand a concept qualitatively different from the concept of the existence of the dead in the Underworld. Here and there we do find a hope that existence itself is not the highest possession, but rather co-existence with God; and that communion with God may possibly lessen or even overcome the loneliness of Sheol. But even this idea is by no means forcefully expressed in the texts under discussion. Rather, it is the experience of Ps. 63 which gives us hope, a psalm of thanks for a divine acquittal:

'I have seen you in the Sanctuary,
   (or: I shall see you)
   beheld your power and glory.
For your grace is better than life.' (63,2f.)

The concept of an eternal life after death was not discovered in Israel until the late Hellenistic period. It seems first to be attested in the Wisdom of Solomon (1st century BC).[3] However, the view of death as the weakest form of life, with its implications for weakened life on the one side and on the other the shadow life of the souls of the dead, must not be seen as a veiling of the inevitable fate which is prescribed for all humanity. Only gods are immortal, and even they only if

[3] O. Kaiser, E. Lohse, *Tod und Leben*, 1977, pp. 7ff.; 68ff.

they have not, as Ps. 82 satirically suggests, been condemned to death:

'Gods you are, all of you sons of the Most High!
And yet in truth, you shall die like men . . .' (82,6f.)

3. Conduct and Destiny

However, there are also ideas about the course of each individual life which concern everyone and which therefore belong to the rules and principles of life. We recently noted the connection which in the Israelite understanding existed between a person's conduct and his destiny. We discussed this in terms of reward, and spoke of the repayment which each deed earned and received. But this is far too modern a concept. The ancient mind thought more in organic categories of the fruit of the evil or good deed, and of the almost natural effect which follows from all dealings, reproducing itself in counter-dealings, with corresponding results. This idea of the connection between a person's actions and their fortunes, which finds its widest acceptance in Wisdom, and has been thoroughly discussed in the context of the Job problem, is known as the 'synthetic' outlook on life (K. Hj. Fahlgren), or 'the government of destiny by deeds' ('die schicksalswirkende Tatsphäre', K. Koch).[4] The wise men and theologians were not always happy with the deep-seated resistance of this compensatory or retributive thinking. Psalms 37; 49 and 73 are, like the Job poetry, obsessed by the question of whether this schema is in principle always valid and usable. They too, find solutions only within the framework of this doctrine which they cannot question a limine.

But it was not only theologians who had to struggle with the problem, and the question of how the personal care and concern of God for man was to be combined with such a

[4] K. Koch (ed.), Um das Prinzip der Vergeltung in Religion und Recht des ATs, 1972.

schematic operation of life; was he merely the guarantor of this order? In everyday life, this pattern could have devastating results, namely when a particular person like Job had been struck by misfortune and the surrounding world more or less automatically asked the aetiological question. This question was asked in John's Gospel for the teaching of later generations: 'Who sinned, this man or his parents, that he was born blind?' (Jon. 9,2). The misery described in the 'biographical' Psalms is in no way traced back to such a rigid concept. The example of Job is well known. The poet there makes a heroic attempt to break the chain of this doctrine.

The psalmists, less free than the Job-poet, and overpowered by their sufferings, are not able to choose the heroic way. But, much to the credit of the community, there remained for them a set procedure, be it the sacred proceedings in the divine court which was designed for such difficult and unclear cases, or be it public atonement, a ritual which had the purpose of restoring the damaged sacral and social integrity of the unfortunate. Each of these models contained its own possibilities for prayer, as the Psalms of the Accused, the Sick and the Suffering bear witness. Both of them have already been discussed in the context of cultic questions. Here we have a society which has created institutions for the alleviation of problems the roots of which lie within itself, namely in the social consensus that each person takes the credit or blame for his or her own destiny. We can see that these institutions were effective from the Psalms of Thanksgiving which, in addition to their didactic function and their element of praise, also had the purpose of emphasising the acquittal, the forgiveness of sins and the 'justice' which had been dealt out, and of carrying these over into a life where such things would by no means be self-evident.

At any rate, these considerations demonstrate that this 'role'-thinking influenced the psalmists' behaviour, and even their language. Hence the efforts to present oneself as a 'penitent' who more than satisfies all the requirements, who more than pays his debt. And here, the so-called oriental exuberance or exaggeration ('All night long I flood my bed, my couch is drenched with tears', 6,6) comes into its own. Hence also the self-labelling (poor, righteous, humble, pious) which would otherwise be quite nauseating, and which can only be understood as a conventional image of self. And lastly, hence the expectation which is implicit in such self-images: the vow of praise already anticipates a positive outcome. What else could sustain and carry the psalmist than this certainty, formulated by Ps. 36: 'In your light we see the light' (36,9)? With this pointer to the element of role-playing in the biographical sections of the psalms, our first circle of observation is complete.

4. The 'We' of the Psalms

When the Psalmists say 'we', what do they mean by it? We now attempt to gain certain insights into the group identity of the Psalms. It is of little help to us to begin with the fixed groups or orders which, we must assume, were behind the psalm-poetry. From the Book of Chronicles we know the names and remits of various guilds of temple singers, to whom sub-collections within the Psalter were ascribed (the Korahites, Asaphites, etc.). However, it is questionable whether their influence on the Psalms themselves ran particularly deep. We should be thinking more of musicians and choral singers who were in some way connected with the temple. Remarkably, the priests stand very much on the periphery in the Psalter, despite the fact that a certain proportion of the poetry is ascribed to them. Did they deliver the oracle of salvation or the promise of answered prayer? We are given no clear answer. Only the Wisdom philosophers can be recognised, as writers of the reflexive psalms and the scholarly hymns. But can they be seen as a fixed group?

It is better to begin with the group identities of which the psalmists themselves speak. But even here, as far as I can see, there is very little definitive information to be gathered. Those who speak their prayers usually are aware of belonging to a group which has come with them to the sanctuary, or at any rate, which celebrates with them. The 'we' group which speaks of its deliverance in Ps. 124 seems to have been of this kind:

'Our soul is like the bird which has escaped the fowler's net;
the net is torn, and we have escaped.' (124,7)

Likewise the categories of 'redeemed' which are described in Ps. 107: those who had previously been lost, imprisoned, sick, shipwrecked, those who should praise YHWH 'in the assembly of the people', 'in the council of the elders' (107,32). Whatever is intended by this term, it is at any rate wider, it means the whole, the 'great assembly' (35,18; 22,22.25), the organised gathering of the whole community. In particular the Todah singers had an obligation before this gathering. We know very little of its nature, and what little we do know is spread over a very wide historical period.

'The pious' (ḥᵃsîdîm) and 'the righteous' (ṣaddiqîm) seem to be the terms employed most frequently by the community to describe itself, along with 'the god-fearing' (yᵉrē'îm). In the case of other predicates like poor, humble, oppressed, etc., it is difficult to tell how far the word still has its full meaning. Even for the three principal terms this is hard to say. Nevertheless, there are overtones which ring through, which once belonged to the basic nuances of the word, overtones like pardoned, justified, reverent, and so forth. But more importantly, these terms form a basis for the negative terms of which the Psalms are full: 'evil-doers' (pᵒ'alê 'āwen), 'godless'

174

(*rᵉšā'îm*), 'fools' (sg. *nābāl*). These are certainly not terms used by the particular grouping of themselves, but rather they are designations which, by contrast with the group's own position express a disassociation, or even a condemnation. From the various ways in which these defamatory terms are used, we must conclude that they do not refer to clearly defined groups.

5. Congregation and Community

We must therefore take account of the fact that the YHWH congregation of the post-exilic period had a serious problem of delimitation. Obviously affiliation and admission to the congregation and its activities played a greater role than has commonly been recognised. At any rate, even then, the political community (province, city and state of Jerusalem, population, etc.) was by no means to be identified with the 'assembly of the righteous', that gathering which built its group identity on the predicates which have been mentioned, and sustained it by marking off clear boundaries.

It is in terms of this endeavour that we are to understand the attempted definitions which seek to describe the stereotype of the godless (Ps. 73; 10), to characterise him (Pss. 14/53; 36) or to define him in opposition to an antetype (Ps. 1). Whether these were developed into usable models or remained mere theological constructions is a question which must remain open.

It is quite surprising that other political and contemporary problems have hardly found a mention in the Psalms. Pss. 74 (lament for the temple), 137 (lament on the exile) and 79 (concerning enemies) are virtually the only ones which take any notice whatsoever of current political issues. Where is there an echo of the Persian era with its enormous problems (Ezra – Nehemiah, structural questions, constitutional

questions, the Law)? Where do we find an impression of the
Hellenistic-Ptolemaic epoch (Hellenistic culture, diaspora
problems, etc.)? Even the Historical Psalms, so eloquent
when discussing the past, fall silent when it comes to the
present (78; 105; 106). Has this to do with the selection of
usable songs and prayers? Or with the concentration on the
personal problems of life? Or with the increasing isolation
(attested in Ecclesiastes and the Books of the Maccabeans) of
the Congregation of the Righteous from the wider community, as Jewish society became more and more heathen?
There are no satisfactory answers.

What we *can* say in conclusion is this: The system of
orientation which underlies almost all the Psalms is the
centripetal alignment towards Zion, towards the temple
sanctuary of Jerusalem. It is this foundational *Qiblah* which is
already expressed in 1 Kings 8 in the deuteronomistic temple
dedication prayer of Solomon (exilic):

'. . . and pray to you towards the land you gave their fathers
towards the city you have chosen, and towards the temple I have
built in your name, then from your dwelling place in Heaven you
will hear their prayers and their supplication . . .' (vv. 48–49)

This was how the psalmist saw his life, and the life of his
congregation, firmly fixed at this central point, and arranged
around it:

'From Zion, the crown of beauty, God shines forth.' (50,2)

Chapter VIII

COSMOLOGY OF THE PSALMS

Every bit as important as the theological traditions and the ways of making sense of life are the assumptions about the nature of the universe which shape what the psalmists say about their world. The writers are, often unconsciously, conditioned by the prevailing system of ideas. They live within its horizons and develop their symbols and images accordingly. Only the hymn-writers manage to raise themselves above the level of 'common knowledge', seeking to draw out new aspects and to discover a clear conception behind their world-view. But even they stand within the limitations of their time, and build on its foundations. And again it is the case that Israel shared the knowledge of the whole ancient world, at any rate as far as untested everyday concepts were concerned. For them, the sun went out in the morning and returned home in the evening – just as the eye experiences and understands it. It is, of course, to be expected that their faith would set the standards by which these observations were to be interpreted and brought within a conceptual system. However, we can only discern this critical view of the world if we first understand the general world-view of the ancient orient.

1. *An Ancient Oriental World Map*

Since all modern attempts to reproduce an ancient cosmology inevitably have their faults, we shall take as the starting point of our observations an ancient oriental sketch-map of the world. The so-called Babylonian world map (Fig. 36) is a clay tablet, 8 × 8 cm, a little damaged, particularly in the lower part. Its origin is in Babylon, from the 6th century BC (the

Fig. 36. Babylonian world map.

period of Israel's exile); however, in its original form, the map may be many centuries older. Its history shows something of the constancy which apparently characterised the ancient cosmological picture. The older form is passed on, even when this is known to have been superceded by more recent knowledge. 'Ancient Israel' – writes O. Keel in the chapter

'Concepts of Universe' of his pictorial commentary on the Psalms – 'appears to have held concepts of the structure of the Universe which, from a technical viewpoint, were very similar to those of the so-called Babylonian world map'.[1] This may be because it is a document containing general knowledge in which Israel participated, or because Mesopotamia, like the civilisation on the Nile, was Israel's mentor in questions of science and culture.

The centre-point of the diagram, where the geographer set his compass, must be taken as a point on the Euphrates south of the city of Bablyon; for Babylon is represented by the long rectangle above the centre, the Euphrates (and the Tigris?) by the band drawn through the middle of this rectangle, stretching southwards from the northern mountains, part getting lost in the southern swamps, and the other part pouring itself into a sickle-shaped arm of sea, obviously the Persian Gulf. Around the central point are grouped in a circle some of the cities and principalities of Mesopotamia. The Tigris is conspicuous by its absence.

Two concentric circles have been drawn with the compass, marking the horizon, the limits of the earth. The inner one shows the edge of the round (disc-shaped) earth, the banks of the 'bitter stream' (the ocean), which in turn has the outer circle as its limit. Outwith the outer circle, arranged like a large star, are isosceles triangles (only partly preserved) which are identified in the accompanying inscriptions as 'districts' or 'islands'; these represent the mountains at the ends of the earth on which rests the great vault of the Heavens (not marked on the sketch).

This is an attempt to picture the whole known world and present it in a cosmological map. It starts with familiar phenomena like the horizon, perceived as circle and centre-

[1] O. Keel, *Die Welt der altorientalischen Bildsymbolik und das AT*, 1984 (4th ed.).

point, and known topographical features, such as cities, mountains, swamps and seas, and forces them *more geometrico* into the pattern of concentric circles. Empirical knowledge, geographical observation and cosmological speculation are combined to produce an impressively simple picture of the universe. The sketch gives no information about the 'upper and lower parts', that is, the three-dimensionality of the world; but no doubt this is contained in the text.

2. *The Structure of the World*

The psalmists had similar conceptions. Israel probably saw itself as being at the centre-point of the world. The old sayings about the 'navel of the world' were certainly known in the Jerusalem temple. At any rate, when one spoke of the 'ends of the earth' and the peoples living there, one did not count oneself among them (Pss. 22,27; 48,10; 59,13; 65,5–8; 67,7). Ps. 48 diverges from this by placing Zion 'in the furthest north' (48,2), in order to proclaim it as the highest and most holy of sacred mountains. It abandons the notion of centrality for the idea of the sanctity of the 'Mountain in the North'.

It is not the psalmists, but Deutero-Isaiah and the author of Job who make use of the technical term for the horizon (*ḥûg* 'circle').[2] This encloses that which is understood by the 'Earth' (*'ereṣ*) or the 'Circle of the Earth' (*tēbēl*). In the course of the centuries the concept may have been extended, the circular form corrected, but it remained the fixed, protective coast-line which separated land from sea. 'You have set a boundary which they (scil. the waters) cannot cross' (104,9). Ps. 104 has the clearest concept. The ocean surrounding the earth (Heb. 'primeval flood', 'great waters', 'sea', 'rivers'), from which it rises like a mountainous island, forms the boundary of the habitable world. As such, it is placed, even in

[2] See my article in the *Theological Dictionary of the OT*.

the pre-exilic period, under the authority of the Anointed, the 'Son of God', the King of Jerusalem. The dominion over the natural world is part of the old ideology of kingship: 'Ask me, and I will given you the nations as your inheritance, the ends of the earth as your possessions'. This verse from Ps. 2,8 belongs to the 'resolution of YHWH' which is delivered to the Davidic monarch at the coronation; and in Ps. 89, God says to the king, 'I have him place his hand upon the sea, his right hand upon the rivers' (89,25). Ps. 72 gives the most precise definition of the realm in which the anointed one is responsible:

'He shall reign from sea to sea,
    from the river to the ends of the earth.' (72,8)

We can read this from the map. The reference is probably not to the Euphrates, but, as O. Keel rightly concludes, the 'Bitter Stream', the Akkadian term for the peripheral ocean.[3] Were similar world maps available at the court and temple in Jerusalem? We may answer this question affirmatively, since this seems to be what lies behind Gen. 2,10–14. Only a very few of the hymn-writers have thought out their cosmological ideas in detail. Beyond the basic assumption of a flat, circular earth, we are told very little. Ps. 136,6, for example, with the words:

'. . . who founded the earth upon the waters . . .'
                            (literally: 'stamped', 'hammered')

Then, of course, Ps. 104:

'He founded the earth on its pillars (foundations),
    so that it should never move again.'

The peripheral mountains are seen as part of the world-structure in their own right:

---

[3] Op.cit. (note 1), pp. 17ff.

'Before the mountains were born,
and the earth and its circle created,
You are God . . .' (90,2)

The 'mountains', also called 'islands' (Ps. 97,1), are the
outermost limit of the earth (Isa. 41,5). They stand like pillars
in the sea, and carry the great vault of Heaven; Ps. 18,7 speaks
of the 'foundations of the mountains', and the parallel text
calls them 'foundations of Heaven' (2 Sam. 22,8), thus giving a
precise statement of their function. The world map describes
the seventh 'district' (below right) as the one where 'the
morning lights up from its dwelling'. This not only points to
the motif-tradition of the sun rising between the mountains
on the horizon, but also reminds us of Ps. 19 where the sunrise
is described: 'Like a bridegroom he rises from his chamber'
(19,5; in Hebrew, the sun is masculine).[4]

The sky has no graphical image on the world map, although
it may be present in the text. Unlike similar symbolic
diagrams from Egypt, this map betrays a shyness about
making a visual image of these upper regions of which a
certain amount was known, but little was seen. Similarly in
the Psalter, the concepts are vague and abstract. Heaven, or
'the Heaven of Heavens' (148,4) is the upper, raised region of
the world, 'the upper chambers' (104,3). It is the divine realm.
Here belong the sun, moon and constellations, along with that
part of the primeval ocean which became 'the waters over the
expanse' (the firmament of Heaven). The ocean above the
firmament (see Gen. 1,6–8) shines blue through the great
dome of the sky. Rain falls when the sluice-gates are open (the
'streams of God', 65,9). Ps. 33 speaks of this with powerful
imagery:

'He gathers the waters of the sea as in a jar (or: dam)
He puts the ancient deep in a storeroom (or: bottle?).' (33,7)

[4] Ibid., Figs. 9–13.

182

The reference is to the ocean of Heaven. In Ps. 29,10 it is called 'the flood' (*mabbûl*). And finally Ps. 104 describes the sky as a tent which has been stretched out, and beomes a dwelling which God has constructed for himself (104,2f.). This poetic imagery replaces the cosmological pattern; but the conventional concepts win through again when it comes to invoking the location and boundaries of the bodies of water on this side of the mountains and beyond them, and 'over the mountains', i.e. above the firmament of heaven (104,6–9).

In this way, the sea forms the third part of the world, alongside heaven and earth; the concepts, however, begin to become confused. Such a threefold division lies behind various statements in the Psalms (e.g. 8,7f.; 33,6ff.; 36,5f.; 69,34; 96,11; 104,2ff.; 135,6; 146,6). The whole edifice of the world, constructed from these three elementary spheres, is surveyed by Ps. 95 first in a vertical, then in a horizontal cross-section:

> 'In his hand are the depths of the earth,
>> his also the tips of the mountains.
> His is the sea – for he made it,
>> his also the firm land – for his hand formed it.' (95,4f.)

To his realm belong also the adjoining regions: the depths of the earth and the peaks of the mountains which reach to the primeval sea; the lower and upper oceans of which the earthly sea is a part; and the firm land where humans dwell. Similarly Ps. 36 sounds out the world of grace:

> 'YHWH, your goodness reaches to the heavens,
>> and your faithfulness to the clouds.
> Your righteousness is like the mountains of El,
>> your justice like the great flood.' (36,6f.:

– i.e. incomprehensible. The 'mountains of El' are the peripheral mountains of the world.

The Underworld ($\check{s}^e$'$\bar{o}l$) is, as has already been mentioned[5], also a cosmic entity. However its position in the structure of the universe and in relation to the other parts of the world is unclear. It does not come into view in the Hymns of Creation, but it is very strong in the Laments. A number of points indicate that the underworld, as the word suggests, was located under the earth. Thus the word 'earth' by itself can indicate this place (e.g. 7,5; 44,25; 143,3). But really we are thinking more of a mythical place, a gigantic grave. For 'the grave' carries the same experiential values which are ascribed to Sheol: deep, dark, silent, forgotten. 'Each individual grave is a miniature "Underworld".'[6] However this last dimension of the cosmic structure remains very much within the psalmists' consciousness, if only to demonstrate the extent of salvation:

'Where can I go . . . ?
        Where can I flee . . . ?
If I climb to the heavens, you are there;
        If I make my bed in the underworld, you are there too.
If I rise on the wings of the morning,
        and settle beyond the farthest sea,
Even there your hand would reach me.
        Your right hand would hold me . . .'
(Ps. 139,7–10, cf. Am. 9,1–3)

The location of the world of the dead within the cosmic structure may be illustrated by a relief on a late classical boundary stone from Susa (12th century BC; Fig. 37). Two snakes encircle the cylindrical stone: at the top we see the snake of Heaven above the symbols of the great gods which in turn are pictured above the band depicting an earthly procession; on the lower part, the far larger dragon-snake encircles a fortress-like building, the towers of which support the earthly world. This lower fortress, flooded by the waters

[5] VII. 2 above.
[6] O. Keel, op.cit., p. 53.

Fig. 37. Kudurru from Susa.

of Chaos, represents the city of the Underworld with its gates, of which the psalmists speak (9,13; 107,18; Jon. 2,6; Isa. 38,10; cf. also Ps. 75,3). Thus the world is divided into three levels, familiar to us also from other texts, the best known being in the prohibition of graven images (Exod. 20,4). Apparently this three-storey pattern was very widely used.

3. Chaos and Cosmos

'He who is enthroned in Heaven, laughs at them' (2,4). Heaven is the domain of God. He dwells there as on a 'balcony' (104,3), or rather, he is enthroned there. The image of a heavenly palace, part of the imagery of the 'King of the Gods' (95,3), influences all the statements concerning the heavenly realm, making them more vivid. To the Royal Palace belongs the royal household, the messengers and hosts ($\check{S}^e b\bar{a}$'ôt), to which, in an extended sense, even the other gods (82,1; cf. 8,5) or former gods and 'Sons of El' (29,1) are occasionally counted. Ps. 148 summons the heavenly powers and bodies to praise; and in first place among them are the 'messengers' ('angels') and 'hosts'.

The earth is inhabited by an abundance of 'creatures' (104,24), people, peoples, animals. The sea, too, is full of living things. *Leviathan*, the sea dragon, and *Behemoth*, a monster of Chaos, dwell here; both are representatives of the powers aligned against God. The basic dualistic principle of an anti-power was never quite lost from Israel's world-picture. It was always there, the ancient hostile power, the power of Chaos which threatened the created world. True, it is only ever presented as a defeated power; but its primeval strength remains a constant threat to the cosmic order, and to the delicate balance in which this world exists.

The power of Chaos is identified with the primeval waters. These in turn are given a mythological tone by the chaos dragon and the sea monster. The conflict between Chaos and cosmos is exemplified in the ancient myth of the battle between the deity and the dragon, a struggle which also belonged to the material of Israelite tradition. The clues point to a Canaanite origin, more precisely to the heritage of Old Jerusalem (the Jebusite period). Since the discovery in 1929 of cuneiform inscriptions from the North Syrian port of Ugarit (Ras Shamra), which have given important insights into the mythological world of the 13th century BC, there can be no doubt about the origin of this mythology, even though the time gap and the geographical distance from Jerusalem throw up regional variations.

There it is the god of the weather, *Baal*, who decided the battle of the second generation gods (the first generation, the high god *El* and his consort, was responsible for the existence of the gods and of the world) against the sea god, *Yamm*, and the god of death, *Mot*, and was able to win kingship and the palace on the mountain in the North. The myth recounts these events and sets out their significance for the present. The texts from Ugarit offer us a lively impression of the richness of mythological tradition in ancient Canaan.

Various psalms, for the most part probably pre-exilic, pass down the mythological motifs which belonged in the Jerusalem temple. Here it is YHWH who wages war against the powers of Chaos and wins the kingdom. Usually this motif of the victory over Chaos is linked with the creation of the world, a combination which again reminds us of Babylonian models (*Enuma eliš*, the creation epic), whereas in the Ugaritic texts the creation does not explicitly emerge in the Baal myth. Be that as it may, the Psalms participate in the cosmic myth.

Ps. 74, a temple lament from the exilic period, recites elements of myth:

'But you, O God, are my king from of old,
   working works of salvation on earth.
You split the seas apart by your might,
   you smashed the heads of the dragon(s) on the waters.
You crushed the heads of Leviathan,
   and gave him as food to the sharks of the sea.
You dug out the springs and streams,
   you dried out the eternal streams . . .
Remember this . . .' (74,12–15.18)

According to Ugaritic sources, the sea dragon *Lītān* (*ltn*) had seven heads; as in Job. 26,13 and Isa. 27,1, he is called a 'coiling' and a 'gliding' (slippery?) serpent. This domesticated monster in the subdued ocean serves, as in a zoo, for the pleasure of God; thus the enlightened hymn 104 (v. 26). Ps. 29 tells us that YHWH has set up his throne on the primeval waters (v. 10). Rahab is the name of the sea dragon in Ps. 89; here again the dragon myth is being cited because Chaos seems to have broken in upon the royal order (vv. 9–14; cf. 65,6f.). And Ps. 95 shows King YHWH as the unshakable rock, against which the 'rivers', the 'great waters', the 'oceans' surge in vain.

Here, as in Pss. 74; 89; 65; 29 and 104, the myth of the dragon fight is beginning to take on a life of its own as a kind of *theologumenon*, while remaining merely a symbol and image for God's warlike dealings with hostile powers of all kinds; these were epitomised by that primeval force. In this way the Psalmists of the post-exilic period were able to use this motif freely for the sake both of poetry and theology (Pss. 33; 77; 46 etc.; cf. also 29; 65; 104 in their final forms). In particular, as Psalms 46 and 93 show us, the battle motif is combined with the motif of the invincibility of YHWH on Zion, on which Israel built many of its hopes.

4. The Mythological World

The points of contact which emerge here with the theological traditions of creation, kingship of YHWH, Zion, David and theophany, raise the question of whether the dragon fight might not also have become part of these traditions. We could answer this question positively on the grounds that the mythical motif shows an affinity to almost all of these traditions: Ps. 104 testifies to the connection with the creation theme, Ps. 93 with the theme of kingship, Ps. 74 with the theme of the temple on Zion, Ps. 89 with the theme of Davidic kingship, and finally Ps. 29 with the theophany theme. As these texts can to some extent be dated, or at least can mostly be reckoned as pre-exilic or exilic (not Ps. 104; but Ps. 74 also deals with creation), a further question arises, as to whether there might not have been in the pre-exilic temple an entire complex of theological concepts which are reflected in particular psalms; from these literary echoes we might propose a theological context which, by analogy with the texts from Ugarit, might be called myth.[7] Such an assumption, which for the time being is hypothetical, would allow us to explain the wider structure of the cult at the Solomonic temple under the monarchy, and would give a more concrete form to our understanding of what is generally known as the sanctuary legend, or the *hieros logos*. Meanwhile, however, we must content outselves with more reliable conclusions, treating the traditions of old Jerusalem themselves and the inheritance of old Jerusalem from the Canaanite period, on their own merits, even if the idea of a synthesis at the old sanctuary in Jerusalem has a certain amount going for it. At any rate, the mythical world, or rather, the world as it is reflected and elucidated by mythology, influenced the world-views of many psalmists. We must take account of this influence, just as much as we do of the restrictions

[7] VI. 1 above.

imposed by particular philosophies of life or historical faith-traditions. For the person reading such psalms, or using them devotionally, the same unavoidable problem arises as for all the creation texts of the Bible. These are founded on contemporary pictures of the universe: how are we to handle such cosmological concepts? An uncritical acceptance and appropriation of these concepts is certainly the worst of all possible solutions. But here we are going beyond the limits which we set for our 'Introduction'.

Chapter IX

RELATIONSHIPS WITH CLASSICAL ORIENTAL PSALMODY

The study of the relationships between the Psalms and comparable poetry of the ancient Orient has become increasingly urgent since large amounts of written material from the major neighbouring cultures has come to light. In quantity these far surpass the psalms known to us from Israel. The Hebrew Psalms soon proved to be a part of classical oriental literature, and in this historical context they came to be seen in a new light. At the same time, scholars had to face the question, what was the *proprium* which was unique to the Biblical Psalms, what distinguishes them from the classical oriental documents, and what was the reason why only the Biblical Psalms enjoyed an unbroken history of use (we return to this in Chapter X), and not the material from Mesopotamian, Egyptian and Canaanite cultic poetry.

Our objective, then, is to explore the nature of these relationships. Comparison is still the best method of defining an object in terms of its own individuality and its own idiosyncrasies. This, however, presupposes the closest possible examination of the counterpart which has been chosen for comparison. Here our study has clear limitations. We content ourselves with (1) a number of general observations on the relationship of the Biblical Psalms to the classical eastern psalms, and (2) a number of examples of concrete textual comparison, in order to convey at least an impression of the possibilities and the difficulties which arise here.

1. *Problems of Comparison*

In comparing the Biblical Psalms with analogous classical

oriental pieces, a number of points must be borne in mind.

1. The Biblical Psalms are for the most part far younger than the corresponding documents of the Sumerian, Akkadian, Egyptian and Canaanite cultures. The inter-dependence, if one exists, or rather, the line of influence, will therefore always be one-directional. Beside this poetry, the Biblical Psalms are late arrivals, written in a period when these neighbouring cultures were in a late phase of their develop-ment. Since the editions of ancient eastern poetry are more interested in the classical period and its forms, a major time gap opens up which must not be overlooked in comparison. Many of the classical documents of ancient eastern cultic poetry belong in the second millenium (Sumerian/Old Babylonian and Egyptian hymns, Canaanite/Ugaritic myths), while Israel's Psalms belong to the first millenium, most of them indeed to the second half of the first millenium (Chapter II). While synchronic comparisons would be particularly interesting, they are seldom possible.

2. The linguistic differences, particularly the different scripts, did not permit an unhindered exchange or flow of material. Which psalm-poet (only the poets come into question, hardly the lay worshippers) could understand Akkadian or read Cuneiform, or decipher Egyptian with its hieroglyphs, or even come to terms with the Ugaritic cuneiform alphabet in order to read the Canaanite/Ugaritic/ Phoenician dialects which just might have been comprehen-sible? How could a literary exchange have been possible? Is it conceivable that the poet of Ps. 104 had seen the sun-hymn of Akhenaton in the grave of Eye in Amarna, or had read a copy or heard a translation? Hardly! (In fact, closer inspection reveals only a few points of contact – contrary to popular opinion.)

3. It is, therefore, clear that literary dependence in the sense of the borrowing and reworking of classical psalms is scarcely

to be expected. This kind of dependence only comes into discussion in the case of two texts: Ps. 29, for which a Canaanite origin is suspected, and Ps. 104, for which a connection with the sun-hymn of Akhenaton is posited. I hold the former to be more likely than the latter.

4. This means that the relationships are restricted to the 'pre-literary', to motifs, images and ideas on the one hand, and to linguistic, oratorical and literary form on the other. These can be inspired either by similar or analogous contexts (*Sitz im Leben*), or by quite different ones. It is in this area of the influences acting on texts that the best possibilities for comparison arise, since the classical documents are often more precise in detail, and being also more numerous, they offer wider opportunities than the Psalms. This is particularly true with respect to their function.

5. For it emerges that the Mesopotamian and Egyptian 'Hymns and Prayers' permit far more exact definitions of their functions; in particular, the context for which they were intended is intimated by the text, the series of texts, or the data concerning the type of text. Thus, for example, form and function can be precisely defined in the Sumerian Divine, Royal and Temple Hymns and the 'Letters to God', as also in the Babylonian/Assyrian 'Prayer-vows', the Egyptian cultic hymns and Hymns of the Dead addressed to the sun-god, or the prayers of 'personal piety'. The same is true of the corresponding Old Testament Hymns and Prayers.

A wide field opens up here for possible observations.[1]

2. *Examples*

2.1   *Hymn to the Sun-God (Sumerian/Akkadian)*

'Invocation.

Utu, when you come forth from the "great mountain",

---

[1] Cf. M.-J. Seux, *Hymnes et Prières aux Dieux de Babylonie et d'Assyrie*, 1976.

when you come torth trom the "great mountain",
"the mount of the spring",
when you come forth from Duku, the place where fate is
decided,
5   when you come forth from the foundation of Heaven,
the place where Heaven and Earth meet,
then the "great" gods approach you for judgment,
the Anunnaki approach you for the pronouncing of
verdicts,
(but) humans, whole nations, await you,
(even) the beast, the four-footed brute, has turned its eye to
your great light.
10   Utu, you are wise and exalted, your own counsellor,
Utu, exalted leader, you are the judge of Heaven and Earth . . .'[2]

To help us understand this, we can draw comparisons with
the famous Old Akkadian cylindrical seal (Fig. 38; c.2200 BC),
which could almost be an illustration of this hymn. The sun-
god Utu (Akkadian Shamash), with glowing wings and sickle-
shaped saw, rises between the Mountains of the World in the
East. The gods approach him, on the right Enki, God of
(fresh) water and wisdom, with his two-faced messenger, and
on the left presumably the 'Lady of Heaven', Inanna, and a
divine hero (Gilgamesh?). The Anunnaki in the text were
originally all the gods, then later, as in this hymn, the gods of
the Earth. Possibly they are represented by the two figures on
the outside, the messenger and the hero. Humans are absent
from the picture, but animals are shown.

Compare this with the ancient cosmological ideas sketched
out in Chapter VIII, and in particular read Ps. 19 which also
speaks of the sun dispensing justice (vv. 5–6).

---

[2] Opening of a Sumerian/Akkadian bilingual text, with Akkadian interlinear
translation. Text translated from the German.

Fig. 38. Picture from an Old Accadian cylindrical seal.

2.2 Oath to Enlil (Akkadian)

For use by the king in the purification ritual *bit rimki* ('bath-house').

'Invocation.
Great and mighty lord,/ mountain of I[gigu],[a]
   Ruler of the Anunnaku,[b]/ judicious prince:
[Enl]il, great and mighty lord,/ mountain of Igigu,
5   Ruler of the Anunnaku,/ judicious prince,
who constantly renews himself,/ whose claim can never be
      changed,
the commands of whose lips, no god/ can resist!
Lord of lords, king of kings,/ bodily father of the great gods,
Lord of destinies and fates,
10   who orders Heaven and Earth,/ lord of all lands,
who enforces justice,/ whose command is unchangeable,
   who decides destinies/ for all the gods!
On your word of command/ humans are born;
   of king and governor/ you name the name.
15 Since the creation of god and king/ rests with you,
   and you can make the weak to be like the strong,/
among all the number of the stars of Heaven,[c]/ I have placed
                              my trust in your, o lord:
   I extol you,/ my ears are turned to you.
Let my destiny be life,/ decree honour for my name;
20   take away misfortune from me/ and give me justice!
Grant me . . ./ and bring me abundant gifts!
May [god] and king/ hold me dear,
   the high one and the prince/ do what I say!

May he who regards me (with envy) come to grief through me,/
in the assembly of all may my word be heard! May the
'Fortune' [Lamassu]^d of prayer, answer and provision/ be
daily at my side!
25 God, I extol you,/ goddess, I seek you,
grant that I, your servant, may live,/ let me become well,
then I will glorify your mighty works,/ I will pay you homage!
This is a prayer of the raising of hands for the god Enlil.'^{3}

^{a} *Igigu* – Babylonian name for the high god of Heaven
^{b} *Anunnaku* – gods of the Earth
^{c} Stars as a symbol of deity
^{d} *Lamassu* – 'Fortune' personified, luck demon and patron deity

The so-called prayer of hand-raising is the most common
Akkadian form of private prayer. Usually connected with a
cultic ceremony (water ritual, burnt-offering or similar), it
forms the ritual lament in which the sufferer or supplicant can
approach the desired deity and present his request. For this
purpose, model texts were drafted in which the worshipper
could add his own name (here: 'I, your servant', elsewhere
often the N.N. formula). The prayer seems to be addressed
indirectly to the high god (here: Enlil or Ellil, Sumerian 'Lord
of the air', 'Chief god of Nippur', Babylonian 'God of the
mountains'), but directly to the personal patron deities ('god'
and 'goddess') who are to present the petition to the High-
god. A prayer of this kind would normally include the
following elements: (1) words of invocation and praise; (2)
presentation of the worshipper; (3) lament concerning some
crisis; (4) prayer for mercy and deliverance; (5) praise and
thanks. These elements can vary. This prayer to Enlil (there
are similar ones to this same god) forms part of the kingly
ritual of atonement and purification, though this may be a
secondary usage. But we can see that it could in fact be used
by anyone, and this is perhaps its original aim.

^{3}Two versions are known, from Nineveh and Sippar. Text translated from the
German.

The most obvious parallels in the Psalter are the Royal Psalms of Lament (18; 89), and in a sense all the laments of individuals which have a cultic framework (e.g. 6; 51; 63; also 8; 33 etc.).

2.3 Prayer to Ishtar

'Invocation. High Ishtar,/ creator of mankind,
    who gives ritual its permanence,/ enthroned on high!
Majestic Ishtar,/ most splendid of the Igigu,
    creator of mankind,/ who keeps all life in order!
5 The glorious Irnina,[a]/ the war-like one are you,
    who make your feud against those who struggle,/ who
    repeatedly suppresses resistance.
The river which brings abundance,/ is neither opened/ nor
    [dammed] up [without] you;
    the channel from which the people drink,/ is neither
    opened/ nor [damned up] [without] you.
Without you, the wicked Gallu/ does not come upon people,
10   without [you], Chum, Lilu, [Lilit][b]/ and the daughters of
    Lilu, cannot approach the sick.
I, N. son of N.,/ whose god is N., and whose goddess is N.,
    your tired and weary [servant],/ have looked upon your face;
Ishtar, who wears the gown and veil[c] of a goddess,/ I have
    [looked] upon your face,
    [have brought]/ my life to you.
15 On your sublime command, which cannot be changed,/
    and your reliable assurance, which cannot be broken:
    tear out the evil "spy",/ the "provider of evil",
    who has entered into me/ and pursues me without ceasing,
    tear him from my life this very day,/ and deliver him up to
    your angry heart!'[d]

[a]Title of Ishtar
[b]Demons
[c]Items of Ishtar's clothing, with obvious sexual connotations

[d]Text translated from the German.

'This prayer belongs, along with other prayers to Ishtar and the gods of the Underworld, to a major ritual for the fighting off of a sickness caused by demons. Lines 9 and 10 declare that the demons only can only gain power if the god first abandons a person. The goddess' gown (line 13) is the furbelowed dress always shown on pictures of goddesses. There is no formula of thanksgiving in this prayer.' (W. von Soden)

The first section is hymnic praise. This is followed by the part of the formula at which the worshipper can add his own name and those of his patron gods. One of the surviving versions was intended for the use of the king. The second half contains petitions for the driving out of evil spirits.

The relationships with the Biblical Psalms of Ill-health lie mainly in the negative. A different aetiology of sickness demands a different response. On the whole, the Ishtar prayer represents roughly that which in the Psalms is rejected as subreligious, or superstitious, but which was obviously present in the popular religion. Cf. Pss.41 (v.8); 91 (esp. 5f.; 10ff.); 16(2ff.?); 58.

2.4 Nebuchadnezzar's Prayer to Marduk (Babylonian)

'Marduk, Lord, wisest of the gods, proud prince! You created me, and entrusted me with kingship over all mankind. I love your exalted form as dearly as my own life. In all the provinces I will not erect any city more majestically than your city Babylon.ᵃ Since, then, I love your fearful godhead, and continually seek your majesty, be compliant with the raising of my hands, hear my prayer! For I am the king, who richly adorns (and) makes your heart rejoice, the astute governor, who richly adorns all your cultic cities! On your command, O merciful Marduk, may the house which I have built endure visibly until distant times, that I may be made replete with its abundance, see old age in it, (and) find satisfaction in my children! May I receive in it a great tribute from the kings of the coastal regions (and) from all people! From the foundation of the Heavens to their highest height, may I have no enemies; may I find no-one who frightens me! May my descendants rule over the black heads[b] in it for ever!'[s]

[a] On his building works, see: D. J. Wiseman, *Nebuchadnezzar and Babylon*, 1985.

[b] i.e. human beings

This prayer comes from an inscription on a building by Nebuchadnezzar II (king of Babylon from 604 to 562; conquest of Jerusalem 587/6). In form and style, similar inscriptions point to a set pattern, according to which such official royal prayers were constructed. As a royal prayer, it expresses both the doctrine of state and the programme of government. In the Psalter, the Royal Psalms from the pre-exilic period are comparable (e.g. 101; 110; 72; also 2).

2.5 Prayer to Marduk and Nabu (Akkadian)

Obverse:

'Sun of his fathers, exalted, the noble Asare,
The giver of length of days, skilled, learned,
It is in your sphere to keep alive and to preserve,
Mankind extols your fitting name.
5   The afflicted and the oppressed heed you,
You [heed] their prayer, you grant offspring,
The peoples of the land persist every day in praising you,
All living creatures magnify your sweet name.
Let there be protection for Nabû-ušebši, the reverent supplicant,
10 That he may gain progeny and descendants, as is decreed for
     the peoples,
That his seed may be established before you for ever.

Eleven lines lacking . . . The beginning of the inscription and the end of the inscription shall be recited twice.'

Reverse:

'Hero, lofty, son of Asare,
Creator of everything that exists, hearer of prayer,

[s] Text translated from the German.

Of shining countenance, counsellor of his fathers,
Irresistible autocrat, heir of Nudimmud,[a]
5   Most fitting of the Igigi,[b] lord of [wisdom], who
      [comprehends] all learning,
The fashioning of heaven and underworld is established in
      your [hand],[c]
You decree a favoured destiny, O . . . Nabû,
Give long life [to Nabû]-ušebši, your slave,
That he may enjoy [good health] and reach a ripe old age,
10   That all [. . .] may praise your prowess in war.

[Ten lines] lacking [. . .]. The beginning of the inscription and the end of
the inscription [shall be] recited [twice].
Colophon: . . .] Nabû(?)-šum-iddina, son of the Doorman.'[6]

   [a] Epithet of Enkis (Eas)
   [b] Gods of the Heavens
   [c] Translation dubious

The tablet, inscribed on both sides, contains prayers in the
form of a double acrostic. The opening syllables of the lines of
both prayers, when read from top to bottom, yield the
following sentence: 'Of Nabû-ušebši, the Priest of the
Invocation (*āšipu*)', while the ends of the lines read from top
to bottom: 'The servant who proclaims your majesty', and
'The praying servant who honours you' – the so-called
acroteleutic, which is not attested in the Biblical Psalms, and
indeed is very seldom found in Akkadian writings.

These are two personal prayers of the invocation-priest
Nabû-ušebši ('Nabu-let-(him)-live'), which he probably
wrote himself and used for his own intercession. The post-
scripts indicate that the prayers were included in the ritual
recitation of a cultic ceremony (most likely secondarily), in
which the name of the copyist(?) in line 13 (reverse) may also
have played a role.

The editor of the modern edition describes the style as

[6] From Korsabad (N.E. of Nineveh). Text from: W. G. Lambert, 'Literary
Style in First Millenium Mesopotamia', *JAOS* vol. 88, 1968.

'sophisticated', and refers to the exquisite words and phrases. No wonder, for the writer subjected himself to an even more rigorous formal regime than the writers of the Alphabetical Psalms. Nevertheless, the two prayers allow personal intercessions to come through. It is long life and descendants (since in a sense they lengthen life) which the writer requests of Marduk, the high god of Babylon, in his capacity as son of Enki, creator of culture and lord of the invocation (obverse, line 3), and of Nabu, son of Marduk, god of wisdom and scholarship.

The Psalms do not give us the names of any of their authors. The attempt to find similar name-acrostics in Pss. 2 and 110 with *Yny'* (Jannaeus) *and his wife* and *Šm'n* (Simeon, after the high priest) has been abandoned. However, poems and prayers which are at once personal and artistic are certainly to be found in the Psalter (III).

2.6 Prayer to El (Ugaritic)

1   'O El! O sons of El!
    O assembly of the sons of El!
    O meeting of the sons of El!
    O Tkmn and Shnm[a]!
5   O El and Ashirat[b]!

    Be gracious, O El[c]!
    Be a support, O El!
    Be salvation, O El!
    O El, hasten, come swiftly!
10   To the help of Zaphon,
    to the help of Ugarit.
    With the lance, O El,
    with the upraised (?)[d], O El.
    With the battle-axe[e], O El.
15   with the shattering, O El.
    Because of the burnt offering, O El,
    because of the appointed sacrifice (?), O El.
    because of the morning sacrifice, O El.'[7]

[7] From Ugarit (Ras Shamra), *c.* 13th century BC. Text from: W. Beyerlin (ed.), *Near Eastern Religious Texts relating to the Old Testament,* 1975 (Eng. tr. 1978), p. 222.

[a] *Tkmn* (or *Trmn*) and *Shnm* – presumably mythological locations
[b] *Ashirat* – consort of El
[c] or: *El is gracious!*
[d] *the upraised axe?*
[e] *battle-axe* – or: *cudgel?*

This very difficult text, which in many places can only be translated with great uncertainty, is understood by some commentators to be a prayer to El, by others, a class-room exercise. It is not impossible that both interpretations could be correct. Here we find ourselves in the same position as with the artificial acrostics. In any case, the content of the text is significant.

The address to the pantheon of gods (1–5) is attested elsewhere, and probably conforms to convention. Among the Biblical Psalms, 29, 82 and 89 have similar conventional salutations. There follow what may be confessional statements concerning El (6–8), and then prayers to El to come to the aid of Zaphon (= Ugarit), presumably in a crisis situation (9–11). The prayer is that he should bring into play divine weapons (12–15), usually the prerogative of Baal(?), and El's obligations to the city are cited (16–18: 'because of . . .').

This prayer, resembling a litany, is strongly reminiscent of the reconstructed version of Ps. 29 (p. 55, see above): similar openings to lines, repeated invocations, the address to the sons of El, 16 mentions of the name of El compared with 18 of YHWH, etc. The uncertainty about interpretation permits no far-reaching conclusions. However, it is important to notice that here El holds the position which in Ps. 29 is given to YHWH, but which in the Ugaritic myths would be passed on to Baal.

2.7 The Sun Hymn of Akhenaton (Egyptian)

'Praise of Re Har-akhti, Rejoicing on the Horizon, in His Name as Shu
Who Is in the Aton-disc, living forever and ever; the living great Aton
who is in jubilee, lord of all that the Aton encircles, lord of heaven, lord of
earth, lord of the House of Aton in Akhet-Aton; (and praise of) the King
of Upper and Lower Egypt, who lives on truth, the Lord of the Two
Lands; Nefer-kheperu-Re Wa-en-Re; the Son of Re, who lives on truth,
the Lord of Diadems: Akh-en-Aton, long in his lifetime; (and praise of)
the Chief Wife of the King, his beloved, the Lady of the Two Lands:
Nefer-neferu-Aton Nefert-iti, living, healthy, and youthful forever and
ever; (by) the Fan-Bearer on the Right hand of the King . . . Eye. He says:

Thou appearest beautifully on the horizon of heaven,
Thou living Aton, the beginning of life!
When thou art risen on the eastern horizon,
5   Thou hast filled every land with thy beauty.
Thou art gracious, great, glistening, and high over every land;
Thy rays encompass the lands to the limit of all that thou
        hast made:
As thou art Re, thou reachest to the end of them;
(Thou) subduest them (for) thy beloved son.
10 Though thou art far away, thy rays are on earth;
Though thou art in *their* faces, *no one knows thy* going.

When thou settest in the western horizon,
The land is in darkness, in the manner of death.
They sleep in a room, with heads wrapped up,
15 Nor sees one eye the other.
All their goods which are under their heads might be stolen,
(But) they would not perceive (it).
Every lion is come forth from his den;
All creeping things, they sting.
20 Darkness is a shroud, and the earth is in stillness,
For he who made them rests in his horizon.

At daybreak, when thou arisest on the horizon,
When thou shinest as the Aton by day,
Thou drivest away the darkness and givest thy rays.
25 The Two Lands are in festivity *every day*,
Awake and standing upon (their) feet,
For thou hast raised them up.

Washing their bodies, taking (their) clothing,
Their arms are (raised) in praise at thy appearance.
30 All the world, they do their work.

All beasts are content with their pasturage;
Trees and plants are flourishing.
The birds which fly from their nests,
Their wings are (stretched out) in praise to thy *ka*.
35 All beasts spring upon (their) feet.
Whatever flies and alights,
They live when thou hast risen (for) them.
The ships are sailing north and south as well,
For every way is open at thy appearance.
40 The fish in the river dart before thy face;
Thy rays are in the midst of the great green sea.

Creator of seed in women,
Thou who makest fluid into man,
Who maintainest the son in the womb of his mother,
45 Who soothest him with that which stills his weeping,
Thou nurse (even) in the womb,
Who givest breath to sustain all that he has made!
When he descends from the womb to *breathe*
On the day when he is born,
50 Thou openest his mouth completely,
Thou suppliest his necessities.
When the chick in the egg speaks within the shell,
Thou givest him breath within it to maintain him.
When thou hast made him his fulfilment within the egg, to break it,
55 He comes forth from the egg to speak at his completed (time);
He walks upon his legs when he comes forth from it.

How manifold it is, what thou hast made!
They are hidden from the face (of man).
O sole god, like whom there is no other!
60 Thou didst create the world according to thy desire,
While thou wert alone:
All men, cattle, and wild beasts,
Whatever is on earth, going upon (its) feet,
And what is on high, flying with its wings.

65 The countries of Syria and Nubia, the *land* of Egypt,
   Thou settest every man in his place,
   Thou suppliest their necessities:
   Everyone has his food, and his time of life is reckoned.
   Their tongues are separate in speech,[a]
70 And their natures as well;
   Their skins are distinguished,
   As thou distinguishest the foreign peoples.
   Thou makest a Nile in the underworld,
   Thou bringest it forth as thou desirest
75 To maintain the people (of Egypt)
   According as thou madest them for thyself,
   The lord of all of them, wearying (himself) with them,
   The lord of every land, rising for them,
   The Aton of the day, great of majesty.

80 All distant foreign countries, thou makest their life (also),
   For thou hast set a Nile in heaven,[b]
   That it may descend for them and make waves upon the mountains,
   Like the great green sea,
   To water their fields in their towns.
85 How effective they are, thy plans, O lord of eternity!
   The Nile in heaven, it is for the foreign peoples
   And for the beasts of every desert that go upon (their) feet;
   (While the true) Nile comes from the underworld for Egypt.

   Thy rays suckle every meadow.
90 When thou risest, thy live, they grow for thee.
   Thou makest the seasons in order to rear all that thou hast made,
   The winter to cool them,
   And the heat that *they* may taste thee.
   Thou hast made the distant sky in order to rise therein,
95 In order to see all that thou dost make.
   Whilst thou wert alone,
   Rising in thy form as the living Aton,
   Appearing, shining, *withdrawing or approaching*,
   Thou madest millions of forms of thyself alone.
100 Cities, towns, fields, road, and river –
   Every eye beholds thee over against them,
   For thou art the Aton of the day over *the earth* . . .

Thou art in my heart,
And there is no other that knows thee
105 Save thy son Nefer-kheperu-Re Wa-en-Re,
For thou hast made him well-versed in thy plans and in thy
strength.

The world came into being by thy hand,
According as thou has made them.
When thou hast risen they live,
110 When thou settest they die.
Thou art lifetime thy own self,
For one lives (only) through thee.
Eyes are (fixed) on beauty until thou settest.
All work is laid aside when thou settest in the west.
115 [But] when (thou) risest (again),
[*Everything is*] made to flourish for the king, . . .
Since thou didst found the earth
And raise them up for thy son,
Who came forth from thy body:
120   the King of Upper and Lower Egypt, . . . Akh-en-Aton, . . . and
the Chief Wife of the King . . . Nefert-iti, living and youthful
and ever.'[8]

ª Cf. Genesis 11 (the confusion of languages)
ᵇ The rain

This text, written by the Pharaoh Amenophis IV (Ach-en-
Aton, c.1364–1347) himself, and discovered in the grave of
Eye at Tell el-Amarna, stands in the tradition of Egyptian
hymns of the sun-cult, a tradition which sings of the course of
the sun across the sky, and follows it in ritual. However, it
breaks with this tradition in that it places the element of light
in the foreground, suppressing the whole complex of themes
connected with night (descent into the underworld, the threat
of enemies). This enlightened stance obviously corresponds to

[8] From Amarna, Grave of Eye, 18th dynasty, c.1350 BC. Text from:
J. B. Pritchard (ed.), *Ancient Near Eastern Texts relating to the Old Testament*,
pp. 369ff.

the new form of address to the 'sun-disc' (Aton), the significance of which comes out in the new theological formulation of the name; 'Re Har-akhti, Rejoicing on the Horizon, in His Name as Shu Who Is in the Aton-disc' (a sentence-name, written in a cartouche; lines 1f.). A tendency towards theoretical monotheism characterises the theology and hymnody of the Amarna period. 'The hymn', writes J. Assmann, 'sees its theme in the worshipful acknowledgement of the beneficent works of God. These it pursues in detail, with its often ingenious expositions of phenomena as proofs of the power of the life-giving energy of God.' No doubt it is the enlightened Wisdom background of this poem as much as the actual motifs which calls forth echoes of Ps. 104, a Psalm which seems to have arisen in a similar milieu. Among the parallels: the nightly hunt of the predatory animals (ll.18f.; Ps. 104,20ff.); in the morning people set out to work (l.30; Ps.104,23); fish and ships (ll.38ff.; Ps.104,25f.); the phrases 'How manifold it is, what thou hast made!' (l.57) and 'How many are your works, O YHWH!' (Ps.94,24); the theme of Heaven (ll.94ff.; Ps. 104,2ff.); the theme of water (ll.73–88 – subsidiary theme; Ps. 104,5–30 – principle theme). These same points of contact, however, could also be made with other hymns. Despite certain similarities of image and tone, the literary dependence of one text upon the other must be ruled out. The two poems are autonomous constructions, each with its own importance.

2.8 Inscription on an Egyptian Votive Stele

A. Accompanying Text

'AMON-RE, the Lord of Thebes,
the Great God, who presides in Karnak;
the illustrious god, who answers prayers,
who answers the voice of the poor, when he is in distress,
5   who gives breath to those who are oppressed.

Give praise to AMON-RE,
to the Lord of Thebes who presides in Karnak,
kiss the earth before the AMON-of-the-City, the Great God,
the lord of the great and beautiful forecourt:
10   may he protect me, that my eyes might behold his beauty!
For the Ka of the artist of AMON, *Nebre*.'

B. The Text of the Stele

'I will give praise to AMON,
I will write hymns to his name;
I give him praise,
as high as is the heaven, and as wide as the earth reaches
5   I proclaim his mighty signs to all who travel up and down the river

Beware of him!
    Proclaim him son and daughter,
        large and small!
        Tell of him to children and to children's children
10   who are not yet born!
        Tell of him to the fish in the river
            and the birds in the sky!
Proclaim him to all who do not know him, and to all who do!
        Beware of him!

15   You are AMON, the lord of the 'Silent ones',
who answers the voice of the poor!
I cried to you when I was in distress,
and you came and delivered me.
You gave breath to him who was oppressed,
20   you delivered me, when I lay in bondage.
You are AMON-RE, the Lord of Thebes,
you deliver those who are in the Underworld;
for you are the one [who is gracious] when we call on him,
it is you who comes from distant parts!

25   Composed by the artist of AMON in Der el-Medine,
Nebre, righteous,
for the son of the artist in Der el-Medine,
Paii, (righteous),
in the name of his lord,

Fig. 39. Stele of Neb-Rê.

30   AMON, Lord of Thebes,
who answers the voice of the poor.

Hymns were composed to his name
because his power was so great:
prayers were made before his face
35   in the presence of the whole land
on behalf of the artist *Nachtamon*, righteous,
when he lay down sick, on the verge of death,
when he was in the power of AMON, on account of his cow.

Then I found that the Lord of the gods had come as the North
    Wind,
40   a breath of fresh air from him;
he delivered the writer of AMON,
Nachtamon, righteous,
the son of the artist of AMON in Der el-Medine,
Nebre, righteous,
45   born of the lady of the house, *Pashed*, righteous.

He[a] says: "Though the servant was willing to commit the sin,
yet the lord is willing to be merciful!
The Lord of Thebes is not angry
for the length of a whole day:
50   he rages for an instant, then nothing remains.
The breeze has turned to us in mercy,
AMON came along with his breath of air.
As surely as your Ka endures, you will be merciful,
and we will never do it again!"

55   The artist in Der el-Medine,
Nebre, righteous, speaks:
"I will furnish this stele in your name,
I will inscribe this hymn to you
eternally on the front of it,
60   for you have delivered for me the artist *Nachtamon*!
Thus I spoke to you, and you have heard me,
now look, I have done what I have promised!
You are the lord of him who calls on you,
who is content with MAAT:[b]
the Lord of Thebes!"

Composed by the artist *Nebre* and his con *Chau.*[b]

[a] i.e. *Nachtamon*

[b] *Maat* – divine order, harmony

This memorial (Fig. 39; limestone 67cm high) reminds us of the case of the artist Neb-Rê from the workers' settlement Dêr el-Medîna near Thebes, whose son Amonnacht lay dying. According to ancient thinking, the cause of the illness was to be sought in an event. It is concluded that the patient has obviously misappropriated a sacred cow of the God Amon, chief god and state god, and god of the city of Thebes. The expiatory prayer of his father to Amon results in the son's recovery. Neb-Rê gives thanks for answered prayer and for the saving of his son with a statue which, being set up in the temple court, publicises the case – an act of penance – and spreads the fame of Amon in hymns of thanks and praise. The analogy with the expiatory and consolatory prayers of the sick in the Psalter is clear. Obviously, Israel and Egypt knew similar forms of ritual activity in the realm of personal piety. With this monument, we might compare Pss. 30; 41; 69; 102; also 40; the memorial stele replaces and expands the oral psalm or hymn, and corresponds to the written form of the psalm on a papyrus scroll (cf. Fig. 39, bottom right-hand corner) or clay tablet which would have been dedicated in the sanctuary as a votive offering (e.g. Ps. 40,7; see Chapter II.2).

❊   ❊   ❊

These selected examples exhibit the possibilities for comparison. They could be continued almost endlessly. However, it will be seen that in this frontier area where the traditions meet, particular care is needed. It is often tempting to draw lines here and there, without taking due note of the geographical-cultural and chronological-historical gaps

[9] Text translated from the German.

involved. Most importantly, the texts to be compared must first be allowed to stand up for themselves with their own characteristics and their own integrity before we can risk setting them together. Nevertheless, a careful reading of the published collections of ancient writings is of inestimable value for our understanding of the Biblical Psalms, for this makes it possible to regard each one within its literary-historical framework, and to judge it by the standards of its time.

Chapter X

THE INFLUENCE OF THE PSALMS

In this chapter we pursue the history of the influence of the Psalms. By 'influence' we do not mean what one can influence, or might imagine oneself able to influence by use of the Psalms. Even the Biblical Psalms were not immune to being drawn into the ideas and practices of magic. There are signs that Ps. 91 ('He who dwells in the shadow of the Most High'), or parts of it ('No harm will befall you', v. 10), was used at a very early stage for the deterring of demons. A small, fragmentary scroll found at Qumran (11QPsAp^a) contained, alongside apocryphal texts, Ps. 91. Use as a charm is highly likely. It is interesting in this connection that, according to the story of the wilderness temptations in Matt. 4, Jesus rejected such a usage. The Tempter suggests this to him in a significantly incomplete quotation from Ps. 91,11f. (cf. Matt. 4,6). 'The scoundrel skipped over these words, "in all your ways", for they went against him' (thus Luther). Jesus rejected it sharply? 'It is also written, "Do not put the Lord your God to the test"' (from Deut. 6,16). In Talmudic Judaism, the 'song against evil spirits', as Ps. 91 became known, was as popular as in the Early Church, where it has frequently been found as an amulet, on papyri, and on house walls, a custom which has continued into our own time on medallions, talismans, and so forth.[1]

The belief in this kind of supernatural influence is not our

---

[1] Cf. P. Hugger, *Jahwe meine Zuflucht. Gestalt und Theologie des 91. Psalms,* Münsterschwarzacher Studien 13 (1971, pp. 331ff.). Here it is recorded that when the Kaiserin Elisabeth of Austria was found murdered in 1898 she was wearing a medallion inscribed with words from Ps. 91: 'Do not fear the horrors of the night, nor the arrow which flies by day.'

theme. Nor is the worshipper's hope that the words of the psalm might elicit a special divine intervention, a theme which lies at the very heart of the whole question of prayer. This cannot be discussed here. Rather, in looking at the history of the Psalter, we ask how people reacted to the influence of the Psalms, what influence the texts had on their behaviour. And even here, we must limit our scope drastically. In principle it could be said that everyone who comes in contact with the Psalms, Jew or Christian, reader or supplicant, poet or singer, reacts to them in some sense. From this multitude of reactions, we must choose a few, whether because they are better researched or better known, or because they leave a particular impression, always with the intention of seeing in the mirror of the influence of the Psalms further characteristics and meanings of these unique texts which we have already regarded from quite a different angle. A number of highlights in the history of the Psalter's reception will be presented and examined. From the outlook of others on the Psalms, we hope to win a fresh outlook for ourselves. The following examples may be rather random and arbitrary. But the intention is to illustrate, not to catalogue.

1. Post-Canonical Psalm Writing

Even at a time when the Biblical Psalter had not yet been closed or given its final form, independent collections of songs and prayers were emerging which were strongly influenced by the style of the Biblical Psalms, which indeed were dependent upon them, although they each had their own distinctive flavour. We may look first at the collection of praise songs and prayers which were found in the first cave at Qumran in 1947 (1QH), and which are called Hodayot after their stereotyped opening formula 'I thank thee O Lord' (*'ôdᵉkâ ᵃdônây*). It is generally assumed that the writer of the songs was the founder of the community himself, the so-called 'teacher of righteousness'. For a date, we are thinking of the 2nd century BC. The thirty-plus songs are built on a loose parallelism. Clearly they are in essence a further development of the Biblical Psalm of Thanksgiving. They take on the free style of these lay prayers, but widen out the scope to include meditative Wisdom. The emphasis on insight and spiritual understanding is combined with apocalyptic speculation.

An example:

'They caused (me) to be
   like a ship on the deeps of the (sea),
and like a fortified city
   before (the aggessor),
5 (and) like a woman in travail
   with her first-born child
upon whose belly pangs have come
   and grievous pains,
filling with anguish her child-bearing crucible.

10 For the children have come to the throes of Death,
   and she labours in her pains who bears the Man.
For amid the throes of Death
   she shall bring forth a man-child,
and amid the pains of Hell
15   there shall spring from her child bearing crucible
   a marvellous Mighty Counsellor;
and the Man shall be delivered from out of the throes.

When he is conceived
   all wombs shall quicken,
20 and the time of their delivery
   shall be in grievous pains;
they shall be appalled
   who are with child.
And when he is brought forth
25   every pang shall come upon the child-bearing crucible.

And they, the conceivers of Vanity,
   shall be prey to terrible anguish;

the wombs of the Pit
   shall be prey to all the works of horror.
30   The foundations of the wall shall rock
   like a ship upon the face of the waters;
the heavens shall roar
   with a noise of roaring,
and those who dwell in the dust
35   as well as those who sail the seas
shall be appalled by the roaring of the waters.

All their wise men
   shall be like sailors on the deeps,
for all their wisdom shall be swallowed up
40   in the midst of the howling seas.
As the Abysses boil
   above the fountains of the waters,
the towering waves and billows shall rage
   with the voice of their roaring;
45   and as they rage,
   (Hell and Abaddon) shall open
(and all) the flying arrows of the Pit
   shall send out their voice to the Abyss.

And the gates (of Hell) shall open
50   (on all) the works of Vanity;
and the doors of the Pit shall close
   on the conceivers of wickedness;
and the everlasting bars shall be bolted
   on all the spirits of Naught.'

                                          (Col. III, lines 6–18)[2]

The fragmentary lines at the top of the column (the first few
scraps are not translated in the English edition: '. . . you have
made my face to shine . . . , . . . for you in eternal glory with
all . . . , . . . of your mouth, and you have saved me . . .')
contain the usual imagery of a Psalm of Lament and
Thanksgiving. The experience of crisis and deliverance evokes
the image of a ship threatened on high seas, a city under seige,

   [2] Text from: G. Vermes, *The Dead Sea Scrolls in English*, 1962, 3rd. ed. 1987
pp. 157f.

a woman overcome by pain. This last image of birth pains
fascinates the writer, and draws him by association further
and further into the vision of a great earthquake which had
seized the present time like a pregnant woman at the end of
her strength. He pictures the world as a womb giving birth,
shaken by convulsions, until the 'man-child', the 'Marvellous
Mighty Counsellor', of prophecy – the allusion is to Isa. 9,6 –
has been born. Surprisingly, the psalmist declines to expound
any particular Messianic interpretation of the prophetic text.
Instead, his thoughts are completely taken up by the idea of
the shaking of the world. He becomes caught up in a whirl of
apocalyptic vision. In the dramatic events of the great
earthquake of the end of time, the images of city and ship
appear again before they founder along with the figure of the
'conceiver of vanity' (symbolising the fallen community) in
the jaws of Hell and in raging Chaos, the gates of the Abyss
finally being barred upon them. What began in the style of a
psalm of thanks ends in an almost surrealistic nightmare of the
final catastrophe.

The so-called Psalms of Solomon, mentioned in some of the
canons of the Early Church, were long thought to have been
lost, but were rediscovered in the 17th century. Since then, a
number of Greek and Syriac manuscripts have turned up. So
far, no trace has been found of the Hebrew original. 'There
are eighteen of these Psalms, which are in form very similar to
the canonical Psalms, but like the Qumran songs are strongly
meditative.'[3] They are heavily influenced both in type and in
style by the Psalms which were (later) included in the Canon,
and are therefore probably to be ascribed to one of the
Pharisaic groupings, either to a single author or, less likely, to
several. The repeated reference to the Romans, and in
particular to Pompey and his death (48 BC) allow us to date

[3] L. Rost, *Einleitung in die alttestamentlichen Apokryphen und Pseud-
epigraphen*, 1971, p. 89.

them to the second half of the 1st century BC. Nothing concrete is known concerning the relationships with the Jerusalem Cult or the Qumran community. Apparently this collection, like the Hodayot, was important only to the group concerned.[4]

The same could be said of the hymns and prayers, likewise an offshoot from the mainline tradition of the Psalter, which grew up in the earliest Christian communities but were never collected. The New Testament makes frequent reference to such early Christian hymnody. Yet only a very few text fragments have been preserved, mostly enclosed in other texts. Examples are John 1,1ff.; Phil. 2,6–11; Col. 1,15–20; Eph. 2,14ff.; 5,14; 1 Tim. 3,16; 1 Pet. 2,21–24. Then there are the 'Psalms of Luke', the 'Magnificat' Luke 1,46–55 and the 'Benedictus' Luke 1,68–79, which are formed in imitation of the Old Testament Psalms. Despite close relations with the Greek tradition of Psalm-writing and frequent citations and imitations, the hymnic style is dominant: the invocation to the *Kyrios Christos* is becoming established. New experiences of grace lead away from the old Psalmody and allow new poetic forms to arise.

In Rabbinic Judaism, three lines of development become recognisable after the suspension of the temple cult. The first was the creation and imposition of a new book of prayer very much in the tradition of the Psalter, designed to preserve the religious community deprived of temple worship. Consequently in the 2nd century the important 'prayer of the 18 benedictions' was formulated, with the *Shema* (Deut. 62,4–9; 11,13–21; Num. 15,37–41) and the accompanying praises, designed to take central position in the worship of the Synagogues. This community prayer was established by the Rabbis as the model of all private piety and prayer.

[4] Cf. D. Flusser, 'Psalms, Hymns and Prayers', in : *Jewish Writings of the Second Temple Period* (ed. M. E. Stone), 1984, pp. 551–577.

As a result – and this is the second line – the Biblical Psalms were pushed back onto the level of ancient venerated holy writings; their former importance for the temple cult was still well known, but they were now used liturgically only in the Passover rite, in the expectation of a restitution in the near future. It was after all in the Passover that a large number of the Psalms of the late temple period were rooted. The so-called 'Hallel' (Ps. 113/4–118) was sung at the blessing of the cup. According to Mark 14,26, Jesus and his disciples sang the small Hallel at the Last Supper. Particularly important after the destruction of the temple, when there was no high priest to invoke the name of God, was the 'Hallelu-Yah', which contained both the name and the praise of God. The Hallelujah Psalms move into the foreground, and with them the whole last third of the Psalter: 'David spoke 103 psalms; but he spoke no hallelujah until he had seen the defeat of his enemies' (bBer9b–10a, an allusion to Ps. 104,35, the first hallelujah in the Psalter). From the Passover, the piety of the Psalms shines into the realm of private life (grace before meals, and so forth).

The third line of development runs parallel to the whole understanding of Scripture. The Psalter was brought into the Torah as Holy Scripture, and serves for the illustration of God's will in the Law. David is cited as the expositor of Moses. 'This gave the utterances of the Torah a poetically mild and emotionally religious note' (thus C. Thoma[5]). In this way, the first step towards the implantation of the Psalms in Synagogue worship had been taken.[6]

---

[5] C. Thoma, 'Psalmenfrömmigkeit im Rabbinischen Judentum', in: *Liturgie und Dichtung* (ed. H. Becker, R. Kaczynski), 1983, vol. I, p. 102.

[6] An example of this is the so-called *Shiwiti*, a votive tablet with the words from Ps. 16: *šiwwitî* etc., 'I have YHWH before me at all times', which was hung up in the synagogue in sight of the worshippers, in order to exhort them to prayer. Colloquially, the word is synonymous with 'piety'.

These three lines can now be traced in the history of Early Christianity. On the first, the Psalter becomes the most frequently cited book in the New Testament, with Ps. 110 (and the phrase 'sitting on the right hand of God') the most quoted individual psalm. The Psalms belong to the writings of the old covenant. They are the Word of God, and they serve for the discerning of God's will, even with respect to Jesus Christ. The events of the passion are seen as the basis of Ps. 22. On the second, the Psalms had a special relation to the festival of Easter which is analogous to the Jewish usage. How close this relation was can be seen from the earliest known Christian Easter liturgy, from the Jerusalem of the 5th century AD, which was recently highlighted by B. Fischer.⁷ Particularly noteworthy here is the fact that the Psalms were assigned both the role of *vox Christi* and *vox ad Christum*, a tradition which is also attested in the exegesis of the Church Fathers (e.g. Augustine). On the third, the Church attempted to expand and complement the Biblical Psalter by the drafting of new hymns and prayers, though only the outlines of this can be seen from the documents of the New Testament and the Early Church. One relatively late expression of this trend is the appendix which was added to a number of Christian glosses on the Psalter. This appendix, found only in manuscripts from the 5th century, not in any from the 4th, contains under the heading OΔAI, 'Odes', anything from nine to fourteen additional pieces: the Song of the Red Sea (Exod. 25), the Song of Moses (Deut. 32), the Psalm of Hannah (1 Sam. 2), the Prayer of Habakkuk (Hab. 3), the Prayer of Isaiah (Isa. 26), the Psalm of Jonah (Jon. 2), the Prayer of Azariah (Dan. 3 LXX), the Prayer of the Three Men in the Furnace (Dan. 3 LXX), the Magnificat and Benedictus (Luke 1); also the Song of the Vineyard (Isa. 5), the Psalm of Hezekiah

⁷B. Fischer, 'Der liturgische Gebrauch der Psalmen im altkirchlichen Gottesdienst', in: *Liturgie und Dichtung* (note 5 above), vol. I, pp. 303–313.

(Isa. 38), the Prayer of Manasseh (Old Testament apocrypha), the Prayer of Simeon (Luke 2), and the Gloria (a 'morning hymn' of the 4th century AD).

2. *Psalmody and Illustrated Psalter*

It has already been mentioned that very little is known about the way the Psalms would have been performed at the time of their writing. This is equally true for the prayer, the song with its music, and the poem. All reconstructions of the actual performance are purely hypothetical. In principle this is also true of all secondary forms of recitation. Nietzsche's statement, 'In the ancient world, people read . . . in loud voices', is still valid, and can be applied both to prayer and meditation (Ps. 1). Songs, however, conform to different rules.

In this context we must take note of a particular phenomenon which presents us with a unique manner of use: Psalmody, the psalm-song. The roots of psalmody go back a long way. It is questionable whether they go back to the time of the temple cult; this must remain open. But in the course of the long process by which the Biblical Psalms were integrated into Jewish and Christian worship, forms of recitation began to emerge, which developed from reading aloud to antiphonic song, to the most complicated musical settings. The accentuation in the Hebrew Bible manuscripts, in effect a Masoretic reading aid, with its special system for the Psalms, stands in the same tradition. From the musical forms which have come down to us, it is possible to see how the intonation of the Psalms grew out of the Latin usage, as a *'saturata oratio'* ('filled speech', Tertullian). The formula to which it was set in the Latin Church held in its 'couplet' structure to the rule of 'Hebrew rhythm' (Nietzsche), *parallelismus membrorum*; it fitted with the psalm-tone of corresponding pitch (*tuba, tenor* < *šōpār*) elastically to the varying lengths of the lines; with its rising opening (*initium*) and its falling close (*terminatio*) it followed the curve of speech melody, creating at the apex in the middle (*mediatio*) a little space for quiet, reflection, and free play. Furthermore, this model, which can be divided up between groups, choirs and soloists, takes account of the antiphonic or dialogue structure of the Psalm texts. It is important to see how psalmody allows each psalm to be handled identically within the framework of possible variations (*differentiae*), and to be used at once as prayer, song and testimony. The melody of a psalm promotes its words; but these can speak for themselves. The solo songs (*tractus*), probably stemming from Jewish synagogue worship, which add much melodic superstructure to the psalmodic framework, were soon incorporated into the celebrations of eucharist and mass. They should be seen as developments of the basic psalm tone (Fig. 40).

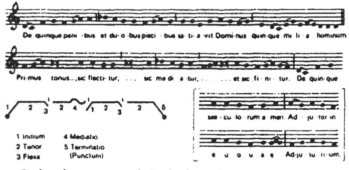

Psalmody: structure of a Psalm formula.

Responsorial Psalmody: Milan liturgy (4th century?). *Fig. 40.*

Psalmody grew up in the Early Church; it spread and became established most particularly in the daily monastic cycle of prayers (*officium*). From there it underwent a development which had a strong influence on the whole history of music.[8]

Also rooted in the monastery was the medieval art of book decoration, which approached the Psalms with particular dedication, and created the illuminated Psalter. In the production of biblical manuscripts, a great deal of love and skill went into illustrating and decorating the Psalter. From the large number of illuminated Psalters, we might choose as examples two of the most important early medieval cycles, both of them Carolingian manuscripts: the Utrecht Psalter (from Utrecht, c. 820–830 AD), and the Stuttgart Psalter (from St. Germain-des-Prés near Paris, about the same time).

'Psalters were used both in the office and for private meditation. They formed a particularly large and valuable group (sc. in the history of book illustration). The magnificent Psalters made for rulers and nobility are known to be as early as the Carolingian period; of the ... pieces exhibited, one belonged to Henry the Lion-heart or his wife ... But towards the end of the 11th century, the blessed Marianus was writing Psalters for poor Regensburg widows, and in the 12th and 13th centuries, the sources mention Psalters in the possession of women of the urban merchant classes ... The Psalter then, as later the prayer book or book of hours, was a particularly common book, being widely used by lay people, and not seldom decorated to the highest artistic standards.' (From an exhibition catalogue)[9]

[8] Cf. A Gerstmeier, 'Die Deutung der Psalmen im Spiegel der Musik. Vertonung des "De profundis' (Ps. 130) von der frühchristlichen Psalmodie bis zu Arnold Schönberg', in: *Liturgie und Dichtung* (note 5 above, vol. II, pp. 91–130.

[9] R. Kroos, in the catalogue of the exhibition 'Die Zeit der Staufer' ('The Staufer period' – Stuttgart 1977). This exhibition gave a unique over-view of the wealth of illustrated psalters from the 12th and 13th centuries.

The illuminated Psalters are impressive translations into visual form of the messages of the Psalms. The abundance of artistic and interpretative work invested in them opens up for us a new line of access to the texts which is of lasting value.

3. *The Psalter – The Little Biblia*

Luther's reforming zeal owed more to the Psalter than to any other Biblical book – the Epistle to the Romans included.

'Before all the Biblical writings, yes far more than any of the New Testament books, he expounded and preached, prayed through and imitated the "little Biblia", the Psalter, and at the great turning points of his life, he let the words of the Psalms meet him and comfort him. Ps. 2,11: *servite domino in timore*, he tells us, he hated as a monk. The references to the "righteousness" of God which Luther found repeatedly in the Psalms (Ps. 9,4ff.; 31,1; 71,2) had thrown him into a crisis of despair, which can still be traced in his lectures on the Psalms. So much the more did he later hold passionately to the Psalter which had caused him so much trouble, praying and singing it continuously as his only song of comfort and joy (especially "his" Psalm, 118, the "beautiful *confitemini*", until that evening when he lay down to his last rest with Ps. 31(30),5: *In manus tuas commendo spiritum meum, redemisti me deus veritatis*. Psalm 130,4: "With you there is forgiveness, therefore you are feared", convinced him time and again that God could only be truly honoured by the belief in justification. Luther knew no better way to thank the Hereditary Marshal of Electoral Saxony, Hans von Löser in Pretzsch, for a holiday than by the dedication of his exegesis on the 147th Psalm, his spiritual "game" which he had "bagged" on the back of the wagon while his host hunted, had cleaned and prepared at home, and now sent complete; but unlike ordinary game, he was also able to keep it completely for himself! Psalm 64, it seemed to him, could have been written against Heinz von Wolfenbüttel, and so he used it as his most powerful weapon in his polemic "*Wider Hans Worst*". This was how the Psalter lived for him, in a thousand connections with his own world; the examples could be continued endlessly.' (H. Bornkamm)[10]

[10] H. Bornkamm, *Luther and the Old Testament*, 1948 (Eng.tr.1969).

4. *Psalm-Song and Song-Psalter*

'At the turn of the 16th century, the genre of the vernacular hymn became productive. Within this genre, the psalm-song proved to be of particular significance in the 16th and 17th centuries. A flood of psalm-songs, and a considerable number of complete Psalters in song style appeared.' (A. Reich)[11]

This is tied up with the central issue of the Reformation. With the re-orientation of the channels of grace from the sacramental act to language-based processes such as proclamation and prayer, linguistic possibilities assumed a prominent position in church and faith. The vernacular song received its place in the church service. The reformers were therefore concerned to produce songs suitable for public worship.

Luther thought first and foremost of setting the Biblical Psalms in song form. He himself composed seven psalm-songs, all of which grew out of the process of psalm translation to which he had devoted himself all his life. Psalm-songs have the advantage of being able to found their linguistic form on the Psalms, taking on their Biblical authority, and connecting with the long tradition of medieval psalmody. They are Scripture reading, sermon, prayer and song all in one, while also being accessible to ordinary people, easily memorised, and as Luther wrote in the preface to the Wittenberg Song-book of 1524, particularly suitable for: 'propagating the holy Gospel, which has increased by God's Grace, and setting it in motion'.

'Even more than Luther, Calvin strove to bring the psalm-song into the centre of the liturgy ... For Calvin, the Psalms were, along with other *Cantica* from the Holy Scripture, the only liturgically permissible church music.' (A. Reich)[12]

---

[11] A. Reich, 'Psalmübertragungen und Umdichtung im Psalmlied des 16. und 17. Jahrhunderts', in: *Liturgie und Dichtung*, vol. I, pp. 659–710.
[12] Ibid., p. 667.

In the course of a year, the Psalter was to be sung twice through. For this purpose, Calvin commissioned the French poet Clement Marot to continue a translation which he himself had begun, on the model of Jerome's *Psalterium gallicanum* (386); Th. de Bèze completed this after Marot's death. The so-called Huguenot Psalter appeared by 1562, two years before Calvin's death. Written in strong homophony, it received a remarkably wide distribution. In just four years it ran into sixty-two French editions. It reached Germany in translations by M. Schede and most importantly by A. Lobwasser (1572/73), where it established itself over a period of seventy years in repeated new translations. The final climax of this movement was the German translation of the Huguenot Psalter by Martin Opitz (1624).

The success of the Huguenot Psalter also influenced the development of the song-psalters which stood in the Lutheran tradition. Following from the important work of Burkhart Waldis (1553), a whole series of psalters appeared which were strongly marked by Lutheran-Orthodox characteristics; but these never achieved the popularity of the Huguenot Psalter. The same could be said of the Catholic song-psalters which now began to appear, of which the psalter published anonymously by W. G. M. Johann Philipp of Schönborn in 1658 deserves special mention on account of its spiritual content.

The earliest English metrical translations of selected psalms were those of Thomas Sternhold and John Hopkins. Their work was incorporated into the Anglo-Genevan Psalter *One and Fiftie Psalmes of David in English Metre* (1556). Complete Psalters included those of Day (1563), with four-part harmonies, and Este (1592), which introduced the custom of naming tunes after places. The most influential English-language song-psalter was the Scots Metrical Psalter. After a number of attempts, the text was established in 1650, influenced among others by the work of Francis Rous. This psalter bore the presbyterian *imprimatur*: 'Allowed by the authority of the General Assembly of the Kirk of Scotland, and appointed to be sung in congregations and families.'[13] For many years no other form of church music was permitted than the unaccompanied singing of these psalms. The texts are often very awkward, because of the constraints of producing a singable, yet strictly literal text of Scripture. Nevertheless, they were extremely popular, and their influence throughout the English-speaking world has been immense. In particular, the 23rd Psalm is better known in this version ('The Lord's my shepherd, I'll not want,/ he makes me down to lie . . .') than in any other. The writing of metrical Psalms, for private use rather than for public devotion, was fashionable among Scots poets in the 18th century. In 1773, James Maxwell published *A New Version of the Whole Book of Psalms in Metre*. Even Robert Burns engaged in this pursuit.

The English Reformation took a different course. Since Psalms were more commonly chanted, metrical psalters were not given such a high profile. A number of versions were made, among them that of Playford (1667), but by the 18th century their use had all but died out. Individual metrical psalms do, however, feature in many Anglican hymn-books, as do some of the finest psalm tunes.

For the further 'history of poetic arrangement' of the Psalter in the German-speaking world, we turn to the important article by H. Kurzke:[14]

[13] R. Roy, 'The Bible in Burns and Scott', in: *The Bible in Scottish Life and Literature* (ed. D. F. Wright), 1988, p. 91.
[14] H. Kurzke, 'Säkularisation oder Realisation? Zur Wirkungsgeschichte von Psalm 130 ("De profundis") in der deutschen Literatur von Luther bis zur Gegenwart', in: *Liturgie und Dichtung*, vol. II, pp. 67–89.

'Among the numerous psalters of the Baroque period, the texts by *Opitz, Hohberg* and *Fleming* (1640, 1675 1631) are outstanding. Their principle readership was no longer the religious community, but the scholarly world. They try out the new linguistic awareness of the Baroque, won from the poetry of the Renaissance, on the familiar models of spiritual poetry. In the 18th century, it is above all *Cramer* and *Mendelssohn* (1763, 1783), and *Herder* (*Vom Geist der ebräischen Poesie*, 1782/3) who contribute to this great tradition. In contrast to the 17th century, which moulded the Psalms in the classical forms of Opitz's *"Poeterey"*, they believed they had found the true and original poetical form of the Hebrew verse. With reference to *Robert Lowth's "De sacra poesi Hebraeorum"*, which discovered *parallelismus membrorum* as the basic formal element of the Psalter, Herder described the poetic structure of Old Testament verse, and gave model translations of many Psalms. Herder rejected rhyme and meter, and thus proceeded down the path which had been marked out by *Klopstock's* free rhythms. The language of the Psalms, as the original poetic language of the human race, therefore contributed in no small way to the development of the literary language of the Classical and Romantic epochs.

But here, this great tradition quite suddenly ceases. Whereas previously religious and poetic interests were closely bound together, the Romantic period saw a division between the sacred and the secular strands of the history of the use of the Psalms. The sacred side was imitative, with no innovative power ... The secular ... reached to the lyrics of the present day.'

5. Psalm Lyrics

The influence of the Psalms on modern poetry cannot be discussed here. We shall limit ourselves to a number of brief references to psalmodic, i.e. psalm-like poetry resulting from the direct appropriation of material, and to important (linguistically creative) adaptations. And here again we are concerned more with the influence exerted by the Psalms than with the importance of the poetry itself. Besides, an 'introduction' like this can only offer a few, perhaps inspiring pointers.

228

I shall make mention of three fields in which the Psalms are active in the modern creative power of literary style, and shall leave it as an exercise for the readers to discover such connections for themselves in the literature with which they are familiar.

1. Modern lyrics in which psalm forms are deliberately taken up, imitated, satirised or criticised. Examples are legion.[15]

2. Songs and hits from all over the world, especially of course the Black American spirituals, a tradition which uses many psalm-texts (e.g. 'By the rivers of Babylon'; 'Hallelujah! An'a hallelujah!'; 'Little David play on yo'harp', and many others).

3. Folk poetry and freedom songs, like the collection of Latin American 'Psalms' published by E. Cardenal, with its own variations on the Biblical Psalm-texts.[16]

With this kind of reception of the Biblical Psalms, we must ask whether we are not doing the ancient texts an injustice when we make them the vehicle, and a very powerful vehicle at that, of a message which may perhaps be foreign to them? Are we not sometimes guilty of a suppression and subjugation of the texts, which goes against the proper purposes of Psalm reception? Even texts, and particularly Biblical texts, have a right to their own life and their own message. It is both a theological and a moral question how we may and should handle historical texts. And it is the so-called historical-critical exegesis which seeks to raise the awareness of such questions, and to sharpen the conscience.

6. Translations of the Psalter into German

'In vain men have . . . struggled with the Book of Job, the Psalms and other songs, to make them enjoyable to us in their poetic

[15] Cf. P. K. Kurz, *Psalmen vom Expressionismus bis zur Gegenwart*, 1978.
[16] E. Cardenal, *Das Buch von der Liebe*, 1971.

form. For the majority who will be moved by them, a simple rendering is still always the best. Those critical translations which contend with the original in fact serve only for the mutual entertainment of scholars.' (J. W. von Goethe).

We conclude by examining a number of translations in an attempt to show which possibilities our modern languages offer for the rendering of the Psalms. As an example we take Ps. 127.

6.1 Excerpts from the Old High German translation of Notker the German (950–1022)

1 Vnser truhten nezímberoe das hûs. ferlorne arbeite sint déro/die
        iz îlton zímberon . . .
        (CHRISTVS nehûote dia ecclesiam)
2 Íu ist ún-núzze fóre táge ûf ze stânne . . .
        Stânt ûf. so ir gesízzent . . .
        Íu chído ih. ir mit sêre brôt ezent.
3 Sô er daz ende gibet sînen hóldôn.
        so chumet daz erbe . . .
        So chumet der lôn. des sunes . . .
        So chumet der lôn des uuûocheres dero heiligun uuúmbo.
4 Also die strâla in des mahtigen hende. so sint dero erscútton súne.
5 Kesah in Got. der sih kérot iro ze gesátonne.
        Saligo den íro lero lustet . . .
        Sie neuuérdent scámeg. so sie ûfen búrgetóre sprechent ze iro
        fienden . . .[17]

If our Lord does not build the house, lost are the labours of those who hasten to build it . . ./ (If CHRIST does not protect the *ecclesiam*)/ It is useless for you to get up before the day . . ./ Stand up, you who sit . . ./ I tell you, you will eat your bread with pain./ So he will give the end to his friends./ thus comes the inheritance . . ./ Thus comes the recompense of the son . . ./ Thus comes the recompense of wickedness from the holy womb./ Like arrows in the hands of the mighty, so are the sons of those who shoot./ (He is) accepted by God, who turns to them for satisfaction./ Blessed

[17] Text: *Notkers des Deutschen Werk* (ed. E. H. Sehrt), 1955, vol. III, pp. 968–970.

are they who crave their teaching . . ./ They will not be ashamed when they speak to their enemies upon the city gate.

The manuscript is in St. Gallen. Dialect: Alemanic. The Latin text and explanations have been omitted. Underlying this translation is an allegorical interpretation. House = Church (1), rising = resurrection (2), 'shot' arrows = apostles, with a Christological orientation, fruit of the womb = son of Mary (3), *CHRISTVS ist daz purgetor'* (the city gate, 5). 'When we survey the prose of the Carolingian period, Notker's use of the German language demands our admiration. Every problem of translation seems to have been solved. Notker handles the source text with total freedom; he was only concerned to capture the sense, and to make it clearly understood. The certainty with which he covers each Latin word with a corresponding German one is admirable. In particular when it comes to the old touchstone of linguistic ability in the scholarly sphere, the translation of abstractions, his mastery of language becomes clear.'[18]

6.2   *M. Luther 1545*

CXXVII

1   Ein Lied Salomo
    Im höhern Chor.
    Wo DER HERR nicht das Haus bawet
    So erbeiten vmb sonst
    die dran bawen.
    Wo der HERR nicht die Stadt behütet
    So wachet der Wechter vmb sonst.

2   Es ist vmb sonst
    das jr früe auffstehet
    vnd hernach lang sitzet
    vnd esset ewer Brot mit sorgen
    Denn seinen Freunden gibt ers schlaffend.

3   Sihe
    Kinder sind eine Gabe des HERRN
    Vnd Leibes frucht ist ein geschenck.

[18] H. de Boor, R. Newald, *Geschichte der deutschen Literatur*, 1949, p. 116.

4 Wie die Pfeile in der hand eines Starcken
  Also geraten die jungen Knaben.
5 Wol dem
  der seine Köcher derselben vol hat
  Die werden nicht zu schanden
  wenn sie mit jren Feinden handeln im Thor.[19]

CXXVII/ A song of Solomon/ in the upper choir./ Where THE
LORD does not build the house/ they labour in vain/who build at
it./ Where the LORD does not guard the city/the watchman
watches in vain./ It is in vain/ that you rise early/ and afterwards sit
long/ and eat your bread with cares/for he gives it to his friends in
their sleep./ See/ Children are a gift of the LORD/ and the fruit of
the womb is a present./Like the arrows in the hand of a strong man/
so the young lads end up./ Blessed is he/ whose quiver is full of
them/They will not be disgraced/ when they deal with their
enemies in the gate.

1 'in the upper choir' – a raised gallery for the choir? (as a translation
  for 'song of ascents'?); 'where' creates a concrete localisation of the
  imagery; alliteration on *w* (cf. Heb. *5*). Note that in the German
  tradition, as in the Hebrew, the heading is part of the first verse. In
  many psalms, the heading takes up a whole verse, or even two (eg.
  Ps 51f.) with the result that almost half the verses in the Psalter are
  numbered differently from the English Bible.
2 A sympathetic depiction of the daily work of a peasant; 'eat . . .
  with cares' instead of 'labour for'; 'his friends' – following Vulgate
  (most Hebrew manuscripts singular); 'in their sleep' connects with
  the image of the day's work. The image in this verse comes together
  very nicely with Luther's *sola gratia*.
3 'gift', 'present' – translates 'wage': building on the theological idea
  in 2.
4 Luther is thinking of the advantage to boys of a firm upbringing,
  the Hebrew text of the advantage to the parent who heads a strong
  family unit.
5 'deal' – or 'negotiate'

Cf. Luther's *Psalmus politicus et Oeconomicus*, and his psalm-song
'*Vergebens ist all Müh und Kost*'.

[19] Text: D. Martin Luther, *Die gantze Heilige Schrifft Deudsch*, Wittenberg
1514 (ed. H. Volz, 1973).

THE INFLUENCE OF THE PSALMS

'When Luther's Bible appeared, it was what the Bible should be, what indeed makes it unique among all human books: a sensation . . .' And yet it grew up in the soil of the Latin Bible. '. . . even Luther himself gave flesh and blood to its wording. Even he, whose German Psalter was perhaps the crown of his achievements in translation . . . recited the Latin text when he withdrew into prayer! Though he may have penetrated the meaning of the Hebrew, he himself thought . . . not in Hebrew, but in Latin.'[20]

6.3   R. Guardini 1950

Psalm 126   Gottvertrauen

1   *Baut* der *Herr* nicht das Haus,
   mühn sich um*sonst, die* daran bauen.

   Hütet der Herr nicht die Stadt,
   wacht vergebens, *der* sie behütet.

2   Nutzlos *ists, wenn* ihr vor Tag euch erhebt,
   tief in der *Nacht noch* (an der Arbeit) sitzt,

   ihr, die ihr esset der harten Mühsal Brot –
   gibt Er es doch den Seinen im Schlaf.

3   Siehe, Gabe des Herrn sind Söhne,
   Gnade von Ihm des Leibes Frucht;

4   Pfeilen *gleich* in des Kriegers Hand
   sind Söhne der jungen Jahre.

5   Selig der Mann,
   der mit solchen den Köcher gefüllt,

   denn sie versagen *nicht*
   im Kampf mit den Feinden am Tor.[21]

[20] F. Rosenzweig, 'Die Schrift und Luther', in: *Die Schrift* (ed. K. Thieme), 1984, pp. 62, 70.
[21] Text: R. Guardini, *Deutscher Psalter* (1950).

233

Psalm 126 Trust in God/ If the *Lord* does not *build* the house,/ they *strive* in *vain, who* built at it./ If the Lord does not *guard* the city,/ he *watches* to no avail, *who* guard it./ *It is* futile *when* you rise before day,/ deep into the *night still* sit (at work),/ *you*, who eat the bread of tribulation – / He *gives* it to His own in their sleep./ See, a gift of the Lord are sons,/ grace from Him, the fruit of the womb;/ *like* arrows in the hand of the warrior/ are sons of the young years./ Blessed the man,/ *who* has filled his quiver with such,/ *for* they do *not* fail/ in the battle with the enemies in the gateway.

Syllables in italics are to be emphasised. Guardini arranges his text in couplets.

1 The complex meaning of *šāw'* is dispersed into three alternative translations: 'in vain', 'to no avail', 'futile'.
2 *'Nacht noch'* – alliteration; added explanation in brackets; *'der harten Mühsal Brot'* – very compact phrasing; verse 2 is seen as a unity, drawing out the parallel between 'day's work' and 'sleep'.
3 'Grace' for Hebrew 'wage'.
4 *'Pfeilen gleich'* – elevated style.
5 'Blessed' has spiritual overtones; 'battle with the enemies' – almost a little too warlike.

Guardini's translation is colourful, rhetorical, rhythmic, a good text for reading aloud, with a tendency towards religious language.

6.4   M. Buber 1953

CXXVII
Ein Aufstiegsgesang Salomos

Will ER ein Haus nicht erbauen,
wahnhaft mühn sich dran seine Erbauer.
Will ER eine Stadt nicht behüten,
wahnhaft durchwacht der Hüter.
Wahnheit ists euch,
die ihr überfrüh aufsteht,
die ihr euch überspät hinsetzt,
die das Brot der Trübsal ihr esset:–

Rechtes,
im Schlaf gibt ers seinem Freund.

Da, von IHM eine Zueignung: Söhne,
ein Sold: die Frucht des Leibes.
Wie Pfeile in des Wehrmanns Hand,
so sind die Söhne der Jugend.
O Glück des Mannes,
der seinen Köcher mit ihnen gefüllt hat!
Die werden nicht zuschanden,
wenn sie mit Feinden reden im Tor.[22]

CXXVII/ A song of ascents of Solomon/ If HE chooses not to
build a house,/ its builders strive at it foolishly./ If HE chooses not
to guard a city,/ the guard watches foolishly through the night./ It
is foolishness to you/ who rise all too early,/ who lie down all too
late,/ who eat the bread of sorrow:–/ The right way,/ he gives it to
his friend in his sleep./

So, a dedication from HIM: sons,/ a remuneration: the fruit of the
womb./ Like arrows in the watchman's hand,/ thus are the sons of
one's youth,/ O happiness of the man,/ who has his quiver filled
with them!/ They will not come to disgrace,/ when they speak with
enemies in the gate.

Lines follow the structure of Hebrew verse. Rhythmic. In
two sections. No verse numbers.

1 'HE' ('HIM') – YHWH; Buber's key-word (*Leitwort*) is *šāw'*,
   translated colourfully as '*Wahnheit*', foolishness, madness.
2 '*Überfrüh*', '*überspät*' – underlining the everyday phrase; '*rechtes*' –
   derived from the structure of meaning, this is set up in polarity to
   the key-word; 'his friend' – singular, following the main Hebrew
   reading.
3 '*Zueignung*' and '*Sold*' – unusual words, giving a deliberate
   alienation. Similarly:
4 '*Wehrmann*'; the style of address in vv. 3–5 is heightened dramatically by the '*da*' in v. 3, and by the interjection '*o Glück*'.

'One might take the view that the limits of what is
permissible in a Bible translation have here been crossed.

[22] Text: *Das Buch der Preisungen*, 1953, p. 188.

235

Certainly, in Buber's own contribution to the fabric, in the contribution of his literary and intellectual style, lie also a weakness and a limitation. But who would wish to insist on this, and demand an accounting of such a successful piece of work? How much is given to us here! Do we really know so precisely the limits of the meaning contained in the Scripture? Who has measured out its depth and breadth? Does Buber not stand within it, despite all that is his own? Even this pathos which no earlier generation had managed to draw out of the psalm, even this is a gift of the Scripture. Buber would agree with us.'[23]

7. Translations of the Psalter into English

Unfortunately, there are no surviving translations of the Psalter into Old English, although such must at one time have existed. Aldhelm, first bishop of Sherborne (c. 700), is said to have translated the Psalms into English, and Alfred the Great (who included an English version of the Decalogue and some of the other Pentateuchal laws in his national law-code) is credited with the translation of part of the Psalter. A number of Middle English versions and paraphrases of the Psalter have come down to us from the 13th and 14th centuries.

The earliest complete English versions of the whole Bible are the two translations associated with John Wycliffe. The first of these appeared in 1384. Other important early translations were the Bible of William Tyndale (1494/5–1536), Coverdale's version (1535), the Great Bible (1540), and the Geneva Bible (1560).

[23] N. Lohfink, 'Bubers Bibelübersetzung, in: *Das Siegeslied am Schilfmeer*, 1965, pp. 260f.

7.1 *Authorised Version (King James Version) 1611*

PSALM 127

A Song of degrees for Solomon.

1 Except the Lord build the house, they labour in vain that build it: except the Lord keep the city, the watchman waketh but in vain.

2 It is vain for you to rise up early, to sit up late, to eat the bread of sorrows: for so he giveth his beloved sleep.

3 Lo, children are an heritage of the Lord: and the fruit of the womb is his reward.

4 As arrows are in the hand of a mighty man; so are children of the youth.

5 Happy is the man that hath his quiver full of them: they shall not be ashamed, but they shall speak with the enemies in the gate.

This is certainly the most influential of all English Bible translations. It is marked by literal translation and a great concern for accuracy, although unfortunately it often rests on a poor Greek or Hebrew text. If it often appears to have a particular power and beauty of expression, this may be less because it conforms to the patterns of the English language than because it has helped to shape them.

Heading: 'For Solomon' – takes the Hebrew preposition l^e as a dedication rather than a mark of authorship.

1 'Build', 'keep' – subjunctive, these are hypothetical cases. But the Hebrew verb is not capable of such subtlety. 'Lord' – the Authorised Version established the principle, adopted by most English translations, of translating YHWH in this way, following the Jewish custom of pronouncing instead the surrogate '*adonai*' (= 'lord'). It is capitalised in order to distinguish it from those cases where the Hebrew really does have '*adonai*'.

2 'Bread of sorrows' – magnificent phrase: this makes the bread into a metaphor for trouble generally; 'He giveth his beloved sleep' (sleep itself is the gift, rather than unnamed gifts being given 'while they sleep') – this is the most literal translation; note that 'beloved' could be either singular or plural.

4 'The youth' – the article is misleading: 'youth' here is an abstract concept.

5 'They' – i.e. the children.

'The Authorised Version was admirably suited for public reading. A study of its prose rhythms suggests that the men responsible for it (not only King James's revisers but their predecessors as far back as Tyndale) had an instinctive feeling for good style. If preachers, orators and writers would spend a little time noting the rhythms of the early English Bible, they would grow discontented with the sentences that please them now.'[24]

7.2 P. H. Waddell 1871

PSALM CXXVII.

Livin folk's ay better nor stane an' lime; an' biggin siclike for a houss till the Lord, 's his ain wark.

A sang o' the Upgaens: for Solomon.

1 An JEHOVAH big-na the houss, they fash for nought, wha big at it; an JEHOVAH keep-na the brugh, he waukens for nought wha keeps waird onto 't.

2 It'll do ye nae guid till steer or light, till bide late at night, eatin yer bread wi' a pingle: *for* till them he loes weel, he gies sleep.

3 Na, bairns are the LORD's heritage; the mither's fraught, *his* fee.

4 Like flanes in the han' o' some mighty wight, sae new-fun folk *maun be.*

5 Blythe be the wight wi' a sheaf o' siclike; no blate sal they be, but sal crack fu' hie, till wha wiss them ill, i' the yett.[25]

big – build	pingle – effort	blate – dull, stupid
brugh – town	bairn – child	crack – converse
steer – plough	fraught – burden	fu' hie – in haste
or – before	flane – arrow	yett – gate
bide – wait	wight – fellow	

This 19th century Scots translation stands in some ways in the Authorised Version tradition, but it is often idiomatic rather than literal. However, words added for the sake of

[24] F. F. Bruce, *The English Bible*, 1961, p. 109.

[25] Text: P. Hately Waddell, *The Psalms: Frae Hebrew intil Scottis.* 1871 (ed. G. Tulloch, 1987).

clarity which are not present in the Hebrew are placed in italics, indicating some concern for accuracy. The italicised heading suggests the main messages of the Psalm for Waddell. These are quite concrete: people are more important than buildings; and building a house for God is his work (i.e. work done in his service). The Hebrew heading is also given. 'For Solomon' reflects the influence of the Authorised Version.

1 'Jehovah' – mixed reading of Hebrew Y(J)–H–W(V)–H and the vowels of *Adonai*. But this is not used consistently: in the heading we read 'Lord', and in v. 3 'LORD'.
2 'It'll do you no good' – circumlocution loses the force of the triple *šāw*'; 'to those whom he loves well' – this is plural, following a minority Hebrew reading (2 Manuscripts).
3 'Mother's burden' (that which she bears) – for 'fruit of the womb'; a marginal note reads 'outcome o' the wame'.
4 'New-found folk' – idiomatic phrase for children; no mention of the father's youth, though a marginal note reads "bairns o' the young"; 'must be' – one suspects that this phrase has only been used to create a rhyme with 'fee'.
5 Rhyme between 'be' and 'hie'; Hebrew makes no mention of haste; 'those who wish them ill in the gate' – the significance of the gate as the location of the law court is well understood here; note how the rhythm accelerates in this final verse.

'As the accepted English translation of the day . . . the Authorised Version will certainly have been the translation best known to Waddell and the one against which he was consciously setting his Scots alternative. Despite his attempts to distance himself from the Authorised Version – the two versions are so different that one senses a deliberate endeavour on Waddell's part not to use the Authorised Version's wording even where it would have made good Scots – the Authorised Version makes its presence felt . . . Yet we should remember that Scottish people were also familiar with another version of the Psalms in English, the Scottish Metrical Psalter. The influence of this version, so important in Scottish worship, may account for one of the stylistic peculiarities of Waddell's prose version, the occasional resort to rhyme.'[26]

7.3   J. Moffatt 1924

127

A pilgrim song, by Solomon.

1   Unless the Eternal builds the house,
       workmen build in vain;
     unless the Eternal guards the town,
       sentries are on guard in vain.
2   Vain is it to rise early for your work,
       and keep at work so late,
     gaining your bread with anxious toil!
       God's gifts come to his loved ones, as they sleep.

      *   *   *

3   Sons are a gift of the Eternal,
       and children are a boon from him.
4   Strong sons born when one is young
       are like arrows in an archer's hands;
5   happy the man who has a quiver full of them,
       he need not fear to face a hostile band.[27]

This is one of the most successful attempts by a single translator to render the whole Bible into English. James Moffatt (1870–1944), a minister of the United Free Church of Scotland, held chairs in both New Testament Exegesis and Church History. The translation is marked by a bold choice of language and a deep understanding of the critical questions involved.

Asterisks mark a clear division between the two halves of this psalm.

Heading: 'By Solomon' – taking the Hebrew preposition as a *lamed auctoris*.

---

[26] G. Tulloch, ibid., pp. xvi f.
[27] Text: J. Moffatt, *A New Translation of the Bible*, 1924.

1 'Eternal' – throughout his entire Bible, Moffat consistently translates YHWH in this way. This has no philological basis, but it may reflect the Jewish reluctance to pronounce the divine name. According to G. Anderson, this 'sounds impressive, but may be judged unsuitable since the concept of eternity has no place in Old Testament thought'.[28]

2 'With anxious toil' – a colourful phrase, later taken up by the Revised Standard Version, to which Moffatt also contributed; 'as they sleep' – most of the English versions take the verse this way.

4 'Archer' – continuing the image of arrows, though the Hebrew is not so specific.

5 reduced to two stichs; 'he' – i.e. the father: this may seem to make good sense ('happy is the man'), but in Hebrew both verbs are plural; 'fear . . . face' – alliteration (the Hebrew verbs 'be ashamed' and 'speak with' both contain the letter *Beth*); 'band' possibly to rhyme with 'hand'?

'As the best qualities of his New Testament translation are seen in the Pauline Epistles, so in the Old Testament they are most evident in the prophetic books. Amos exhibits with particular effect his ability to transmit the urgency and passion of the prophetic message, both in stern denunciation and in solemn dirge. He is less successful in his translation of the Psalms, where the poetic structure is often unaccompanied by the poetic spirit, no matter how clearly the sense is conveyed. His terse, matter-of-fact style is well suited to much of the Wisdom literature . . .

In spite of the blemishes which have been noted, Moffatt's translation of the Old Testament is a remarkable achievement. The merits of his rendering far outweigh its defects.'[29]

---

[28] G. Anderson, 'James Moffatt: Bible Translator', in D. Wright (ed.), *The Bible in Scottish Life and Literature*, 1988, p. 50.
[29] Ibid., pp. 50f.

7.4 Jerusalem Bible 1966

PSALM 127   V 126

Trust in Providence

Song of Ascents   Solomon

1   If Yahweh does not build the house,
    in vain the masons toil;
    if Yahweh does not guard the city,
    in vain the sentries watch.

2   In vain you get up earlier,
    and put off going to bed,
    sweating to make a living,
    since he provides for his beloved as they sleep.

3   Sons are a bounty from Yahweh,
    he rewards with descendants:
4   like the arrows in a hero's hand
    are the sons you father when young.

5   Happy is the man who has filled his quiver
    with arrows of this sort;
    in dispute with his enemies at the gate,
    he will not be worsted.

A Roman Catholic translation. The Psalms are numbered according to the Hebrew system, but the numbers from the Vulgate are given in smaller print in the margin (V 126). A heading is added which rightly draws out the theme of providence from v. 2 as the major theme of the whole Psalm. The Hebrew heading is also given. No preposition is used with the name of Solomon; similarly, 'David' in Ps. 124, but rather inconsistently, 'Of David' in Ps. 131 and others. The text is divided into four stanzas.

1   'Yahweh' – the most probable vocalisation of YHWH; the indentation in this stanza differs from the other three, drawing attention to its internal structure (the exact grammatical parallel between the two pairs of lines picks up on a pattern in the Hebrew – but the Hebrew is not quite so neat); 'masons' and 'sentries' – a

refreshing change to 'builders' and 'watchmen'. But note that the Hebrew only has one sentry.

2 'Earlier' – than what? Hebrew does not have a comparative form here; toiling for bread is taken as a metaphor for earning a living.

3 'Bounty' – an unusual word for such a colloquial text; similarly 'worsted' (v. 5); 'descendants' – the image 'fruit of the womb' (like 'seed') can look to distant generations, but in view of v. 4 it seems more likely that the reference here is to the immediate generation, to sons and daughters.

4 'Sons you father' – the second person pronoun from v. 2 has been carried over.

5 'At the gate' – a very helpful footnote adds: 'The city gate, at which all business matters and disputes are settled'.

This translation reads pleasantly enough, and strays less than some from the basic text.

7.5 New English Bible 1970

127

1 Unless the LORD builds the house,
 its builders will have toiled in vain.
 Unless the LORD keeps watch over a city,
 in vain the watchman stands on guard.

2 In vain you rise up early
 and go late to rest,
 toiling for the bread you eat;
 he supplies the need of those he loves.

3 Sons are a gift from the LORD
 and children a reward from him.

4 Like arrows in the hand of a fighting man
 are the sons of a man's youth.

5 Happy is the man
 who has his quiver full of them;
 such men shall not be put to shame
 when they confront their enemies in court.

A translation into literary English.

Heading – not translated: the introduction explains that these are 'almost certainly not original'.

1   Interesting use of tenses: 'builds' (present indicative, as opposed to
    Authorised Version 'build') implies that building is currently taking
    place, so the result 'will have toiled' is put in the future perfect (but
    then, why not 'will have stood'?).
2   no mention of sleep – a footnote gives notice of an unintelligible
    Hebrew word at the end of this line (although this is the only
    occurrence of the spelling šn', most scholars accept it as a variant on
    šnh, 'sleep').
3   'gift' – for 'inheritance'.
5   'in court' – an explanation rather than a translation (the reader is
    therefore not required to know that the city gate functioned as a
    law-court).

The New English Bible attempts a 'high style' and a
'timeless language' with mixed success. It has a tendency to
opt for controversial readings.

7.6   Today's English Version (Good News Bible) 1976

127   In Praise of God's Goodness

1   If the LORD does not build the house,
      the work of the builders is useless;
    if the LORD does not protect the city,
      it is useless for the sentries to stand guard.
2   It is useless to work so hard for a living,
      getting up early and going to bed late.
    For the LORD provides for those he loves,
      while they are asleep.
3   Children are a gift from the LORD;
      they are a real blessing.
4   The sons a man has when he is young
      are like arrows in a soldier's hand.
5   Happy is the man who has many such arrows.
    He will never be defeated
      when he meets his enemies in the place of judgment.

Hebrew heading not translated, though part of it is
rendered in a footnote: 'By Solomon', taking the Hebrew
Lamed to indicate authorship. A new heading is added,
accentuating the positive side of the Psalm's message.

2 'Work for a living' – interprets the image of toiling for bread; 'get up', 'go to bed' – colloquial wording typifies this translation; note that the order of ideas in this verse has been altered.

3 'They are a real blessing' – very weak translation.

5 'Arrows' – repeating the word in this verse may give added clarity, but the image of the quiver is lost; 'never be defeated' – a more substantial claim than 'not be disgraced' (it is possible to lose a case, yet retain one's dignity); 'the place of judgment' – following the interpretative rendering of the New English Bible; the structure of stichs seems to break down in this verse.

The assumption of this translation is that 'Today's English' means a simplistic linguistic niveau with a very limited range of vocabulary. The most frequent complaint is that both accuracy and beauty are sacrificed for the sake of clarity.

7.7 The New International Version 1978

Psalm 127
A song of ascents. Of Solomon

1 Unless the LORD builds the house,
    its builders labour in vain.
  Unless the LORD watches over the city,
    the watchmen stand guard in vain.

2 In vain you rise early
    and stay up late,
  toiling for food to eat –
    for he grants sleep to those he loves.

3 Sons are a heritage from the LORD,
    children a reward from him.

4 Like arrows in the hands of a warrior
    are sons born in one's youth.

5 Blessed is the man
    whose quiver is full of them.
  They will not be put to shame
    when they contend with their enemies in the gate.

Heading translated in full; 'Of Solomon' captures the ambiguity of the Hebrew prepositional prefix.

2 'He grants sleep to those . . .' – sleep itself is the gift, a relief from the toil of the day – but a footnote gives the other possibility: 'for while they sleep he provides for . . .' Of all the translations examined here, this is the only one to acknowledge both possibilities.

3 'Heritage', 'reward' – the same words which were used by the Authorised Version, revealing the New International Version's debt to the language of the Authorised Version.

5 'They' (plural) – as in the Authorised Version, it is the sons who will not be put to shame.

Probably the most balanced Protestant translation available in modern English, the New International Version retains much of the familiar style of the classical English translations, yet achieves a very readable style. It is able to take account of modern scholarship, but is cautious in translating disputed texts.

7.8   Other Important English Translations

A number of other translations should be noted:

The Douai translation (the standard Roman Catholic version, comparable in some ways to the Authorised Version).

Roland Knox, *The Holy Bible translated from the Latin Vulgate in the light of the Hebrew and Greek* – 1949 (New Testament 1945).

Revised Standard Version – 1952 (based on the American *Revised Version*, which in turn is a revision of the Authorised Version).

J. Gelineau, et. al., *The Psalms: a new translation* (1963). A Catholic translation, intended to be sung in worship. These Psalms attempt to render in English the rhythm of the Hebrew.

J. E. McFadyen, *The Psalms in Modern Speech*.

P. Levi, *The Psalms*, translated for Penguin Classics (1976), with a useful introductory section on the nature of Hebrew verse.

H. Mowvley, *The Psalms introduced and newly translated for today's readers* (1989), with an introductory note on each Psalm.

Chapter XI

EXPOUNDING THE PSALMS

As soon as the Psalter came to be counted among the Holy
Scriptures, having reached more or less its final form, it was
not only prayed (cf. 102,1), read and studied (cf. 1,2), sung and
performed (cf. the headings, and the general terms ψαλμός,
ψαλτήριον) but it was also expounded. This was the
beginning of a long, unbroken chain of exegesis which sought
to elucidate and keep alive for each generation the words of
these songs and prayers, as their archaic style and language
threatened to push them back into obscurity. The age of the
commentary had dawned. From the almost unmanageable
abundance of this literature which has gathered in the course
of time, we choose a few examples in order to learn what kind
of contribution each epoch has made to the exegesis of the
Psalms, and to discover how perspectives have changed in the
course of this long history.

1. *Early Jewish and Early Christian Commentaries*

The earliest known commentary (in the proper sense of
textual exegesis) on the Psalms was that of the Qumran
community. Or at any rate, the oldest surviving fragments of
commentaries on at least *some* Psalms originated there: e.g.
the *Pešer* on Ps. 37 from the fourth cave (4QpPs37).[1] Together
with the commentaries on the Prophets (1QpHab, 4QpNah,
4QpZeph), it shows that the Qumran Essenes already had a
tradition of exegesis, and that the Psalms belonged to the
category of texts worthy of exposition. This exposition runs
along the lines of apocalyptic interpretation: the material

[1] E. Lohse, *Die Texte aus Qumran*, 1981 (3rd edn.), pp. 269ff.

contained in the Psalms is seen as future prediction, and is related to the contemporary situation of the interpreter, who believes himself to be living in the 'end-times'. The commentary employs the *'pesher'*-procedure. Verse by verse, the text is quoted, and an interpretation is offered, beginning with the formula: 'its meaning' (*pšr/w*). Eg. 37,11:

> '"But the meek will inherit the land, and will delight in the abundance of peace." Its meaning relates to the Community of the Poor, who have taken upon themselves the time of anguish, who will be delivered from all the snares of Belial; afterwards, they will delight...' (II, 9–12)

The Community of the Poor is Qumran, Belial is Satan. The alphabetical structure of the Psalm is not acknowledged, not at any rate in the surviving text. If earliest Christianity had found time to write a Commentary on the Psalms, it would probably have looked similar to Qumran's *pešer*. This assumption may be drawn from the analogies which exist between the two movements, particularly with regard to their use of the Psalter, and is supported by comparable passages of the New Testament: Rom. 3,10ff.; Acts 2,25ff.; 4,25ff.; Heb. 1,5ff.; 2,5ff.; 10,5ff.; 1 Pet. 3,10ff.

2. The Early Church

Psalm exegesis in the Early Church suffered from a general ignorance of the Hebrew language. It was only Origen and Jerome who concerned themselves with the *hebraica veritas*. But even they, like almost all expositors of the period, were dependent on the 'Greek Truth', with all the weaknesses which were inherent in this from the beginning. Certainly, a number of the Church Fathers wrote commentaries, or at least 'introductions' to exegetical questions, as for example, Origen (180–254) and Athanasius (295–373). But the only outstanding work of this kind was the collection of sermons by Augustine (354–430), '*Enarrationes in Psalmos*' (416 AD).

'The afflictions from which the earliest Psalm expositions suffered are in general the same for both Greek and Western exegetes. In addition to their inadequate linguistic knowledge of the under lying text, we must reckon with their unmethodical procedure, their deliberate overloading of the prophetic character of the Psalms . . . , their unhistorical perspective, within which all distinction between the two testaments disappears, their misleading predisposition towards allegory . . . But never has the Church immersed itself in the Psalms with such delight as it did then, tirelessly singing them by day and by night; never has it used them more successfully, even in martyrdom. In those days it was quite usual to know 'the whole David' by heart . . . What the Early Church failed to achieve with ink in the expository field, it more than made up for by preserving the power of the Psalms in its blood.'[1]

3. The Middle Ages

Among the Medieval interpreters of the Psalms appear such names as Alkuin (735–804), Walahfrid Strabo (807–847), Bruno von Würzburg (†1045), Peter Lombard (†1160), Richard de Saint-Victor (†1173), Albertus Magnus (c.1206–1280), Thomas Aquinas (1225–1274), Nicholas of Lyra (c.1270–1349). They receive and hold in trust the heritage of the Early Church. The fruits of their labours lie more in the general theological field of hermeneutics. The exposition of the Psalms seems to have become a hermeneutical paradigm for them. With the possible exception of the mystics, their interpretative insights scarcely surpassed those of the earlier period. Nevertheless, medieval exegesis is important for two reasons. Firstly, it served as a vehicle for our inheritance from the Early Church, preserving very many insights, gathering them carefully and passing them on. Secondly, it developed a variety of expositional techniques, including the gloss and the scholium, which, being grouped around the text itself, were

[1] F. Delitzsch, 1894 (reprinted 1984), p. 43.

being grouped around the text itself, were intended to make the access to the text simpler. As an example of this kind of commentary, we might take the hand-book of practical Psalm exposition, written by Benedictine monks in early medieval France (7th century), which, significantly, was entitled '*Glosa psalmorum ex traditione seniorum*', and which drew particularly on the work of Augustine, Jerome and Gregory. This '*glosa*' was still being copied in the 15th century.

> 'Seen as a·whole, the glossing consists of two different elements. Firstly, there are short explanations of words, usually appended to particular words in the text with *id est*, or *hoc est*. And then there is the real exposition of the text, often sub-divided between *secundum historiam*, what the words actually say, and *secundum sensum*, occasionally expanded to *secundum sensum moralem*, the allegorical meaning or moral teaching of the text.'[3]

Another classical example is the '*Commentarius in Psalmos davidicos*' by Peter Lombard, following the technique of interlinear and marginal glossing which had been developed by Anselm of Laon (1050–1117). This is a catena commentary which became the standard work for the whole medieval world ('*glossa ordinaria*', 1135/37).

> 'The most elegant, and perhaps also the oldest form of the chain reference commentary is the "marginal catena": in a carefully marked space in the middle of the page, the writer paints in the sacred text, and then writes his interpretation on narrower lines in the broad margins which far exceed the area of the text itself . . . The second major form of the chain reference commentary had short groups of verses of the sacred text followed by the corresponding explanations.'[4]

Real progress, giving exegesis a new impetus, came from the Jewish expository literature. Aided by their knowledge of the Hebrew language, which had improved thanks to the new

---

[3] H. Boese, 'Die alte "glossa psalmorum ex traditione seniorum"', *Vetus Latina* 9, 1982, p.35.

[4] H. Lietzmann, *Catenen*, 1897, pp.9–11.

work done on grammar in the 10th century, these commentators were able to dig deeper into the psalm texts and draw out results which greatly benefited first Humanism and hence the scholarship of the Reformation. In particular we should mention the commentaries of:

> Saadja Gaon (892–942) from Sura, with its Arabic translation and notes by Abraham ben Meir ibn Esra (1092–1167) of Toledo.
>
> R. Solomon ben Isaaq (known as Rashi; 1040–1105) of Troyes, which is included in all editions of the Talmud.
>
> R. David Kimchi (1160–1235) of Narbonne.
>
> R. Moses ben Maimon (Maimonides; 1135–1204) of Cordoba.

4. *Humanism and Reformation*

It was the German humanist, Johannes Reuchlin of Pforzheim (1455–1522), who laid down new standards in psalm exposition. He concerned himself systematically with the Hebrew language, wrote a textbook on the subject, and published a commentary on the seven Psalms of Expiation under the title *'In septem psalmos poenitentiales hebraicos interpretatio de verbo ad verbum et super eisdem commentarioli sui, ad discendum linguam hebraicam ex rudimentis'* (1512); roughly translated: '[Introduction] to the seven Hebrew Psalms of Expiation, [and] exposition from word to word and explanations beyond this, in order to learn the Hebrew language from its rudiments'. The 'philological method of exegesis' (H.-J. Kraus) was making its way into the study of the Psalms.

Martin Luther (1484–1546) made the exposition of the Psalms the cornerstone of his exegetical work.[5] His published commentaries included: *'Dictata super Psalterium'* (1513–16); *'Operationes in Psalmos'* (1519–21/1530); the Summa on the Psalms (1531) and the great lectures on the Gradual Psalms

[5] According to H. Bornkamm, *Luther und das alte Testament*, 1948, pp. 230ff., Luther's psalm exegesis occupies roughly 2500 pages in the Weimar Edition.

(1532–33). As soon as he took up his post as lecturer *in biblicis* in 1512, Luther set about a series of lectures on the Psalms (1513–16). A recently discovered fragment of his early exposition of Pss. 4 and 5 shows strikingly how far he had already come in his development of a new understanding of Scripture. We may cite an extract from the scholium, and the conclusion on Ps. 5:

'1. No-one can pray a Psalm without first making the words of the Psalm his own. But they become his own when he has the same feeling and the same spirit in which they were spoken. If he does not have these, and prays, he is like someone who plays a role in a comedy, where certainly the words are real, but the matter is fictional. For what the shipwrecked mariner actually says sounds quite different from what the actor portraying him or the mask says, even though it be the same words. The former speaks his own, the latter alien words, and naturally the feeling is different. For the former, the words correspond to the fact, for the latter they are feigned. Now since the words of the Psalms and of prayer are words of the humble and the sinner, if someone pretends to be "justified", he speaks not his own but alien words, and displeases God as much as a mocker. However, this can only be confirmed and guaranteed by the evidence, and cannot be clearly known, whether we have their spirit, for the words of prayer are understood so symbolically that, even if they had not been uttered, they would shape our spirit or form it accordingly, so that – according to Augustine – even though they might appear to have been expressed by us, they could not have been better formed than the way they have been formed.'

'So we see how this Psalm both reveals what we are to seek, and also prays, teaching us the manner of our seeking, so that no-one might think that this has been said to him in order that he might work through his own power, but rather so that he might recognise that he cannot do it, and so learn to say to God "give what you command, and command what you will"; not like the arrogant and self-assured who say: "I have done, and I do, and I will do what you command, so give me in return what you have promised". For even if they do not speak aloud in this way, yet they behave in their self-confident tepidness and in the denial of their life as though by their deeds they wish to say: "We have faced everything, achieved everything, completed everything".'[6]

In the same class we have the Psalm expositions of John Calvin (1509–1564). His '*commentarii in psalmos*', which appeared in Geneva from 1557 (in French from 1558) in many editions, is a masterpiece in its drawing together of the philological, historical and theological aspects. His knowledge of the Hebrew language, acquired in Paris, Basel and Strasbourg, gave him access to the linguistic style and structure of the texts. '*Comprendre l'intention de chacun de ceux qui ont composé les Psaumes*' – i.e. '*mens rsp. consilium auctoris*', was how he expressed the aim of exegesis. For him this meant nothing other than the '*sensus verus*' of Holy Scripture.

> 'The fact that Calvin, in this relentless conclusion, focused all his attention on the sensus historicus has had a remarkably powerful impact on the history of Biblical research . . . The way was being prepared for historical-critical research.'[7]

Other reformers, too, produced commentaries on the Psalms: e.g. Johannes Bugenhagen (Basel, 1524, with a preface by Luther), and Martin Bucer (1529, with the remarkable rendering of the tetragrammaton YHWH as '*Autophyes*'; *a se et per se existens*). In particular, the ground was prepared by new editions of the Hebrew Bible. The Psalter was the first of the books to appear in print (Boulogne, 1477), followed by the Pentateuch (1482), and finally the whole Old Testament (Soncino, 1488). Luther was able to draw on the 1494 edition from Brescia. In 1522, there appeared the '*Psalterium ex hebreo diligentissime ad verbum fere translatum*', by Felix Pratensis (†1558), the editor of the first 'Rabbinical Bible' in

---

[6] H. Beintker (ed.), *Die reformatorischen Grundschriften*, 1983, vol. II, pp. 25; 53.

[7] H.-J. Kraus, *Geschichte der historisch-kritischen Erforschung des Alten Testaments*, 1969, p. 15.

Venice (1516/17). As a baptised Jew, Pratensis was concerned to pass on the Jewish heritage of Medieval exegesis.

5. The Enlightenment

'In the period of the Enlightenment, we look in vain for great expositors.'[8] Whereas in the age of orthodoxy knowledge was collected and amassed producing many-volumed super-commentaries (we might mention works ranging from S. Robert Bellarmin, 1611, to Johann Heinrich Michaelis, 1745), the enlightened 18th century brought forth new ideas which certainly provided some impetus, but did not until the turn of the next century begin to set down commentaries. It was Johann Gottfried Herder who rediscovered the 'Spirit of Hebrew poetry' (1782–83), heralding a new movement in exegesis. His Hebrew Humanism draws attention to the historical being, the uniqueness and the individuality of this poetry of the ancient Orient, into which the expositor must immerse himself, with which he must empathise. Only with Ernst Friedrich Karl Rosenmüller's 'Scholia in Psalmos' (1798–1804) and Wilhelm Martin Leberecht de Wette's 'Commentar über die Psalmen' (1811) was Herder's Programme set in motion.

6. Historical–Critical Exegesis

Rosenmüller and de Wette marked the beginning of the great classical commentaries of the 19th century, which introduced modern Psalm scholarship: F. Hitzig (1835–36), H. Ewald (1839–40), E. W. Hengstenberg (1842–47), J. Olshausen (1853), H. Hupfeld (1855–62), F. Delitzsch (1859) . . .

The course of the history of scientific research on the Psalms has often been charted, and need not be traced out here. The focus of interest of historical–critical work on the

[8] Ibid., p. 128.

texts, and hence also the methodological apparatus, shifted successively from the historical aspect to the philological, to the religious–historical, to the cultic–historical, to the formal-historical, to the literary–critical. It is the fruits of these labours which this Introduction to the Psalms has sought to describe.

7. A Selection of Modern Commentaries

(Raised numbers indicate most recent editions. Raised letter [e] indicates an English translation.)

F. Delitzsch	1859, [e] 1887/9	E. J. Kissane	1953/4
F. Baethgen	1892, [3] 1904	G. Castellino	1955
B. Duhm	1899, [2] 1922	H. Lamparter	1958
A. Ehrlich	1905	H. C. Leupold	1959
E. G. Briggs	1906/7	H. -J. Kraus	1960, [5] 1978
F. Staerk	1911 [2] 1920	A. B. Rhodes	1960
R. Kittel	1914 [5.6] 1929	A. Deißler	1965, [4] 1971
A. Bertholet	1923	M. Dahood	1966/70
E. König	1926	J. H. Eaton	1967
H. Gunkel	1929 [e] 1967	A. A. Anderson	1972
H. Schmidt	1934	D. Kidner	1973/75
A. Weiser	1935 [e] 1962	L. Jacquet	1975
M. Buttenwieser	1938	G. A. F. Knight	1982/3
B. Gemser	1949	P. C. Craigie	1983
E. A. Leslie	1949	C. Westermann	1984
E. Podechard	1949/54	E. Gerstenberger	1988
W. O. E. Oesterley	1953		

8. General Works on the Psalms

S. Mowinckel, *The Psalms in Israel's Worship*, 1962.
J. A. Lamb, *The Psalms in Christian Worship*, 1962.
P. Drijvers, *The Psalms: their structure and meaning*, 1965.
H. H. Guthrie, *Israel's Sacred Songs: a study of dominant themes*, 1966.
B. W. Anderson, *Out of the Depths: the Psalms speak for us today*, 1970.
J. H. Eaton, *Kingship and the Psalms*, 1976.
G. H. Wilson, *The Editing of the Hebrew Psalter*, 1985.
P. D. Miller (Jr.), *Interpreting the Psalms*, 1986.

W. G. E. Watson, *Classical Hebrew Poetry*, 1986.
C. Westermann, *Praise and Lament in the Psalms*, 1987.
T. Longman, *How to read the Psalms*, 1988.

SOURCES OF ILLUSTRATIONS

Fig. 1. M. H. Goshen-Gottstein (ed.), Aleppo Codex, Jerusalem Bible Project, The Hebrew University, Jerusalem 1976, p. 483.

Fig. 2. J. A. Sanders, Discoveries of the Judean Desert IV, The Psalms Scroll of Qumran 11QPsᵃ, OUP, Oxford 1965, plate xvii. Courtesy of the Israel Department of Antiquities and Museums.

Fig. 3. R. Kasser/M. Testuz, Papyrus Bodmer XXIV, Bibliotheca Bodmeriana, Geneva 1967, plate 36 (=supplement, p. 36).

Fig. 4. Diagram by the author.

Fig. 5. See Fig. 2. Op.cit., plate vi.

Fig. 6. G. Cornfield/G. J. Botterweck, Die Bibel und ihre Welt, G. Lübbe Verlag, Bergisch Gladbach 1969, Fig. 577. With kind permission of Professor Cornfield.

Fig. 7. O. Kreel, Die Welt der altorientalischen Bildsymbolik und das AT, Benziger Verlag Zürich, Cologne, 1972 (3rd edn., 1984), No. 475, p. 327.

Fig. 8. See Fig. 6. Op.cit., Fig. 581. With kind permission of Professor Cornfield.

Fig. 9. See Fig. 7. Op.cit., No. 475a, p. 326.

Fig. 10. Drawing by D. Seybold, based on the catalogue illustration: Frühe Phöniker im Libanon. 20 Jahre Ausgrabungen Kamid el-Loz, von Zabern, Mainz 1983, Fig. 1 (111; 86ff.).

Fig. 11. M. Avi-Yonah, E. Stern (ed.), Encyclopedia of Archaeological Excavations in the Holy Land, vol.

III, The Israel Exploration Society and Massada Press, 1977, p. 838.

Fig. 12. Op.cit., vol. III, p. 843.

Fig. 13. See Fig. 7. Op.cit., No. 470, p. 325.

Fig. 14. U. Winter, Frau und Göttin, Exegetische und ikonographische Studien zum weiblichen Gottesbild im alten Israel und dessen Umwelt, Universitätsverlag Freiburg/Schweiz, Vandenhoeck & Ruprecht, Göttingen 1983, No. 514.

Fig. 15. C. Uehlinger, Hebräische Lieder, Schweizerisches Katholisches Bibelwerk, Freiburg (Switzerland) 1982, cover illustration.

Fig. 16. See Fig. 7. Op.cit., No. 474, p. 325.

Fig. 17. See Fig. 7. Op.cit., No. 472/3. p. 325.

Fig. 18. D. Seybold and R. A. Stucky, Tribune d'Eschmoun, Antike Kunst Beiheft 13, Basel 1984.

Fig. 19. A. Chambon, Tell el Far'ah. L'âge fer. Editions recherches sur les civilisations publiées sous la direction de Henri de Coutenon, Paris 1984, plate 63,2.

Fig. 20. See Fig. 11. Op.cit., vol. IV, OUP, p. 1103.

Fig. 21. Drawing by D. Seybold, based on S. S. Gafni, Die Einzigartigkeit des Alten Testaments, Hänssler Verlag, Stuttgart 1983, p. 293, and other sources.

Fig. 22. See Fig. 14. Op.cit., No. 386.

Fig. 23. B. Reicke/L. Rost (ed.), Biblisch-historisches Handwörter-

buch, vol. II, Vandenhoeck &
Ruprecht, Göttingen 1964, p. 1259f.
Fig. 24. Op.cit., p. 1259f.
Fig. 25. D. Seybold; see Fig. 21.
Op.cit., p. 287.
Fig. 26. D. Seybold; see Fig. 21.
Op.cit., p. 293.
Fig. 27. See Fig. 23. Op.cit., p. 1259f.
Fig. 28. See Fig. 19. Op.cit., plate 63.
Fig. 29. See Fig. 23. Op.cit., p. 1259f.
Fig. 30. Illustrated Bible Dictionary,
IVP, Leicester 1980, p. 1037.
Fig. 31. Op.cit., p. 1039.
Fig. 32. See Fig. 7. Op.cit., No. 447,
p. 313.
Fig. 33. DTV Atlas zur Musik (2nd
edn.), Deutscher Taschenbuch
Verlag, Munich 1978, p. 162.
Fig. 34. S. Moscati, Die Phöniker,
Essen 1975, p. 483.
Fig. 35. See Fig. 11. Op.cit., vol. III,
p. 787.

Fig. 36. See Fig. 30. Op.cit., p. 168.
Reproduced by courtesy of the
Trustees of the British Museum,
London.
Fig. 37. A. Moortgat, Die Kunst des
Alten Mesopotamien, Die
klassische Kunst Vorderasiens,
Verlag M. Du-Mont Schauberg,
Cologne 1967, p. 231.
Fig. 38. B. Brentjes, Alte Siegelkunst,
E. A. Seemann Verlag, Leipzig
1983, p. 87.
Fig. 39. E. Brunner-Traut, Die Alten
Ägypter, Verlag W. Kohlhammer,
Stuttgart 1976, plate 45, p. 139.
With kind permission of the
archives of the Preussischer
Kulturbesitz, Berlin.
Fig. 40. See Fig. 33. Op.cit., p. 18c.

INDEX OF BIBLE REFERENCES

Prepared by Bernhard Seybold. Includes all psalm references discussed in the text. (Interpretations in *italics*, verse numbers in brackets. *h* = *heading*)

DATE DUE

Made in the USA
Lexington, KY
28 January 2012